Knowledge, Dexterity, and Attention

Contemporary cognitive science clearly tells us that attention is modulated for speech and action. While these forms of goal-directed attention are very well researched in psychology, they have not been sufficiently studied by epistemologists. In this book, Abrol Fairweather and Carlos Montemayor develop and defend a theory of epistemic achievements that requires the manifestation of cognitive agency. They examine empirical work on the psychology of attention and assertion, and use it to ground a normative theory of epistemic achievements and virtues. The resulting study is the first sustained naturalized virtue epistemology, and will be of interest to readers in epistemology, cognitive science, and beyond.

ABROL FAIRWEATHER is Lecturer in Philosophy at San Francisco State University. He has edited several volumes on virtue epistemology, including (with Linda Zagzebski) *Virtue Epistemology* (2001), (with Owen Flanagan) *Naturalizing Epistemic Virtue* (2014), and (with Mark Alfano) *Epistemic Situationism* (2016).

CARLOS MONTEMAYOR is Associate Professor of Philosophy at San Francisco State University and the author of *Minding Time: A Philosophical and Theoretical Approach to the Psychology of Time* (2013) and (with H. H. Haladjian) *Consciousness, Attention, and Conscious Attention* (2015).

D1554499

Knowledge, Dexterity, and Attention

A Theory of Epistemic Agency

Abrol Fairweather

San Francisco State University

Carlos Montemayor

San Francisco State University

CAMBRIDGE
UNIVERSITY PRESS

CAMBRIDGE
UNIVERSITY PRESS

University Printing House, Cambridge CB2 8BS, United Kingdom

One Liberty Plaza, 20th Floor, New York, NY 10006, USA

477 Williamstown Road, Port Melbourne, VIC 3207, Australia

314-321, 3rd Floor, Plot 3, Splendor Forum, Jasola District Centre, New Delhi - 110025, India

79 Anson Road, #06-04/06, Singapore 079906

Cambridge University Press is part of the University of Cambridge.

It furthers the University's mission by disseminating knowledge in the pursuit of education, learning and research at the highest international levels of excellence.

www.cambridge.org
Information on this title: www.cambridge.org/9781107461574
DOI: 10.1017/9781316105849

© Abrol Fairweather and Carlos Montemayor 2017

First published 2017
First paperback edition 2018

A catalogue record for this publication is available from the British Library

ISBN 978-1-107-08982-2 Hardback
ISBN 978-1-107-46157-4 Paperback

Contents

Acknowledgments   *page* vii

Introduction: Why Only Agents Are Knowers   1
    I.1   Aims and Motivations   1
    I.2   Dexterity, Attention, and Integration   5
    I.3   A Brief Summary of Chapters   7
    I.4   A Tension in Virtue Epistemology   11
    I.5   Virtue Theoretic Epistemic Psychology   13
    I.6   The Attention-Assertion Model   17
    I.7   Methodology in Epistemology   18

1 Epistemic Virtue, Reliable Attention, and Cognitive Constitution   27
    1.1   The Argument from Attention   27
    1.2   Dispositions and Epistemic Abilities   33
    1.3   The Situationist Challenge   38
    1.4   Knowledge of Syntax   44
    1.5   Knowledge of Logic   47
    1.6   Arguments against Consequentialist Epistemic Norms   48

2 Meta-epistemology and Epistemic Agency   53
    2.1   On the Role of Motivational States   53
    2.2   The Direction of Attention: Self or World   54
    2.3   Cognitive Needs   57
    2.4   The Desire to Assert: The Content of Epistemic Motivation   59
    2.5   Epistemic Needs and the Grip of Epistemic Norms   60
    2.6   Frege on the Grip of Assertion   64
    2.7   The Frame Problem and Virtuous Insensitivity   66
    2.8   Some Concerns about Internal Normative Force   69

3 Success Semantics and the Etiology of Success   72
    3.1   The "Because of" Requirement for Knowledge   72
    3.2   Greco's Contextualist Etiology   74
    3.3   Causality: Folksy, Metaphysical, and Psychologically Constrained   79
    3.4   Success Semantics and the Etiology of Success   81
    3.5   Peirce, Wittgenstein, and Ramsey: Reliability and Assertion 85
    3.6   The Norm of Assertion   86
    3.7   Assertion and Action   90

4   Epistemic Agency   94
    4.1   Tensions between Credit, Agency, and Automaticity   94
    4.2   Sosa's Judgments and Functionings: Personal and Sub-personal
          Success   98
    4.3   Mental and Epistemic Action   100
    4.4   Resolving the Tension   104
    4.5   Language and Agency   109

5   Assertion as Epistemic Motivation   112
    5.1   Attention and Communication   112
    5.2   Dispositions to Assert and Successful Communication   114
    5.3   Forms of Assertoric Force and Forms of Epistemic Attention   118
    5.4   Factivity, Credit, and Social Environments   123
    5.5   Epistemically Virtuous Halting Thresholds and Assertable Contents:
          The Case of Epistemic Modals   128
    5.6   Retraction and Virtuous Sensitivity   132
    5.7   Conclusion   136

6   Curiosity and Epistemic Achievement   138
    6.1   Epistemically Virtuous Curiosity   138
    6.2   Basic Principles of Curiosity   141
    6.3   Curiosity and Halting Thresholds   143
    6.4   Curiosity and Virtuous Insensitivity   148
    6.5   Attention, Curiosity, and Creativity   151

7   Collective Agency, Assertion, and Information   156
    7.1   Collective Epistemic Agency and Cognitive Integration   156
    7.2   Collective Agency and Reliable Social Communication   160
    7.3   Social Epistemology and Collective Assertion   163
    7.4   Collective Attention and Collective Motivation   166
    7.5   Reflection, Explicit Judgment, and Reliability   170
    7.6   Complex Collective Agency   173

Bibliography   178
Index   189

Acknowledgments

Our book examines a version of reliabilism that appeals to abilities. Both of us have benefited from either exchanges with or the direct mentorship of the main proponents of the proposals this book focuses on, Alvin Goldman and Ernest Sosa. Their contributions to epistemology are invaluable and we are personally in debt to them.

The psychology and philosophy of attention is a critical aspect of the proposal we defend. Montemayor would like to thank the constant support and advice of Zenon Pylyshyn. The Object Group was a wonderful opportunity to learn about the philosophical implications of the incredibly interesting and complex evidence on attention. Montemayor is particularly thankful to Randy Gallistel, Rochel Gelman, Harry H. Haladjian, and Fuat Balci, who participated and helped organize the Object Group.

This book is the result of a 5-year collaboration, which started in earnest when we co-taught a seminar on naturalized virtue epistemology at San Francisco State University during the fall of 2011. We benefited from presentations by Mark Alfano, David Copp, and Peter Graham in that seminar, which have helped this project mature in many ways. Thanks to the students who participated in that seminar and a different version of the seminar that Montemayor taught in Spring 2015. Particular thanks are due to Spencer Horne, Christopher Masciari (both of whom gave us valuable feedback), Rebeka Ferreira, and Jennifer White.

A critical development during our collaboration was the presentation of a paper at the Pacific Division meeting of the American Philosophical Association in Seattle, in 2012. We would like to thank Adam Morton for organizing this session and for giving us valuable feedback, as well as Lauren Olin and members of the audience. This paper was also presented at the workshop Cognitive Perspectives on Mind and Language at UNAM. We thank Ángeles Eraña, Maite Ezcurdia, Eduardo García Ramírez, Claudia Lorena García Aguilar, and members of the audience at the Instituto de Investigaciones Filosóficas.

We also benefited from feedback at the Philosophy Department at Oregon, where we presented material on dispositions and linguistic skills in December

2013. We are particularly thankful to Colin Koopman for his valuable feedback on the Ramsey and Peirce material. We are also thankful to Cheryl Misak, who we met through Colin, for sharing her manuscript on the Cambridge pragmatists with us.

Thanks to audience members at the Bellingham conference on curiosity in March 2015, specifically to Dennis Whitcomb for organizing it and for his feedback, and also to Ilhan Inan for co-organizing it. The feedback we received there helped us structure material that mattered for the project as a whole.

Montemayor has benefited from constant discussions on new findings in cognitive science with Ezequiel Morsella and the members of his Action and Consciousness Laboratory. The quality and intensity of the conversations at Morsella's lab, combined with his sophisticated views about how action influences attention and consciousness, were very useful in developing some ideas in this book.

Both of us would like to thank Allison Keiko Allen for helping us proofread the manuscript. Allen is a member of Morsella's lab and a student and collaborator of Montemayor.

Finally, Montemayor would like to thank Victoria Frede for her support and love. Fairweather would like to thank his daughter Barbara for her patience and support as well.

Introduction: Why Only Agents Are Knowers

I.1   Aims and Motivations

The aim of this inquiry is to defend a theory of epistemic agency specifically suited for a virtue reliabilist theory of knowledge, but many of our conclusions will be significant for other areas of epistemic psychology. The fundamental motivations and commitments of this inquiry are presented below, putting our cards on the table at the outset. These will cluster around two main principles: the attentional turn and the continuity of agency. We will defend an epistemic psychology that takes attentional states and processes, rather than propositional attitudes, as the fundamental unit of analysis in epistemology. We thus call for an attentional turn in epistemology, particularly in accounts of the psychology of the subjects evaluated by epistemic norms. We also see epistemic agency as continuous with fundamental forms of cognitive (but not necessarily epistemic) agency. We examine many implications of both commitments throughout this work, but our primary dialectical aims can be stated clearly here. The broadest aim of this inquiry is to understand the phenomenon of epistemic agency in terms of selective attention and to identify current debates in epistemology that can be informed by an epistemic psychology grounded in attention from the outset.

A more specific and perhaps "chancy" claim we defend is that knowledge requires agency. Once we take the attentional turn, we see that cognitive agency is actually non-mysterious and rampant in our intellectual lives, suggesting that the main issue epistemologists should debate is "*which* form of epistemic agency is necessary for knowledge?" rather than "is *any* form of epistemic agency necessary for knowledge?" We affirm a continuity between the forms of cognitive agency that manifest in attention and the forms of agency that are under discussion in current debates in epistemology. In conjunction with the attentional turn, the continuity of agency thesis should provide an understanding of epistemic agency that is non-mysterious and particularly useful for virtue reliabilist theories of knowledge. Each chapter to follow will examine specific points of contact between the psychology of attention (and related issues in psychology) and a number of specific debates in epistemology impacted by an attentional turn.

The theory of epistemic agency defended here is intended equally for psychologists as for epistemologists and is inevitably a hybrid product. The primary subject of analysis in epistemology (processes of forming and revising belief) is a psychological phenomenon, so it is well understood that epistemologists have something to gain by consulting the best relevant theories in psychology. We continue this familiar tradition, but here with a clear and restricted focus on the psychology of attention. Psychologists also have an interest in developing more "theorized" accounts of the concepts and theories at work in fundamental research in their field, and philosophers are often very useful companions here. We aim to speak to the interests of theoretically minded psychologists as well as epistemologists working on the Gettier problem, lotteries, and fake barns in the theory defended here.

The resulting hybrid theory is presented as a form of naturalized virtue epistemology. Because we give a voice to psychology from the very start in the attentional turn, less time and interest will be given to famous thought experiments in epistemology and we will not aim to defend necessary and sufficient conditions for knowledge at any length. Instead, we extend work in the psychology of attention selectively to issues in analytic epistemology that are most usefully informed or impacted by this work.

The current work is fundamentally an endeavor in epistemic psychology. It's older and perhaps wiser cousin, moral psychology has long been recognized as an important area of philosophical inquiry (Anscombe, 1958; Flanagan, 1991; Sinnott-Armstrong, 2007). Moral psychology seeks to explain the underlying psychology of the subjects to which we apply norms of moral praise and blame in ways that facilitate improvements in these very norms. Likewise, epistemic psychology seeks to understand the underlying psychology of the subjects of *epistemic* praise and blame in ways that facilitate improvements in these very norms. This will be useful in part because any epistemic theory with a plausible and theoretically productive psychology will, *ceteris paribus*, have greater explanatory power than any equivalent theory lacking an adequate epistemic psychology. In virtue epistemology, epistemic psychology will often provide *constitutive* elements for theorizing about knowledge, justification, understanding, wisdom, and other epistemic achievements. At a minimum, we want *epistemic oughts to be constrained by psychological cans*,[1] and for this we need an epistemic psychology to determine whether any proposed theory of epistemic oughts can be psychologically realizable by realistic epistemic cans.

The principles of epistemic psychology defended throughout will often do more than constrain normative theory construction; they will provide constitutive

---

[1] For a very interesting discussion of epistemic oughts and epistemic cans, see Neta (2014). Neta argues that certain (functional and essential) epistemic cans actually entail certain epistemic oughts.

elements of epistemic normativity within the virtue theoretic model adopted here. Virtue theory, whether in ethics or epistemology, has a unique way of integrating descriptive psychology and normativity because the dispositions of an agent that constitute a virtue are, by that very fact, normatively significant; otherwise, these dispositions could not constitute a virtue properly speaking. Virtues are always good in some relevant sense, but they should also be psychologically real dispositions in actual human beings.

The specific feature of epistemic psychology of central interest throughout the current inquiry is *agency*. This is the most important, and perhaps most poorly understood, area of epistemic psychology. The perspective in current epistemology with perhaps most to gain from an adequate psychology of epistemic agency is perhaps reliabilist virtue epistemology. We argue that virtue reliabilism will prosper by incorporating the account of epistemic agency defended here. We will show how sufficient agent-level credit is due to an agent for manifesting a reliable *cognitive constitution*, and this in turn is understood as an integrated set of attentional (and thus agential) cognitive dispositions. Importantly, we argue that, with an attentional turn, even basic epistemic achievements like reliable perception or the deliverances of a capacious memory will be agential, and will thus underwrite the distinctive value virtue epistemologists associate with achievements that manifest agency. Returning to the older cousin of epistemic psychology, one important project in moral psychology is to determine which psychological models are presupposed by various ethical theories, and whether these models are empirically or explanatorily adequate. This will be a general aim of epistemic psychology as well, and we take on empirical adequacy directly in Section 1.3. Virtue epistemology (explained further below) has a special, constitutive role for psychological properties of agents, so the contribution psychology makes to epistemology is substantive here. Specifically, the cluster of dispositions that constitute an epistemic virtue in the agent are *sources of epistemic value* in virtue epistemology. We explain this cluster of dispositions in terms of attention, so it will be various forms of attention that function as sources of epistemic value on our account. Below, we introduce fundamental principles of virtue epistemology and begin constructing the epistemic psychology defended throughout.

Virtue epistemology has two distinct (and perhaps rival) forms: virtue reliabilism and virtue responsibilism. Responsibilist virtue epistemology focuses on traits like open-mindedness, conscientiousness, intellectual humility, and the like, and there is little doubt that virtues of this kind require appropriate motivational states of their possessors. Virtue reliabilism emphasizes the truth conduciveness of cognitive capacities and abilities such as vision, memory, basic communication, and basic forms of inductive and deductive reasoning ("hunchy" but reliably reasoning). While responsibilists have clear accounts of the necessary motivational states required to manifest virtue, the demand for motivation appears too strong to capture basic epistemic achievements, precisely those of interest to virtue reliabilists. Virtue reliabilists have a harder time than responsibilists in pinning down just what a relevant motivational state will be, or if any is required for knowledge at all. Accurate vision, a capacious memory, and competence in basic forms of inductive and deductive reasoning are often successful with little or no conscious reflection or deliberate intent, so it is not surprising that properly locating the epistemic role of motivations poses a greater challenge to virtue reliabilism than it does in virtue responsibilism. Motivations of some sort are built into the very concept of any positive character trait in a way not required for the manifestation of our more basic and reliable psychological capacities and abilities. The most sustained account of epistemic agency for virtue reliabilism is Ernest Sosa's recent *Judgment & Agency* (2015). While there are many points of symmetry, we argue that our account of epistemic agency is more empirically plausible and better serves the normative needs of a psychologically informed virtue reliabilism than Sosa's account. This will be the focus of Chapter 4. While Sosa focuses on reflection and "second-order alethic affirmation," we explain person-level epistemic agency in terms of the *integration* of psychological processes rather than reflection upon them. Whether or not second-order affirmations are necessary for fully praiseworthy knowledge in Sosa's sense has important implications for the explanatory burden carried by any adequate epistemic psychology. We argue that agency (in the sense we defend here) is necessary for knowledge, but that agency can be shown through actions that involve little or no internal reflection at the time because attention is typically world directed. World-directed forms of attention will be essential to our argument against requiring that epistemic motivations be full-blown epistemic intentions. Both empirical and folk ways of understanding attention will agree that we typically attend to what lies outside the self, although there are times when human life affords or demands time for deliberate reflection of course.

In the chapters to follow, we introduce a number of new figures into current debates in virtue epistemology. These will include Frank Ramsey, Iris Murdoch, Philippa Foot, Christine Korsgaard, and Imogen Dickie, as well as philosophers working on the nature of attention including Wayne Wu, Chris Mole, and Declan Smithies. In different ways, each philosopher has useful contributions to offer to epistemic psychology. Injecting these new voices into virtue epistemology should be good for the field as a whole, even for a virtue epistemologist who does not ultimately accept the theory of epistemic agency defended here. Virtue epistemology has faced recent empirical challenges from "epistemic situationism" (Alfano, 2013; Olin and Doris, 2014; Fairweather and Alfano, 2017). Epistemic situationism is the view that research in social psychology calls into question the very existence, reliability, or praiseworthi-

any cognitive traits constitutive of any cognitive character we might be said to possess. We examine this challenge directly in Chapter 1.3, where we will argue that our proposed epistemic psychology can clearly stand up to the challenge from epistemic situationism. In the process, we also introduce a number of relevant empirical sources regarding animal and human communication. Robust epistemic abilities can be found here. We utilize models of assertion and communication in Chapters 2, 3, and 5 to define fundamental forms of epistemic motivation and epistemic achievement. The resulting account is supported not only by philosophical work on assertion but also by important findings in psychology showing that attention is paradigmatically modulated for speech, communication, and action. These are the processes and systems that we are primed and disposed to manifest whenever we think about our environment, which is where we spend most of our waking time. The success of most of our actual cognition depends essentially on doing this well, and thus on being disposed to do it well. A proper psychology of assertion, communication, and attention will provide useful resources for epistemologists interested in theorizing about epistemic agency and the value of knowledge in terms of the kind of credit generated by success due to agential cognitive integration.

I.2   Dexterity, Attention, and Integration

In this section, we will briefly explain how our understanding of attention and intellectual ability constitutes a kind of dexterity, and how this, in turn, constitutes an epistemically important form of cognitive integration. We argue that epistemic agency is a matter of proper integration rather than conscious reflection and endorsement, as many perspectives from Descartes to Sosa would have it (see Chapter 4 in particular). This large shift implicated in the attentional turn might appear burdensome to epistemology rather than instructive. Fortunately, there is a considerable amount of research on attention in psychology that presents different forms of integration to work with. Psychologists working in the tradition of "activity theory" have always understood successful cognition as involving a dexterity of the mind that is analogous to the bodily dexterity necessary for successful action. This mental dexterity is also seen in contemporary research models on attention in psychology. Complex actions involve action-guiding attentional processes that must be fast, well integrated with motivational states, and sensitive to the immediate external environment. This is an essential form of integrated attention in human cognition. The Russian "activity theorists" (e.g., Dobrynin, 1966; Leontiev, 1978) developed a lineage of psychological research on forms of attention that involve coordinating complex skills whose operation does not require any exhausting voluntary demands or any form of reflectively endorsement. This ease is especially characteristic of skillful expertise.

Attention theorists call this highly skilled attention "*postvoluntary atten-tion*," a notion based on the work of Bernstein (see Dormashev, 2010). *Dexterity and Its Development*, by Nicholai A. Bernstein (1950), presents a framework for the motor skills required for reliably satisfying needs, and finding complex and layered solutions to well-defined problems. For instance, riding a bike at a high speed or juggling several balls requires well-integrated adroitness, slight and very precise movements. Skillfully engaging in an activity that requires dexterity requires integrating and being efficiently direc-ted by an ongoing understanding of the changing motion, speed, color, and shape of things in the environment.

Motor skills fundamentally require epistemic and attentional abilities in order to reliably keep track of and integrate relevant facts and *only* the relevant facts. This is the ability to successfully ignore irrelevant information. A moment's distraction by what is irrelevant to a given task may mean failure in some cases. More importantly, ignoring the right information prevents cognitive overload. Capacities that enable us to avoid cognitive overload have considerable epistemic value. Agency accomplishes this because the needs, interests, and motives that explain and rationalize an action will entail that vast amount of information an agent might otherwise consider is irrele-vant, given the interests of the action now being taken. Many of the epistemic skills required for motor control, communication, and assertion are processed unconsciously or without explicit judgment, and this might appear to under-mine any claim that knowledge requires epistemic agency. However, as we will show, the fact that many parts of these activities are unconsciously or automatically processed does not preclude their being agential, and in many cases *the automaticity of a process in an agent is actually an indication of success and creditworthiness*. Professional sports, instrument playing, rock climbing, among many other activities require a dexterity that happens auto-matically, and the experience reported by subjects when they perform these activities is one of selfless and effortless participation in the performance, not conscious reflection on rules, norms, or reasons.

In order to understand how epistemic agency actually works in the majority of regular life activities, it is essential to understand these kinds of goal-directed yet significantly automatic cognitive skills. Dexterity requires the coordination of different types of abilities: process-based abilities (modular), assessment-based abilities (reflective, inquisitive, speech-act like), and integration-based abilities (agential). We will argue that epistemic agency is constituted by the forms of goal-directed cognitive integration (and thus cognitive dexterity) required for reliably normative assertion. The forms of attention necessary for reliable asser-tion hold an important place in human psychology. This is quite different from emphasizing the kind of cognitive dexterity or skill required for reflective justification, which is an important form of cognitive dexterity as well.

The ability to integrate processes emphasized by the activity theorists does not require conscious, reflective introspection. In many cases, introspection actually reduces the success of an action, and the same is likely true for successful cognition. Even when the operation of a skill or capacity is sub-personal, sub-personal processes are typically caused by (and rationalized by) some conscious state (e.g., an occurrent or easily accessible belief about the point of one's current behavior). These sub-personal processes are parts of integrated larger processes that are both person level and largely automatic. One thing we aim to do with considerable care is to explain how this is the case and how this principle from epistemic psychology informs normative theorizing in epistemology. We examine the relation between automatic and non-automatic elements of person-level agential processes in detail in Chapter 4, challenging Sosa's account of epistemic agency in the process.

I.3   A Brief Summary of Chapters

We briefly explain each of the chapters in the current work below. The remainder of this introduction will go on to explain the distinction between responsibilist and reliabilist forms of virtue epistemology, present the "direction of analysis" thesis characteristic of virtue theories in general, and defend the necessity of an *agency-based* reading of this thesis. Now we offer a concise summary of each chapter before returning to these issues.

In Chapter 1, we defend a fundamental turn to attention in epistemic psychology, examining recent work in the philosophy and psychology of attention, and then respond to empirical and normative challenges to the attentional turn. Relevant work by Wayne Wu, Imogen Dickie, Mark Alfano, and Selim Berker is discussed. We present an initial account of the attention-based epistemic psychology to be defended and refined throughout this work, and we defend our account of cognitive constitutions that manifest cognitive agency against both empirical and normative challenges.

Giving a bit more detail, we will argue that the properties of agents that constitute sources of epistemic value in virtue epistemology must be seen as agential properties, the properties in virtue of which some process constitutes an exercise of agency. This argument is based on the current way attention is generally understood in psychology, in particular selective attention (where we actively attend to something for a reason or purpose). Selective attention is partly if not wholly constitutive of many important forms of epistemic agency and is one of the cornerstones of reliable human cognition. Attending to one object over time, tracking different objects at the same time, and tracking different objects at different times are all forms of active and integrated attentional achievements. We will call this *the argument from attention*. We then examine a number of issues in disposition theory, defending novel accounts of "virtuous and vicious masking," and beginning to develop an account of an "agential cognitive constitution" (ACC) in terms of dispositions and their proper manifestations. In the last two sections, we examine the empirical challenge to virtue reliabilism from epistemic situationism, and the axiological challenge to consequentialist epistemic norms, respectively. Since we defend a form of virtue reliabilism, it will be important to show that neither of these challenges goes through. In both cases, the role we give to agency in attention enables an adequate defense.

In Chapter 2, we examine the nature and role of epistemic motivation, including both the affective and intentional content of such states, "self-directed" and "other directed" forms of normative attention, internal normative force in epistemology, and assertion as the prime epistemic aim. Relevant work by Iris Murdoch, Philippa Foot, and Christine Korsgaard is discussed. We argue that epistemic motivations aiming at normative assertion provide a psychologically plausible basis for internal epistemic normativity within a virtue reliabilist framework, and that epistemic motivations have additional epistemic value in the forms of ignorance and inattention they sustain.

Giving a bit more detail, we turn to meta-epistemic issues regarding the interpretation of motivational states in epistemology and connected issues regarding internal normativity and the ground of normative force for epistemic evaluations. In different contexts, Imogen Dickie and Iris Murdoch develop accounts of world-directed motivational states that do not involve introspective, conscious representation and are much closer to needs and desires than to intentions to act. We apply this thinner and world-directed account of normative attention to epistemic motivation, and this marks a fundamental difference in the way we understand epistemic motivation than Ernest Sosa does, although the most direct examination of this awaits until Chapter 4. We go on to show that many of the theoretical resources brought by accounts of internal reasons in ethics can be captured in epistemology by non-reflective motives of the sort favored by Dickie and Murdoch. We include discussions of Philippa Foot and Christine Korsgaard in an examination of the way epistemic norms get a normative grip or purchase on agents due to their interests in ways that interest-independent epistemic norms cannot account for.

Chapter 3 examines difficulties in explaining the "because of" relation that properly connects an agent to their achievements such that the achievement is due to the abilities of the agent and is thus a success credited to the agent. Relevant work by John Greco is the primary focus, but we introduce work from F. P. Ramsey and C. S. Peirce pointing in a different direction for understanding etiological requirements for knowledge. We argue against Greco's contextualist analysis of the "because of" relation and motivate a re-direction of analysis toward F. P. Ramsey and C. S. Peirce, developed more completely in Chapter 4.

Giving a bit more detail, we examine the vexing "because of" relation throughout the chapter. This is the relation that connects an agent to their successes in a way that makes the success both sufficiently non-lucky and sufficiently creditable to them as an agent. In a tradition going back to Aristotle, an act of virtue (the act that the virtuous person would perform) which manifests the settled virtue in the agent is better than an act of virtue alone, without a source in the good character of the agent. In the former case, the success is due to or because of certain excellences in the agent and is thus creditable to them in a way that the external success alone is not. This etiology for success is also emphasized by most virtue epistemologists, but with complex issues in mental causation and action in play, it has proven difficult to say just what is required here. We critically examine John Greco's contextualist account and argue that it faces serious difficulties. In its place, we defend a modified version of Ramsey's "success semantics." Roughly, this tells us that a belief has positive epistemic standing if acting on it in conjunction with some desire would result in the satisfaction of that desire. There are many epistemically significant points brought together in our concept of an "epistemic Ramsey success," but one important aspect is that the relevant success (satisfaction of the desire) is due to *integrated* and world-involving abilities of the agent. This normative structure, the epistemic Ramsey success, is compatible with, and unifies, earlier points about attention, dispositions, world-directed motivation, and internal reasons.

Chapter 4 examines fundamental tensions between agency, credit, and automaticity, with specific emphasis on Sosa's recent *Judgment & Agency* (2015). Relevant work from Ernest Sosa, Imogen Dickie, and Wayne Wu is discussed. We argue that the attentional model of epistemic agency defended in Chapters 1–3 adequately resolves the tension above through forms of integration rather than second-order affirmation as in Sosa's account.

Giving a bit more detail, until recently, there has been no fully developed account of epistemic agency in contemporary virtue epistemology, but Ernest Sosa's *Judgment & Agency* (2015) certainly provides this. While there is far more common ground than disagreement with Sosa's account of judgment, we argue against the essential role played by "second-order alethic affirmations" on his account. Sosa's emphasis on "alethic affirmation" has much in common with our emphasis on assertion, so we are largely party to a common cause, but we are able to clearly capture the nature and value of epistemic agency by appeal to the forms of integration accomplished by attentional agency without appeal to second-order alethic affirmations. In order to defend our account against Sosa's, we rely on helpful points from G. E. M Anscombe who explains how practical knowledge does not require consciously reflective attention and we apply some of these helpful points to our disagreement with Sosa.

In Chapter 5 we argue that the epistemic capacities for opening and closing inquiry characteristic of attentional routines are also fundamental in linguistic communication, particularly with respect to the speech acts of assertion and retraction. Relevant work by Kent Bach & Robert Harnish, Sanford Goldberg, John MacFarlane, Friederike Moltmann, John Turri, Robert Stalnaker, and Seth Yalcin is discussed. An important goal of this chapter is to highlight the similar cognitive structure, based on the agent's cognitive constitution, between perceptual and communicative epistemic successes and to identify specific epistemic achievements involved in successful communication.

Giving a bit more detail, this chapter is devoted entirely to assertion and expands on our characterization of an epistemic Ramsey success. We focus on the effective motivations and recognitional capacities of speakers involved in conversation as a way of articulating some detailed functioning of the form of epistemic agency defended in Chapter 4. We emphasize the reliability and pervasiveness of communication skills, which are a paradigmatic example of epistemic capacities. The basic abilities and shared assumptions of speakers that make linguistic communication possible are world involving, predictive, and inferential. We use the account of basic motivations defended in Chapters 3 and 4 to explain communication as an epistemic achievement, one which integrates a number of cognitive skills in response to subtle cues in the environment. We then focus on the assertion and retraction of claims to illustrate detailed ways in which epistemic agency creates epistemically reliable forms of attention, as well as "virtuous insensitivity" to irrelevant information.

Chapter 6 is devoted to curiosity, an obviously important topic in epistemology, but one which has received surprisingly sparse treatment in mainstream academic literature. We present a theory of epistemic achievements based on the reliable and responsible satisfaction of curiosity. The process of virtuously sating a curiosity underwrites a unique and important epistemic standing that is important to account for in virtue epistemology. The work of Ilhan Inan is prominently discussed. Assertable contents are used to specify the normative epistemic thresholds for satisfying curiosity.

Giving a bit more detail, curiosity is a fundamental motivation in our intellectual life and is thus easily relevant to a proper understanding of epistemic agency. We develop an account of "virtuously satisfying a curiosity" and focus on three important abilities we call "reliable halting," "responsible halting," and "virtuous insensitivity." We typically think of curiosity as "spotlighting" some item of interest, and indeed it manages to do that, but largely by making us insensitive to a vast amount of information which, were we to be sensitive to it, would render us incapable of succeeding in the focused inquiries necessary to answer the questions we are most interested in. This is a vital psychological function of curiosity, and fulfilling this function involves a unique and important set of epistemic virtues.

Chapter 7 extends the attention and assertion account defended thus far to work in social epistemology and collective epistemic agency. The work of Miranda Fricker, Margaret Gilbert, and Philip Pettit & Christian List is discussed. Two central problems are addressed, one concerning reliable communication in economic markets and reliable communication among collective agents in general. Further implications regarding moral masks on collective epistemic goods, the structure of legal systems, and the foundations of democratic discourse in reliable communication are discussed.

Giving a bit more detail, we conclude our current project with an examination of social epistemology and collective communicative epistemic virtues. It emphasizes the reliability of collective assertions and collective virtues in the context of communal action (in the case of animals) and economics (in the case of humans). We argue that the assertion and attention model defended in previous chapters can explain collective epistemic agency and properly distinguish epistemic collective agency from other types of collective action.

Throughout the book, we assume that epistemic success depends on epistemic agency and that we can gain considerable understanding of why this is the case from contemporary work in the psychology of attention. In the remainder of this introduction we justify this claim, which is defended and developed in detail in the chapters just described.

I.4 A Tension in Virtue Epistemology

As mentioned, virtue epistemology has traditionally been divided between responsibilist and reliabilist forms. These are commonly differentiated according to the types of dispositions that constitute the virtues under each approach: character virtues and competence virtues, respectively. While our perspective is decidedly virtue reliabilist, our primary concern is not to defend one of these traditional forms of virtue epistemology over the other. It is common to claim that responsibilist virtues essentially include motivations, but competence or faculty virtues do not.[2] We argue that the kinds of virtues typically of interest to so-called virtue reliabilists have necessary motivational components as well.

Rather than responsibilist or reliabilist virtue epistemology, let us distinguish between motivational and non-motivational virtue epistemology, relying on an intuitive grasp of what an epistemic motivation is for now (paradigmatically, but perhaps mistakenly, this would be a "desire for truth"). Motivational theories will require a specific motivation for manifesting

---

[2] Baehr (2011) defends this claim, and Greco and Turri (2011) discuss this as a point of contention. Ernest Sosa's most recent work (2015) is a thorough defense of an essentially motivational virtue reliabilism because of his requirement that any fully apt epistemic performance must manifest an *intention* to alethically affirm. We will discuss his account at length throughout, in particular in Chapter 4, in discussing epistemic agency.

intellectual virtue, non-motivational virtue theories will not. Motivational theories have the advantage of conferring praise on their possessor in a clear way. Beliefs will acquire epistemic value when they manifest an epistemic virtue on this view because manifesting a good motive is a praiseworthy thing to do. However, it appears equally clear that there are cases of knowledge that do not require virtuous motivations, and this supports a nod to a non-motivational account. Simple knowledge from perception and memory (Baehr, 2011; Brendel, 2009) appears to require only well-functioning cognitive equipment in appropriate circumstances, not any overt motive or aim to be accomplished. Any strict requirement that knowledge must manifest motivation thus appears too demanding.

While the requirements for non-motivational virtues are less psychologically demanding and can be used to explain simple knowledge, they do not appear to confer sufficient *praise or credit* on their possessor. This presents a host of problems because "credit for success" is central to many proposed solutions to the value problem and is central in responses to cases of epistemic luck (Greco, 2010; Sosa, 2007; Zagzesbki, 1996).[3] As we will see below, any epistemic theory that accepts the direction of analysis (DA) characteristic of virtue epistemology is committed to the claim that certain properties of agents are sources of epistemic value. But not just any property of an agent will suffice here; we need intrinsically praiseworthy properties of agents (like a praiseworthy motive) to do this kind of theoretical work. Well-functioning cognitive equipment is epistemically advantageous, but this is because of the results brought about and is thus more clearly accounted for by (belief-based) consequentialist epistemic norms.[4]

This is a real challenge. It extends to both of the major forms of virtue epistemology because it challenges the viability of any attempt to ground a theory of knowledge on the virtues. Elke Brendel (2009) nicely frames this challenge below. On the side of non-motivational virtues we have this problem:

> Intellectual virtues differ greatly in the conscious, voluntary control we have over them … if a person S has no control over the manifestation of a certain cognitive faculty in a certain situation (or only a very low degree), it seems inappropriate to say we praise S for forming a true belief on the basis of such a cognitive faculty. (ibid. 334)

There is a problem of insufficient credit for reliable success because many true beliefs are formed with little or no conscious, voluntary control. On the side of motivational virtues we have this problem:

---

[3] Pritchard's (2012) anti-luck virtue epistemology denies that virtue reliabilism can adequately handle cases of epistemic luck without commitment to an independent anti-luck condition. A success may be in fact "from ability" but insufficiently safe, as all too easily it would have been false.

[4] Teleological accounts of epistemic standings generated from properly functioning cognitive processes can be found in Graham (2014) and Neta (2014).

For some virtue epistemologists ... intellectual motivation plays a significant role in the formation of a true belief that properly aims at truth ... it seems to me that such a demanding requirement can lead to a counterintuitive and intellectually over-loaded concept of knowledge. Even if it is true that sensory stimuli can be overridden by background information controlled by a "desire for truth," most perceptual beliefs are spontaneously formed without an explicit aid or control of an epistemic motivation. (ibid. 336)

There is a problem of over-intellectualizing knowledge facing responsible success because of the spontaneity and automaticity of perceptual beliefs. If this is indeed the situation, then it appears that no virtue epistemology can be both sufficiently psychologically undemanding and sufficiently credit conferring. We show that the worry raised for motivational virtue epistemology arises only if one is working with an overly intellectualized account of epistemic motivation to begin with. Much of this book is devoted to articulating a non-intellectualized account of epistemic motivation which still does the work necessary for sustaining a theory of agent-level epistemic achievements and abilities whose manifestations are sufficiently creditworthy.

I.5   Virtue Theoretic Epistemic Psychology

With the above tension between motivation and credit in mind, we set out some essential principles of virtue epistemology that provide some common ground between most responsibilists and reliabilists, and which will inform the inquiry to follow. This will be instructive for the reader seeking useful background on virtue epistemology, and it might be a review for readers thoroughly familiar with the field. A defining commitment of any virtue epistemology is that person-level epistemic excellences, i.e., their epistemic virtues, are sources of fundamental epistemic value. The nature and value of other epistemic properties, such as justification, rationality, and understanding, are defined in terms of epistemic virtues (see Battaly, 2008). An epistemic agent is thereby constitutively involved in his or her epistemic success because some fundamental epistemic value necessary for epistemic achievement is generated by the agent's virtues and vices. This normative structure is common to virtue theory in both ethics and epistemology.

To fix ideas, we can follow Blackburn (2001) who says that virtue theorists affirm a right to left reading of (1) and (2) in ethics and epistemology, respectively.

(1) An action is the right action to perform in the circumstances if and only if a virtuous agent would perform it in the circumstances.

(2) A true proposition is known to be true by an agent S in circumstance C if and only if S in C exhibits epistemic virtues in accepting it (ibid. 17).

In both cases, the right to left reading gives what we can call "an agent-based norm." Any epistemic theory that accepts (2) must locate the bearers of epistemic value in properties of an agent because virtues and vices are properties of agents. The lexicon available to describe and explain an agent's epistemic value-bearing properties will thus include states of character, skills, abilities, tendencies, and habits. We say that a theory of epistemic normativity is agent centered to the extent it whole-heartedly endorses a right to left reading of (2).

Kantians or consequentialists will give explanations that are left to right and will say that we have an antecedent (or independent) understanding of a right action in (1), and the equivalence simply "gives us a fix on what is true of a virtuous agent, that is all" (ibid. 16). Something gets on their list of virtues only by satisfying some virtue-independent norms or standards (see Battaly, 2008; Fairweather, 2001). By contrast, a virtue theorist, as Blackburn puts it, "will say that we have a conception of what virtue would have us do, and in the light of that we fashion our concept of the balance of benefit over harm, or a concept of what it is right to do" (2001, 17). This order of explanation will also hold true for epistemic virtues and other epistemic goods, such as justification, knowledge, understanding, and the like in (2).

Any commitment to a virtue theoretic (right to left) order of explanation in epistemology is significant because this makes epistemic psychology central to epistemic normativity. These points are often captured by the claim that virtue theory has the distinctive "direction of analysis" described as follows:

DA: Some epistemically normative properties of beliefs depend on epistemically normative properties of agents; a belief cannot have a certain positive epistemic status unless it is appropriately related to the relevant agent-level properties.

Some version of this principle is appealed to as constitutive of virtue epistemology by Greco (2010), Turri (2011), Zagzebski (1996), and Battaly (2008). We say "some fundamental normative properties" above because truth is epistemically valuable as well, and that does not have to be an agent-centered normative property. So long as an epistemic achievement as a whole has some essential agent-centered features, it will be an agent-centered epistemic achievement. The relevant sense of "depends on" will be a very significant issue as well and will be a focal interest throughout this inquiry (see Chapter 3). A commitment to DA is not yet a commitment to virtue epistemology because "the normative properties of agents" must be cognitive dispositional properties. Narrowing the relevant properties in DA to include only *cognitive dispositional* properties should give us the minimal commitments for a virtue epistemology.

DA*: Some epistemically normative properties of beliefs depend on normative cognitive dispositional properties of agents.

The dispositional properties of epistemic agents are now at the center of epistemic theorizing as sources of epistemic value. This is an original and exciting aspect of virtue epistemology, but it is now particularly important to provide a clear and plausible epistemic psychology of these cognitive dispositional properties. Which disposition types will constitute the epistemic value-generating features of agents (capacities, skills, traits)? How must a belief be related to these features of the agent in order to receive positive epistemic standing from being so related (the "because of" relation)? What is epistemic agency? How are implicit psychological states or processes involved in manifesting epistemic agency?

Let us call a theory that aims to answer these and similar questions a "virtue theoretic epistemic psychology" (VTEP).[5] The cognitive dispositions examined throughout this work are all available material for the construction of a VTEP. We utilize these in defending an account of an agent's *cognitive constitution* that will serve the needs of virtue reliabilists. On our account, an entailment of premise 2 and DA* is that some of the total epistemic value of an epistemic achievement (such as knowledge) is grounded in the value of an agent's cognitive constitution. How much and what kind of epistemic value will depend on the details of a given VTEP. We provide a detailed account of the forms of epistemic achievement and epistemic value engendered by the attentional turn defended here in each of the chapters to follow.

An important distinction for our purposes is between what we call merely agent-based and fully *agency*-based VTEP. Agent-based views are psychologically weaker than agency-based views; all of the latter will be instances of the former but not the other way around. The essential question for virtue epistemology for our purposes is how we should read the dispositional properties of agents in DA* and 2 above. In particular, should an epistemic theory demand that these cognitive dispositions involve agency or motivation? A commitment to DA* and 2 alone is compatible with a yes or no answer. Answering this question, which we can see is at the heart of DA*, gets us right back to the tension noted above between agency, automaticity, and credit.

We will defend a theory of epistemic motivation that explains how cases of simple knowledge are sufficiently creditable to an agent because of the role played by epistemic motivation as defined here. It is undeniable that many of our cognitive capacities function reliably without introspection or conscious effort.[6] With this in mind, considering the principle for right action in

---

[5] Perhaps the best approximation to a complete epistemic virtue psychology in virtue epistemology is Sosa (2015).

[6] Evidence in psychology shows that human intentional action may occur automatically and implicitly (Hommel, 2010). A substantial body of evidence shows that introspection is unreliable (see Kornblith, 2010, for review). Finally, evidence shows that motor control for action is highly reliable and unconscious (Rosenbaum, 2002). Collectively, the psychological evidence strongly

Blackburn's 1 above, it is certainly plausible to worry that the combination of a right to left direction of explanation and allowing purely automatic (wholly non-agential) epistemic virtues will result in a deficient theory of epistemic normativity, specifically in being able to credit the agent for their success as noted by Brendel. In such a case, we do not have enough (or not good enough) value to bring across in our (so-called) virtues to sufficiently explain the goodness of any actions they bring about. How can knowledge be explained in terms of processes that completely bypass agency? Put in terms of DA*, one worry is that the automaticity of reliable cognitive dispositions entails that there will be insufficient normative properties in play to properly account for the greater epistemic value of knowledge over merely true belief.

The agency-based reading we favor requires that any virtue constituting disposition in DA* must include some agential element. Achieving epistemic goods such as knowledge, justification, understanding, or wisdom will thus require manifesting epistemic agency. This is a strong claim, and we will be at great pains to defend it throughout in our accounts of epistemic attention in Chapter 1, internal normativity in Chapter 3 and the nature of epistemic agency in Chapter 4. Throughout, the essential role of epistemic motivation comes in in integrating cognitive abilities. The exact content of epistemic motivation will directly concern us in Chapters 2 and 5. So long as an adequate theory of epistemic agency is available, any epistemologist that commits to premise 2 and DA* will receive a considerable theoretical yield in their VTEP by accommodating it. Motivational states have multiple psychological functions and provide a particularly attractive way to explain how epistemic value is generated and transferred under DA*. The right account of epistemic motivation should be a very useful theoretical tool for the "success from ability" genus that most virtue reliabilists endorse, but it has been responsibilists that have used motivations in a serious way.[7]

A commitment to agency-based VTEP also means that epistemic achievements take *world to mind* success conditions.[8] The traditional objects of

suggests that a minimal kind of agency that does not rely on reflection or explicit intentions must play a central role in epistemology. For the importance of such minimal notion of agency, see, for instance, Bach (1984) and Montemayor (2014). A major goal of this book is to provide a thorough account of epistemic agency that satisfies not only the requirement of being compatible with – and actually supported by – the empirical evidence, but also with the normative constraints of epistemic virtue.

[7] Sosa and Greco are virtue reliabilists with important things to say on motivations, subjective justification, and agency. We will discuss their views in detail.

[8] The distinction between these two "directions of fit" was first developed in detail by Searle (*Speech Acts*), but the distinction owes to Anscombe. Briefly, a psychological state type has mind to world direction of fit if it succeeds only when a state of the mind comes to represent the way the world is (as with beliefs). A psychological state type has world to mind direction of fit if it succeeds only when a state of the world comes to fit the way the mind represents it as being (as with desires).

evaluation in epistemology are beliefs, and these are typically defined as having mind to world success conditions. Beliefs succeed when the mind comes to fit the way the world is, but motives and intentions succeed when the world comes to fit the way the mind represents it as being. This would be an interesting shift in the structure of epistemic normativity, but what exactly is engendered herein? This is an important issue that deserves further attention in its own right than we can provide here, and we will not give any sustained examination in its own right. However, we arguably exhibit this shift in the account defended between Chapters 1–4, as most of the philosophers that shape our views in these chapters clearly have something like this in mind. We assimilate world to mind success conditions for agential epistemic norms through a modification of F. P. Ramsey's "success semantics," in 3.4 and further in Chapter 5 focusing on the kind of successes that underwrite reliably successful assertion and communication.

I.6   The Attention-Assertion Model

The epistemic psychology we begin to defend in Chapter 1 is grounded in the psychology of attention. Research in the cognitive sciences shows that attention is one of the most fundamental features of cognition (see Hommel, 2010). Michael Graziano (2013) argues that attention is the key to how the brain models and schematizes information for action and cognition, including consciousness itself, which is conceived by Graziano as an "attention schema." Attention is certainly fundamental for the integration of information that allows for action and cognition. No plausible epistemic theory can overlook this deep fact of our psychology. Importantly, incorporating the nature of attention into a VTEP has deep epistemic repercussions because it is also widely agreed that attention exhibits a form of cognitive agency. Understanding the nature of attention that modulates and guides assertion should be very useful for contemporary philosophical work in the theory of knowledge (as well as philosophy of mind and language).

We can now be very specific on this point: *facts about attention define the sources of epistemic value recognized in DA* above.* Recent cognitive science gives us the important datum that attention is paradigmatically modulated for communication and action. These facts bear directly on important issues concerning epistemic normativity at the very center of virtue epistemology, and the theory of knowledge more broadly. The nature and structure of epistemic value, for example, whether it is agential, is determined by the facts about how attention modulates and guides cognition. This gives a VTEP a targeted role for an empirical element that is very useful for reliabilist virtue epistemology. We will also extend this work on the nature of attention to account for "agential cognitive constitutions" (ACC). This will be a set of integrated dispositions whose manifestations are agential and cognitive – belief states that are explained by the agency of the subject. Norms for evaluating these manifestations will come from philosophical and scientific work on assertion and communication. The manifestation of an ACC (given in terms of attention) is an epistemic success if an assertoric norm is satisfied by that manifestation. The attention-assertion model (AAM) will thus unify the psychology of epistemic achievement with a normative theory of assertion. Empirical and philosophical work on the nature of attention will be doing much of the work all the way through, as will become clear in Chapter 1.1.

I.7   Methodology in Epistemology

We do not engage with as many thought-experiments and "cases" as do many epistemologists. The type of epistemic theory we seek here does not primarily aim to "get things right" in the way that many epistemic theories in the current literature do. This is not to abjure the importance of this methodology in epistemology, nor to eschew any accountability to the challenges it presents, but we opt instead to share this theoretical space with investigation into psychologically relevant perspectives on epistemic psychology. We will clarify the broader methodology that motivates the current inquiry below.

There are at least two plausible epistemic methodologies that pass on giving a central place to the analysis/counterexample/thought experiment/intuition methodology seen in much contemporary epistemology. Both epistemic naturalism and the knowledge-first approach defended by Williamson (2000) deny that "handling cases" such as barn facades, cleverly painted mules, gusts of wind, implanted thermometers, stopped clocks, and the like have any central place in epistemic theorizing. At a minimum, no naturalistic approach to knowledge will leave questions about the best supported account of cognition hostage to these kinds of thought experiments, and empirical results must be given authority to drive some elements of epistemic theory in any robustly naturalistic epistemology, irrespective of the results of thought experiments. The knowledge-first approach overtly rejects the analysis/counterexample methodology in epistemology as well. For this approach, it is no surprise that proposed analyses of knowledge seem to invite more and more counterexamples because knowledge cannot be analyzed or decomposed into elements, such as belief plus safety and justification, as assumed by the analysis/counterexample methodology. It is the other way around. It is because we know things in the first place that we can get a grip on the notions of belief and justification.

This book can be read as defending a form of *naturalized virtue epistemology* (NVE) because of the central role given to empirical theories of attention and communication, but this naturalistic commitment comes in a very limited and targeted form explained below. A properly focused and restricted naturalism will provide invaluable benefits to virtue reliabilist accounts of knowledge. Perhaps surprisingly, this will improve our understanding of the normative dimensions of epistemic virtue. We now canvass a few broad issues involved in pursuing an NVE and will describe the main commitments of the very specific form that we defend in this book.

We do not intend to explain the full complexities of naturalism in general, and we do not rest the account of epistemic agency defended here solely on the ultimate fate of any specific tenet of naturalized epistemology *per se* (much is already in place with any commitment to premise 2 and DA* above). In the most general sense, naturalism is a commitment to explaining and understanding the world without invoking any super natural entities or powers. Put another way, it is a commitment to the principle that the world is roughly the way it is described as being according to the best available natural sciences (including at least physics, chemistry, and biology). The essential move here is a simple and important form of what we can call *naturalistic deference* as the authority to set the canons of truth (in some domains) is given to the natural sciences. As the sciences themselves revise the canons of truth, the commitments engendered by naturalistic deference will be revised accordingly. This is an uncontroversial and very general characterization of naturalism, and it is not our interest to pursue the general issue of naturalism any further here.

Naturalism in any particular domain of inquiry simply limits epistemic deference to a specific subject matter: consciousness, ethics, free will, or in our case, epistemology. Epistemology naturalized thus defers to the relevant sciences to illuminate issues of knowledge. This is perhaps where the obvious and uncontroversial commitments of naturalized epistemology end and many distinct paths emerge. Which sciences and for what reasons? This is a question about the motivation for, and content provided by, naturalistic deference. What role is left for autonomous epistemic theorizing given naturalistic deference? This is a question about the *depth* of deference. Which aspects of knowledge are particularly suited for naturalistic analysis and which are not? This is a question of the *scope* of deference. Scope is where our NVE will make very specific commitments and we aim for a deep commitment in that particular area, namely the psychology of attention and communication. We can see the limits of our approach by contrasting it with Quine's understanding of epistemology naturalized.

The most familiar figure in naturalized epistemology is W. v O. Quine, due to the influence of his famous essay "Epistemology Naturalized" (1969). Quine clearly endorses the naturalistic deference noted above and argues that empirical psychology is the relevant area of science to which we defer in epistemology. With respect to scope, Quine appears to advocate that all issues in epistemology are deferred to some area or other of psychology. This would be maximal deferential scope for epistemology. Regarding the depth of deference, Quine is often read as advocating "replacement naturalism" which eradicates all normativity from epistemology because empirical, and presumably non-normative results in psychology take their place in what remains of epistemic theory. Empirical psychology does not just constrain or inform traditional epistemic theory here but would replace and entirely constitute what was hitherto epistemology. While a full understanding of a Quinian naturalized epistemology will include considerable nuance to sharpen the blade here, Quine is often read in ways that support a maximal depth and scope in naturalistic deference. Needless to say, this is seen as a very controversial position.

Whatever the correct interpretation of Quine, there are more modest ways of pursuing naturalized virtue epistemology. One can accept a less restrictive relation between a philosophical theory and the science to which it defers, sometimes called "cooperative naturalism," and one might seek to naturalize some aspects of epistemic theory without committing to full Quinian scope for all aspects. This would limit the scope and depth of naturalistic deference and allow one to avoid extreme forms of naturalism.

To some extent, we will follow Quine and advocate a robust deference to psychology, but this will be very limited in scope. In fact, the scope is very specific and we are already in a place to see it: we need a proper psychological characterization of the subject referred to in DA*, the possessor of epistemic virtues. While the contribution from the psychology of attention and communication will be robust, depth of deference here will also be limited because we advocate a form of virtue epistemology, and the fundamental commitments of this perspective must be preserved in any naturalized version of it. For example, the normative structures for defining epistemic standings and sources of value given in DA* above must remain in place. The target phenomenon for naturalistic deference for our purposes is *cognitive agency*. Utilizing recent work in psychology, we explain cognitive agency in terms of the forms of agency manifest in attention. Facts about attention are the facts about cognitive agency, and we go on to develop an empirically grounded account of *epistemic agency* from these resources. While quite limited in scope, this deference to the psychology of attention will turn out to be incredibly fruitful.

The details of human psychology will be very important to get right for any epistemic theory that endorses DA* or its ilk. Virtue epistemologists thus have good reason to develop an empirically adequate epistemic psychology. Many philosophical accounts of doxastic agency focus on the issue of whether beliefs are chosen in the way that actions are, or whether one can simply form a belief by willing to do so, as one can raise one's arm by willing to raise it. These debates are not without merit, but they are fundamentally different when driven by empirical deference to work on attention.

As noted above, we look to a clear and very specific place for empirical illumination – attention. What is particularly important for our purposes is that attention, as understood in psychology, is typically an agential and goal-directed process or state. Attention paradigmatically involves purpose-driven selection and guidance that engages tacit processes in ways that will be very helpful for epistemic theorizing about epistemic agency.

Deference to research on attention demands that assertion, communication, and action will be salient in explanations of epistemic virtue, specifically in characterizing the intentional content of states of epistemic agency and the forms of epistemic success they support. The science of attention clearly shows that *attentional states are modulated for communication, and action*. This is not strict necessity for any form of attention, as there are attentional states that wander or are undirected, but the most important form of attention in human cognition is selectively aimed at assertion, communication, and action. We argue that these paradigmatic aims of attention (communication and action) should shape or constitute theorizing about epistemic agency.

We believe that our account is also well suited to meet the cases and thought experiments that populate the contemporary literature, even though that is not our primary methodology and we will spend little time on this here. As a nod in this direction, we conclude this introduction by discussing a well-known thought experiment, namely *Truetemp*. One aim in discussing Truetemp is simply to highlight the importance of epistemic agency in the current literature in epistemology. Another aim is to exhibit how the view defended here is equipped to respond to the now diverse set of thought experiments and cases epistemic theories are expected to survive these days. There are multiple versions of Truetemp in the literature. Here is the original version from Keith Lehrer's (1990):

Mr. Truetemp, undergoes brain surgery by an experimental surgeon who invents a small device which is both a very accurate thermometer and a computational device capable of generating thoughts. The device, call it a tempucomp, is implanted in Truetemp's head so that the very tip of the device, no larger than the head of a pin, sits unnoticed on his scalp and acts as a sensor to transmit information about the temperature to the computational system of his brain. This device, in turn, sends a message to his brain causing him to think of the temperature recorded by the external sensor. Assume that the tempucomp is very reliable, and so his thoughts are correct temperature thoughts. All told, this is a reliable belief-forming process. Now imagine, finally, that he has no idea that the tempucomp has been inserted in his brain, is only slightly puzzled about why he thinks so obsessively about the temperature, but never checks a thermometer to determine whether these thoughts about the temperature are correct. He accepts them unreflectively, another effect of the tempucomp. Thus, he thinks and accepts that the temperature is 104 degrees. It is. Does he know that it is? (ibid, 163)

In this fanciful case, Temp has a device implanted in his head which feeds him true beliefs about the temperature of the room (Lehrer, 1990). Beliefs about the ambient temperature of the room are just "popping into his head" but this turns out to be a very reliable process for forming beliefs about the temperature because of the unknowing presence of the tempucomp. Initially, this was raised as an objection to simple process reliabilism because Temp is, *ex hypothesi*, reliable in his beliefs and reports about the temperature but intuitively does not know the temperature of the room.

Why doesn't Temp know here? Understanding the answer to this question is the valuable and difficult aspect of the thought experiment. One thing that is clear is that Truetemp's success in Lehrer's case is not sufficiently due to his cognitive abilities in a way that is creditable to him, despite his reliability. We would say that Temp's success in true belief does not exhibit the cognitive integration necessary for epistemic agency, and that he does not know for this reason.

Compare Temp's formation of beliefs about temperature with typical cases where one consults a thermometer, and, importantly, *one has a desire to know the temperature*. In the original Truetemp case, this motivation is not present. Lehrer says that Temp is "puzzled about why he thinks so obsessively about the temperature, but never checks a thermometer to determine whether these thoughts about the temperature are correct" (ibid.). This is important for us because motivations are not playing the cognitive role in Temp's cognition that they typically play in human knowledge. As we discuss in the next chapter, motivated attention is what creates the cognitive integration necessary for epistemic agency. If we grant this much, we can see that Temp is clearly defective in terms of agency, and this is clearly part of what our intuitions are responding to when we agree that he does not know. Truetemp lacks knowledge because his true beliefs are not cognitively integrated in the ways defended at length throughout this work.

Duncan Pritchard (2012) offers a slightly different version of Temp in order to show the limits of two master intuitions that jointly guide virtue-theoretic assessments of knowledge, an anti-luck intuition to address Gettier cases and what he calls the "ability" intuition, that knowledge is a form of success from ability. In his version of the case, Temp actually consults a thermometer in the room which he has no reason to judge as unreliable and thus has a motivation to know the room's temperature. The key difference is that the thermometer is broken, fluctuating slightly between correct and incorrect readings, and here is also a hidden agent that changes the temperature in the room through a thermostat to match the unreliable reading of the thermometer every time Temp forms a belief about the temperature by consulting it. All of Temp's beliefs about the temperature of the room are thus guaranteed to be right because of the epistemically benevolent agent in the room, but Pritchard argues that Temp's true beliefs do not qualify as knowledge.

The underlying point demonstrated by this example is that no modal principle of the sort required to eliminate knowledge-undermining luck will be able to specify the kind of direction of fit that is required for a belief to satisfy the ability intuition. That is, in satisfying the relevant modal principle one ensures, across a suitable range of possible cases, that there is the right kind of correspondence between belief and fact; but what one does not ensure thereby is that a certain relationship between belief and fact obtains, one that cases like Temp indicate is essential to the manifestation of cognitive success which is the product of cognitive ability. Pritchard notes that a stable modal correspondence between belief and fact (mind to world success conditions) is not enough to ensure that the two are connected in the way required for knowledge (world to mind success conditions). We see the source of the problem in the absence of a clear motivational element in the standard understanding of the ability condition. Without this, Temp's performances may be reliable in many contexts yet fail to integrate motives, skills and beliefs in the way that agency brings about. For Temp to count as a knower on our account, his epistemic success must be explained by his epistemic agency. Temp wants to know the temperature, in Pritchard's example, but his motivation manifests successfully because of someone else's abilities, and thus manifests not because of his abilities, properly integrated, but because of the benevolent agent's abilities. Using the language of the metaphysics of dispositions, the manifestation of ability is not authentic because it is the result of a fink, and as we argue in Chapter 1.2, finks are incompatible with epistemic credit.

We now argue that we can provide a psychologically grounded safety condition for knowledge that does the work of Pritchard's modal account. This will be significant if successful because Pritchard claims that virtue epistemology alone (through an ability condition) cannot adequately handle luck, so he defends an independent safety condition in modal rather than psychological terms.

Modal safety conditions seek to delimit a set of nearby and faraway possible worlds that will support an account of "ability-relevant" successes and failures without appeal to any further ground. Here is Pritchard's account:

SF*: S's belief is safe if and only if in most nearby possible worlds in which S continues to form her belief about the target proposition in the same way as in the actual world, and in all very close nearby possible worlds in which S continues to form her belief about the target proposition in the same way as in the actual world, the belief continues to be true.

From this, we can adduce the additional claims that (1) a faraway success is a good-luck success, (2) a faraway failure is a bad-luck failure, (3) a nearby success is a success from ability, and (4) a nearby failure is either a failure despite ability (due to a mask or malfunction) or an indication of a lack of ability. Neither 1 nor 2 supports person-level epistemic appraisals because luck is the dominant factor, but 3 and 4 do support person-level epistemic appraisals, both positive and negative.

Only the nearby success (3) generates positive epistemic status beyond true belief (which 1 has as well). One condition of adequacy for modal safety principles is whether they properly support intuitively clear knowledge ascriptions. We claim that any psychologically grounded and equally adequate way of distinguishing lucky from non-lucky success is, *ceteris paribus*, preferable to a (ungrounded) modal account. One reason such an account would be preferable is that it provides us with a psychologically realistic explanation of why epistemic success is non-lucky. This gives a psychologically grounded account of safety greater explanatory power than a merely modal account. Another reason is that a psychologically grounded account is more elegant and parsimonious than an account which, as Pritchard claims, must seek an "independent anti-luck condition." An independent anti-luck condition is independent of anything contained in or entailed by an ability condition (that success must be due to ability). Motivations are components of epistemic abilities on our account, and the theoretical gain they bring can thereby be claimed for an ability condition. This is particularly important because Pritchard argues that virtue epistemology alone cannot provide an adequate theory of knowledge without an independent safety condition. If abilities include motivations, and motivations provide an adequate grounding for safety, then no independent condition is necessary. Robust virtue epistemology (with motivations) is viable.

To provide the needed psychological grounding, we utilize a modification of F. P. Ramsey's "success semantics," developed at length in Section 3.4. For now, let's understand this as follows: a belief (p) has positive epistemic status if, in conjunction with some desire (d), acting on p and d would reliably satisfy d. That is, a belief is successful when acting on that belief would reliably satisfy a relevant desire. We will have much more to say about this in form of success, but we can easily define sets of possible worlds to distinguish lucky from non-lucky success with just this much. Let's say that an environment in a possible world is ability-relevant if an ability-appropriate motivation would reliably succeed in that environment and world. An epistemically virtuous agent must reliably form successful ability-relevant motivations in these environments, and this demand on the agent will need to be spelled out carefully. A virtuous agent will manifest two achievements here: the reliability and efficacy of their motive in relevant environments and the formation of the relevant motivation itself. Together, this means *an epistemically virtuous agent will reliably form a reliable epistemic motivation.*

The above account is psychologically grounded because the set of ability-relevant environments and worlds is defined in terms of the success conditions for epistemic motivations. Filling out the account of safety suggested by the above considerations will ground theorizing about luck in the very psychological facts that are also constituents of abilities. These psychological facts will then presumably obtain in any state of affairs that satisfies the ability condition. If this can be done, this will show that Pritchard's argument against robust virtue epistemology fails because a sufficient safety condition is met in the satisfaction of the ability condition as understood here. Pritchard might retort that the argument strategy used here only works if the psychologically grounded account can actually retain all the benefits brought by the best modal account. If it does not, any advance in explanatory power and simplicity would have to be weighed against any theoretic losses elsewhere. However, suppose even the best psychologically grounded account does not capture all the theoretical advantages of Pritchard's modal account. We argue that this is actually a loss for Pritchard's account because it entails that his theory of safety and luck avoidance cannot be reconciled with the best available psychological explanation. If his luck-avoiding principles cannot be realized in actual human subjects, then it is psychologically implausible (and violates ought implies can desiderata). These cases would have to be seen as failures that are not relevant to ability attributions to human subjects as we know them. If his luck-avoiding principles *can* be psychologically realized, then this way of accounting for them has the additional theoretical advantages noted above compared to Pritchard's account and is thereby preferable to the modal account itself.

The consideration of Truetemp, as with many "cases" in epistemology, requires us to examine questions in epistemic psychology. There is no guarantee that the attentional turn here will fully answer cases like Truetemp, but it should bring useful perspectives to bear on debates that have not been motivated on this aspect of epistemic psychology.

We conclude this introduction by highlighting the central concept under discussion in this work: attention. Imogen Dickie (2011) argues that appropriate forms of attention ground demonstrative reference and satisfy anti-luck conditions in philosophy of language. Demonstrative reference is a luck-eliminating cognitive achievement on her account because of the kind of attention involved. Dickie uses these elements of attention for semantic purposes (although she has a very "epistemic" semantics), while our aims are more narrowly in virtue epistemology and epistemic agency. We have a good bit of respect for her account and a good bit of common ground that we will explore in later chapters. We finish this chapter by considering how our understanding of agency, attention, and luck can be illuminated by taking a page from her work in philosophy of language to point the way toward a more complete response to Pritchard in the debate above and to presage the examination of agency in attention in the next chapter.

Imogen Dickie (2011, 2015) argues that perceptual demonstrative reference is a luck-eliminating success. Dickie says that luck elimination for truth-apt states like believing "that is F" requires eliminating all "non-Fx" possibilities. Much of this is accomplished very quickly by attentional anchoring because so many possibilities become irrelevant in light of the cognitive commitment registered in anchoring. An essential skill is therefore anchoring in ways that make the unnecessary things irrelevant. This is an essential epistemic virtue examined in further detail in Sections 2.7 and 6.4.

Conjoining Dickie's point above with principles we have committed to thus far, we now have the following three claims on the table going forward:

1. Knowledge requires epistemic virtue (virtue epistemology)
2. Epistemic virtue requires epistemic agency (our main thesis)
3. Epistemic agency is a luck elimination process (combining Dickie's about reference with the psychology of attention).

From 1, 2, and 3, it follows that

4. Epistemic virtue is luck eliminating

and of course that

5. Knowledge is luck eliminating.

The fact that our account of epistemic virtue entails 5 is, of course, good news. 4 is important because it gives us a clear source of agent-based credit for success. A non-lucky success will be due to the luck-eliminating powers of epistemic virtues on our account, and these will be epistemic motivations and expressions of epistemic agency generally. Thus, we credit an agent for not only getting the truth but also for getting the truth through an agential luck elimination process. *Epistemic motivations do more than express an agent's epistemic values (what they epistemically care about); they secure success by eliminating luck.* An agent's epistemic reliability is therefore partly due to their own luck-eliminating abilities. This is a creditworthy kind of reliability, and we hope to provide the epistemic psychology to support and explain it here.

1   Epistemic Virtue, Reliable Attention, and Cognitive Constitution

In this chapter we defend a fundamental turn to attention in epistemic psychology, examining recent work in the philosophy and psychology of attention, and then responding to empirical and normative challenges. Relevant work by Wayne Wu, Imogen Dickie, Mark Alfano, and Selim Berker is discussed. We defend an initial account of an attention-based epistemic psychology that manifests fundamental forms of cognitive agency.

1.1   The Argument from Attention

This section sets out the basic commitments of an epistemic psychology grounded in the psychology of attention rather than propositional attitudes. We argue that attention is essential to knowledge and that attention is essentially agential, defending a shift in epistemic psychology from propositional attitudes to modes of attention as the basic unit of epistemic evaluation.

We argue that any adequate virtue theoretic epistemic psychology (VTEP) must be agential. Simply put, knowledge requires attention, attention is a form of agency, and thus knowledge requires agency.

1. If S knows that p, then S has actively attended to p, or p was available to S for active attention. (Achieving knowledge requires attention to a content.)
2. Attention is selection for cognition and action.
3. Selection constitutes or requires agency.
4. Therefore knowledge requires agency.

(1) is intended as a platitude, similar to the truism that knowledge that p requires belief that p, captured now with the psychology of attention rather than propositional attitudes. This shift to attention as the primary object of analysis is perhaps the most important commitment of the current inquiry, as we will examine the implications of shifting to an attentional epistemic psychology throughout the next four chapters. It will be important for our account to show that (1) holds even when a good bit of cognitive processing is tacit, or non-attended to, and that this is compatible with a state or process being person level and praiseworthy.

Let's examine two types of counterarguments to (1). (2) states that the relevant sense of "attending to" in 1 is a kind of selection. 1 thus requires some sort of selection to occur for knowledge. A counterexample would then be a case where something is known, but nothing has been selected. Given 2, this would be a case of knowledge without attention, and 1 would be false. Imogen Dickie (2011, 298) gives the example of "unattended peripheral vision," which represents certain features of a person's visual field sufficient for recall and action but where there is a deliberate move to *ignore* that part of one's visual field (to *not* select it). There are also cases where the objects of attention are "forced upon us" and seemingly not chosen or selected. If there is attention without selection in these basic kinds of cases, and these forms of attention can produce knowledge, the connection between knowledge and agency is lost. We will address cases of (apparently) nonselected states of knowledge in detail in this chapter, and most directly in Chapter 4, on epistemic agency. A proper understanding of attentional processes will show that many are largely automatic, but essentially involve agent-level selection and mental agency nonetheless.

A more pervasive problem, examined throughout this inquiry, is selection with no awareness involved. If there is no awareness in selection, selection would appear to be non-agential, so even if attention is always involved in knowledge, this would not ensure that knowledge is agential. Dickie (2011, 299) again provides relevant examples. Blindsighters lack conscious awareness in all or most of their visual field, but can nonetheless reliably identify certain properties of objects in their blind field, and can successfully (physically) grasp them. This appears to be a case of *selective* and reliable processing of information, and plausibly a way of coming to know things, but one which does not require conscious awareness of them. A relevant, but less extreme, case is brief perceptual contact where there is no overt awareness of an object, but where "the mind nevertheless registers this information with the structured characteristics of selective processing (for example, binding features as features of a single thing)" (ibid.). This is often accessible information and is easily explained by priming effects.

Both objections focus on the role of conscious awareness, in the first case claiming that it is not sufficient for selection and in the second case that it is not necessary for selection. It will take some doing, but we will provide a clear account of how and when conscious awareness must be involved in the attentional processes necessary for knowledge in Chapter 4. We argue that epistemic agency allows for a good bit of tacit processing, and that both types of cases above are clearly accommodated. The interested reader can find the criterion for when a manifestation of epistemic agency must involve conscious awareness in Chapter 4, in the section Resolving the Tension, the account leading to and supporting the criterion is developed throughout Chapters 1 to 4. We now examine the view that attention is selection for action in greater detail.

Premise 2 says that attention is a form of selection, and premise 3 adds that selection makes attention agential. We are here relying on a specific understanding of attention, but it is very well supported empirically.[1] A number of philosophers following recent developments in cognitive science see attention as the central psychological phenomenon, and that attention is some form of selection of a target to promote the completion of an aim, task, goal, action, utterance, or the like. To attend to something is to select it (and some features of it) from among a field of candidate targets for some purpose, task, or aim.

Attentional states are nearly always characterized as *integrated states*: "attention is the mechanism that broadcasts information into the global workspace ... the global organization of specific mechanisms in the service of action, reasoning and verbal report" (Smithies, 2011, 253). Chris Mole (2011) describes attention as "cognitive unison," integrated neural mechanisms serving the same cognitive task. Desimone and Duncan (as cited by Smithies, 2011, 253) describe attention as "an emergent property of many neural mechanisms working to resolve competition for visual processing and control of behavior." Psychologists often describe attentional states as "whole organism states," as opposed to sub-personal cognitive processes or modules that might be *constituents* of person-level states (Allport, 2011). It is, after all, the person that pays attention or attends to something, not their eyes, ears, or cognitive modules.

The claim that attention involves selection for action is one of the best established principles in psychology, though there are competing accounts of the details. What we need to understand and explain here is how this feature of attention is related to epistemic agency. Wayne Wu (2011) nicely articulates the basic connection between attention and agency. He first notes that awareness is not the same as attention. To show this, he introduces a hypothetical species of creature that has the ability to consciously represent a number of objects but does not have the capacity to attend to any one of them.

Imagine a creature that is capable of awareness of a manifold of objects but which lacks attention. That is to say, the creature can be simultaneously aware of objects in what we can call its sensory manifold but given that it lacks a capacity for attunement, each object is equally salient to the creature. (Wu, 2011, 107)

Such creatures lack the capacity to fix upon any one of the items represented in their visual field. In this case, there is conscious representation, but no capacity

---

[1] For example, consider feature-based attention: the central role of feature-based attention is the ability to highlight certain features for selection, as in the "visual search" task (Wolfe, 1994). This kind of attention can be modulated toward features in the visual scene to increase the likelihood that they will be selected for further processing (e.g., Bacon and Egeth, 1997). This is the basis of cuing and priming effects, which are more efficient at facilitating selection than top-down processes, as when one is looking for a feature (see Theeuwes, 2013). If one looks at the literature on other forms of attention, one quickly realizes that selection is the most distinctive feature of attention.

for attentional anchoring (what Wu and others call "attunement"). Human beings clearly possess the capacity that these creatures lack, and we exercise it constantly to guide cognition and action. We argue that the ability to anchor and guide attention is a capacity for mental agency. In addition to the active movement of the mind, which selects a target, any act of attending is paradigmatically modulated for some task or goal of some kind. While attentional states are typically goal directed, the goal state will not always be consciously represented, in particular not in skillful and virtuous activity. We attend to what we do because so attending will provide an answer to a question, solve a problem, or provide some other epistemic good.

The goal (or task) directed nature of attention is described by Wu (2011) as the process of solving "many-many problems."[2] For Wu, at any given moment, an agent exists in some "behavior space" or other: "A behavior space identifies the behavioral possibilities for a particular subject at a time and is constituted by multiple potential input-output linkages" (ibid. 100). To act is to select a task-appropriate path through this space of possibilities, where some specific input selection guides intermediate activities toward an output selection. The "problem" is to narrow the many available paths through a behavior space to one. In his example, a person has the intention to kick a ball, and there is a football and a basketball in the person's field of view. Her behavior space has four possible paths, and she must select one in order to act. She can kick the football with the right leg, kick the basketball with the right leg, kick the football with the left leg, or kick the basketball with the left leg. Selecting one of these links between input options (basketball or football) and output options (kick with left leg or kick with right leg) is necessary in order to act at all. The bodily action of kicking the ball requires solving this many-many problem. Importantly, and this is a point we will discuss much further, Wu says "there is no requirement that the states at issue be conscious. This allows for the possibility of unconscious action" (ibid.).

The many-many problem above is analogous to the kind of problems that attentional states must solve throughout our waking life. As William James puts it, the mind must continuously solve the persisting problem of "what to think next." Initiating, guiding, and completing mental or bodily action requires anchoring attention in a certain part of a represented field at many stages, as well as integrating anchors with guidance mechanisms that aim at task completion. This is a form of mental agency (anchoring) that the imagined species above does not possess. But agency is not just selecting an anchor; it is temporally extended throughout the attentional process, the guidance processes triggered by anchoring, and the output selection for task completion.

---

[2] While he does not apply this to epistemology, this is a promising way to think about knowledge (and epistemic achievements generally) – knowledge is a true belief formed by a properly guiding solution to a many-many problem.

We argue that this form of mental agency (anchoring and guidance by solving many-many problems) is necessary for knowledge because attention is necessary for knowledge. Achieving states of knowledge requires anchoring, and subsequent integrated guidance and output selection, and thus manifest agency.

Attentional processes can be understood and evaluated in terms of what Ernest Sosa (2011, 2015) calls "performance normativity." Just as a belief can be evaluated according to how well or poorly it meets the aim of truth (is it accurate and adroit with respect to its aim?), an attentional process can be evaluated according to how well or poorly it achieves the particular goal or task it is directed toward. To this extent, Sosa's normative structure is consonant with empirical understandings of attention, but there are important differences that will emerge. The aim grounding evaluation for belief, as Sosa understands it, is truth, but truth is here a principle that organizes an objective critical domain (in this case, the epistemic evaluation of belief). On our account, the aim according to which an agent's attentional states are evaluated is internal to the psychological state itself, as an agent's goals determine what they attend to, and this in turn determines the guidance and output selection processes that follow. The structure of attentional states provides a basis for their rational evaluation, as with the structure of action. Attention thus provides us with a basis for internal normativity, a point we develop at length in Chapter 2.

We closely examine Sosa's recent account of epistemic agency, as developed in his rich book *Judgment & Agency* (2015), in Chapter 4 and argue that his account is ultimately not compatible with the best relevant psychological work at critical junctures. To anticipate, the heart of the issue is how to understand cognitive integration. What is it for a mental state or process to be cognitively integrated with another? Sosa's account of judgment requires second-order affirmations for the full achievement of knowledge. Being about another mental state is one way for mental states to be integrated with others. However, this is not how most successful cognition typically works, especially in common and basic epistemic achievements. Epistemic agency requires integration, but integration does not require second-order reflection. We will explain what it does require in Chapter 4.

The agential elements of attention, though subtle, can be seen in even the most basic belief formation involving perception and memory. Say we are looking for our keys in the house, and in the process we form various beliefs about where the keys are and are not, or how likely they are to be in various places, as we move about the house. Simply representing a region of the environment will not be sufficient for forming a belief here. (Otherwise we are like the aforementioned species that represents but does not attend.) We need to attend to some specific region with the aim of determining whether a specific item is in that region. Anchoring attention in this task-specific way triggers guidance mechanisms that lead to the formation (or suspension) of a belief about the location of our keys (they are here, they are not here, they are likely to be somewhere near or far) in a relatively automatic fashion. Even simple perceptual beliefs of this kind require the agentive act of attending to regions, features of regions, and the selection of targets, which then recruits appropriate information and guidance mechanisms.[3]

In another case, you might want to predict what beer a colleague will order at a pub where you have plans to meet. Searching memory, you recall that every time you have seen them at a public house they have a Guinness in hand, and you thus predict they will have a Guinness with you as well. Here, we have to not only search for drinking-relevant memories but also focus on the type of beer, rather than the type of glass or clothing involved in previous events, how intoxicated your colleague got, who else had been invited, or the purpose of the meeting. Doing this successfully requires not only attending to certain memories and excluding many others but also searching for the specific *features of these contents* that are relevant to the cognitive task at hand. While this is often described in terms of salience, locating a salient content is not just shining the bright light of interest and concern on something; it also, and indeed more fundamentally, requires preserving a far-reaching blindness to what is not salient. (We discuss this in detail in Chapter 2.) Agency thus requires blindness, precisely because it requires attention, and this will help us understand why agency requires automaticity. We explore an epistemic virtue, which we call "virtuous insensitivity" and which reliably produces task-appropriate attentional blindness, in Chapters 2, 3, and 6.

We will have a lot more to say about attention and agency throughout this book, but this is an initial defense of premises 2 and 3. If these preliminary considerations are correct, then the conclusion of the argument above that

4. Knowledge requires agency, is easily obtained. We can add now a further claim:

5. Any virtue epistemology adequate to explain the achievement of knowledge must substantively appeal to *agential* virtues (i.e., must have an agency-based VTEP).

Any virtue theory for knowledge that accepts 2 and direction of analysis (DA*) above will have to accept 5. This is shown by the agential nature of attention and the fact that attention is necessary for knowledge. We clearly account for the role of tacit and automatic states, which might be seen to cause difficulties for our view, in the chapters that follow, especially Chapter 4.

---

[3] The above example involves "spatial attention," which can be allocated selectively to empty space or objects in space, independent of feature-based attention, and it can obtain the gist of a visual scene through the reliable encoding of the spatial layout of objects (Carrasco, 2011; Cave and Bichot, 1999; Chica et al., 2013).

Attention is both a fundamental and agential part of our cognitive life, and these agential properties generate an important and distinctive form of epistemic value. To understand the details of this form of epistemic value, we need to understand the details of epistemic agency beyond what has been defended here. That is the primary aim of the current and following chapters, culminating in the account of epistemic agency defended in Chapter 4 and the investigation into the nature of assertion in Chapter 5. While many details remain to be explained, this provides an initial defense of our turn to an attention-based epistemic psychology.

1.2   Dispositions and Epistemic Abilities

This section integrates a commitment to cognitive dispositions with the attention-based epistemic psychology defended in Section 1.1, and distinguishes between culpable and non-culpable dispositional masking. Relevant work by David Lewis, Ruth Garret Millikan, and Ernest Sosa is discussed, largely for expository purposes. We argue that, with the move to attention defended in Section 1.1, the dispositions that constitute an agent's cognitive constitution will manifest agency.

As argued above, any VTEP must be disposition based and agency based. We have begun to account for the agential element; we now examine the dispositional element. This will be important because some normative aspects of knowledge are determined by the metaphysical structure of dispositions in general and of virtue-constituting dispositions in particular. We need to understand how the proper *manifestation* of attentional dispositions can account for both the anti-luck and agent-credit desiderata for knowledge. Sosa (2015, 29) and Turri (2011) argue that worries arising from deviant causal chains can be avoided by requiring that a true belief must be a proper manifestation, rather than a mere causal consequence, of an appropriate cognitive disposition. Cases involving "the mimicking of fragility when a fine wine glass is zapped upon hitting the hard floor" are not instances of the glass *manifesting* fragility (Sosa, 2015, 29). As Sosa describes the case, the zapper is activated when the glass will shatter, but this shattering is not a true manifestation of the fragility of the glass even though the fragility of the glass is a cause of the glass shattering. Manifestation is a particularly important relation in virtue epistemology because we want to say that a success that is properly *due to an agent's abilities* merits epistemic credit. Knowledge will be a success that manifests an agent's cognitive constitution, not one that is simply causally related to their constitution in some way. Below, we examine the dispositional nature of epistemic agency as understood here and then defend a couple of novel points about virtuous and vicious forms of masking. The "simple conditional analysis" of dispositions says that an object is disposed to M (manifest) when in conditions

C if and only if it would *M* if it were the case that *C*. This is subject to numerous counterexamples involving masking, finking, or mimicking the manifestation. A mask prevents a disposition from manifesting even when the antecedent condition is satisfied. A powerful poison has the dispositional property to kill you, but if you take an antidote, you mask its manifestation. However, the venom is still poisonous even though *M* does not obtain when *C* does. The same point holds for the dispositional property of fragility when bubble wrap prevents the manifestation of shattering of a vase when it strikes a hard surface. Masks are thus an objection to the simple conditional analysis, which requires that antecedent conditions *entail* their manifestation.

Since Lewis' (1997) proposal, it is generally accepted that the manifestation of a disposition must occur because of some intrinsic features of the object (in our case, an epistemic agent). This will help us get a fix on the basis of agency in the agent, and thus the basis of epistemic credit. We get a start on this below by defining a "well-constituted cognitive constitution" in dispositional, agential, and normative terms. Epistemic success will be understood as the manifestation of this cluster of dispositions. This is a first approximation to what we will call a "normative cognitive constitution" (NCC):

Normative cognitive constitution: An agent is epistemically well constituted when she is disposed to integrate cognitive states, is disposed to manifest attention to relevant evidence, and is led to epistemic entitlements or some occurrent state of positive epistemic standing when her constitution manifests.

Attention integrates a cognitive system based on what is selected, so it recruits specific causal processes and chunks of information and not others. When "relevant evidence" becomes salient for a cognitive system, epistemic entitlements will result from proper selection guidance processes.[4] These entitlements make manifestation normative. We attribute significant epistemic credit to those who reliably produce accurate information *because of their internal capacities*, more so than the credit given for the possession of accurate information by chance or luck. This kind of credit and the success itself are both explained in terms of agents manifesting an NCC, where it must be the internal capacities of the agent that cause an occurrent manifestation (*M*), if *M* is a true manifestation of an NCC.

We highlight a few features of dispositions that are particularly relevant to epistemic evaluation. Recalling the discussion of masks above, one can distinguish between *culpable* masks and *non-culpable* masks. The culpable masking of a disposition is where a disposition fails to manifest in normal conditions because of the presence of some internal or external property that *should not in*

---

[4] We will have much more to say about what is involved in making a property of the environment or content of thought epistemically salient, especially in the context of conversation and assertion (see especially Chapter 5).

fact mask the disposition but succeeds in doing so nonetheless. Normatively speaking, this is an epistemic failure because the presence of the (de facto) masking condition should not, *ceteris paribus*, actually impede dispositional manifestation in what are otherwise normal conditions. This occurs, for example, when a person lets something unimportant "get to them" and this prevents their abilities from successfully manifesting in the task at hand. Jealousy, random memories, and distracting glimpses in our visual field can affect us in this way.[5] When these factors diminish success (compared to a person with the relevant ability that is not impeded in that way) in otherwise normal conditions, this will be a normatively significant failure and too many failures of this kind count against the possession of the relevant ability, disposition, or epistemic virtue.

Culpable masking involves a range of cases where attentional and agential abilities are not successful because of the presence of a condition that should not interfere in the success of a person with the relevant ability but which succeeds in impeding virtue manifestation in otherwise normal conditions. Of course, any apparent failure of this kind might turn out to be a case of non-culpable masking upon further investigation. If we achieve a greater understanding of the relevant ability or disposition in hand, the presence of the (de facto) impeding condition above may turn out to be an expected impeding condition, in which case we have learned something new about the precise operation of the relevant ability.

Non-culpable dispositional masking does not count against the possession of virtue. This occurs when the presence of some internal or external variable is expected to prevent the manifestation of the disposition and it actually does. There are cases where a non-culpable mask obtains in a situation, but where an agent is able to manifest the disposition nonetheless (e.g., withholding any thoughts of retaliation toward someone that is currently embarrassing you in public). This no doubt merits praise for the agent with respect to that disposition (it is possessed *very* robustly in such a case), although they would not be to blame for failing to manifest in such cases.

Some failures of dispositional manifestation, both culpable and non-culpable, occur when an agent is not adequately disposed because of a poorly integrated cognitive constitution. For example, having the right capacities to perceive color, Bob *always* asks Jasmine about the color of objects (and she is reliable on these matters), but he does not form beliefs about colors in her absence, impeding his own reliable performance in situations where Jasmine is not present. While the relevant parts of Bob's internal constitution are fine – he can see color reliably

---

[5] Arguably, this is what situationist scenarios show – our (putative) traits are constantly masked in ways they should not be, so much so that we cannot justify the practice of personal trait attribution. We meet the challenge of epistemic situationism in the next section.

because of his perceptual capacities – he is imposing a mask on his belief-forming capacities that disengages his otherwise well-functioning perceptual capacities from the formation of his perceptual beliefs. His beliefs about color will be reliable when Jasmine is present, but his own cognitive capacities for visual processing are not integrated in his belief formation the way that is appropriate for a person with Bob's cognitive constitution. Bob's color beliefs should come from his own visual system unless there is a reason to get them elsewhere, as there might be certain occasions when relying on our own visual system would be unreliable. This kind of dispositional failure comes from a self-imposed lack of integration. This is one form a culpable mask can take.

Not all masks are bad; there are also *virtuous masks*. For example, Bob always ignores evidence about the subatomic structure of cars, tables, and chairs while driving on the highway, as well as ignoring Zeno's paradoxes of motion. Even if these propositions were to be true, and even justified, they do and should play very little role in the manifestation of Bob's beliefs about macroscopic objects and the current condition of his environment. Bob successfully masks the normal manifestation of these theoretical beliefs: he withholds judgment about the fundamental structure of cars and highways, and ignores any paralyzing incompatibility between what he thinks and what he sees.

Selective attentional abilities can constitute forms of virtuous masking by inhibiting attention to irrelevant information. Interestingly, it seems that true belief involving cognitive *finks* and *mimics* is incompatible with assigning credit because both involve external manipulations that produce the manifestation condition artificially. These are not instances of a disposition actually manifesting. In the case of a fink, the manifestation is systematically produced by a different object, as in the case of the electric wire, which always activates a different wire every time it is measured for electricity. Sosa argues that credit and anti-luck conditions for knowledge are secured only by manifested, not mimicked, dispositions.

Much more will be added to NCC as we proceed, but we will finish this section with some observations about the distinction between abilities and dispositions based on the work of Ruth Millikan (2000). Cognitive integration has been used as a criterion to distinguish between mere information processing and mental representation (Burge, 2010), unconscious processing and conscious content (as in higher order theories), and sub-personal information and a robust first-person perspective (Rudder-Baker, 2013). In epistemology, however, this criterion has not played the central role that it should. One of the few authors who explicitly use cognitive integration in their characterization of epistemic achievements is John Greco (2010).[6] Greco utilizes a requirement for

---

[6] Henderson and Horgan (2011) also discuss cognitive integration, but not as explicitly related to its centrality in virtue epistemology as in Greco (2010).

cognitive integration to prevent cases of reliable but "strange and fleeting processes" from counting as instances of knowledge. Despite reliably manifesting true beliefs, cases such as "Truetemp" (Lehrer, 1990, 163–164; Pritchard, 2012), epistemically serendipitous lesions (Plantinga, 1993, 199), and clairvoyant powers (Bonjour, 1980, 63) are all cases of nonintegrated success. These are also successes that are not creditable to the agent, largely for the very reason that they are not integrated. While this is indeed a good way of avoiding traditional objections to reliabilism, Greco does not use cognitive integration to distinguish abilities from dispositions, in general, or to characterize abilities in terms of *agency*, in particular. Millikan (2000) draws a crucial distinction between merely successful dispositions and abilities. Most important for our purposes, Millikan draws this distinction in terms of *cognitive integration*. To this extent, our account is consistent with Millikan's. Cognitive abilities require integration on our account because attention requires integration. Some dispositions will not be integrated in the same way as others, for example, the basic modular dispositions themselves that abilities integrate. But Millikan includes more in her understanding of abilities than we do. For instance, she writes:

In general, the conditions under which *any* ability will manifest itself are the conditions under which it was historically designed as an ability. These are the conditions under which it was learned, or the conditions in which it was naturally selected for. (Millikan, 2000, 61)

Millikan says that such conditions are evolutionarily determined (abilities were designed for specific tasks). This evolutionary selection distinguishes abilities from other dispositions an agent has.[7] Although this is an important distinction, we believe it is too restrictive to account for epistemic virtues. A given agent may acquire a disposition to be defensive about their knowledge of ancient history or to challenge the opinions of anyone perceived as close minded, but these presumably will not be abilities in Millikan's sense. In any case, our account incorporates her general distinction as follows: abilities are a proper subset of dispositions – those that qualify as cognitively integrated. Some modular component of an ability will be a cognitive disposition, but not an ability, when the component does not itself exhibit the kind of integration that an ability must.

What sets abilities apart as a unique type of disposition (both innate and learned) for Millikan is that they were selected for success in the conditions that were historically relevant for their development. Perhaps some of the dispositions we will privilege as epistemic virtues here will be mere dispositions for

---

[7] Since we characterize these abilities in terms of attention, this evolutionary thesis entails that different tasks involve different kinds of attention. For a review of the empirical literature that supports this thesis, see Haladjian and Montemayor (2015).

Millikan. However, we will base our account on the latest findings in psychology and on the theory of speech acts, which we believe is a very relevant ground for the kind of abilities of interest to epistemologists. Unlike Millikan, who aimed for her account to provide a theory of conceptual-referential capacities, we focus on traditional epistemic achievements like knowledge, justification, and understanding and broader issues in meta-epistemology regarding the role of motivation in a normative epistemic theory. These latter issues are the focus of the following chapter.

We can now be more specific about the way in which we use the criterion of cognitive integration. Like Greco, we use it to distinguish cases of mere dispositions to succeed (i.e., those involved in Truetemp or brain lesion cases) from abilities. On our account, this distinction rests on whether or not forms of motivation and agency are causally efficacious in manifesting successful outcomes. We use cognitive integration requirements on knowledge to characterize the most important normative properties of epistemic agents. These include the forms of integration necessary for successful attention to the external environment and to shifting contexts of communication. Integrating and becoming integrated with other cognitive processes are essential powers of the primary objects of epistemic evaluation, namely, epistemic agents and their attentional states.

To sum up, we argue that agential properties are the intrinsic causal basis of one or more of the dispositions that define an agent's cognitive constitution, and this partly explains why their manifestation generates positive epistemic standing. These basic features of cognitive dispositions give us a start on explaining how agents can be sources of epistemic value in DA* and why the manifestations of these dispositions acquire positive epistemic standing. In the next section, we address the challenge from "epistemic situationism," which claims that no cognitive dispositions can simultaneously meet standards for both empirical and normative adequacy.

1.3   The Situationist Challenge

This section presents and rebuts a challenge to the disposition-based epistemic psychology defended in Section 1.2 from epistemic situationists. Relevant work from Mark Alfano, John Doris & Lauren Olin, Gerd Gigerenzer, Adam Morton, and David Henderson & Terence Horgan is discussed. We argue that our account successfully rebuts the situationist challenge to virtue reliabilism and we provide additional arguments against situationists in Sections 1.4 and 1.5.

Extending previous work in which we criticize situationism in epistemology (Fairweather and Montemayor, 2014a), we here demonstrate that the reliability of the basic epistemic abilities we defend here, including inferential ones, are not threatened by the situationist challenge. The situationist claims that cognitive traits and abilities do not exist are not reliable, or are not praise-worthy. If this is correct, then there is little hope for offering an adequate virtue reliabilist epistemology of any kind, including the one we propose. We certainly believe that epistemically reliable cognitive dispositions exist, and here we support this view against the challenge of epistemic situationism.

We will focus on the challenge to inferential epistemic capacities raised by Mark Alfano (2013, 139–156). We examine a variety of reliable inferential capacities required for accurately representing features of the environment. Because of differences between ethics and epistemology, which we examine further in the final section of this chapter, we remain neutral with respect to situationism in ethics and will exclusively criticize situationism in epistemology. We propose a naturalistic response to Alfano's challenge to virtue reliabilism that will explain the nature and norms of inference in terms of assertion-like dispositions which reliably satisfy basic epistemic needs. One key to our defense will enlist the Bounded Rationality research program started by Herbert Simon and recently developed by Gerd Gigerenzer (2008), according to which fast and frugal heuristic reasoning is usually the optimal solution to problems that require the reliable selection of options for action and decision-making in real time.

The following is Mark Alfano's (2014) situationist argument against relia-bilism about inference, put in terms of an inconstant triad:

(a) *non-skepticism* (most people know a good bit),

(b) *virtue epistemology* (knowledge requires true belief from intellectual virtue), and

(c) *cognitive situationism* (empirical results in social and cognitive psychology). Any empirically adequate and non-skeptical virtue epistemology must affirm all three. However, since cognitive situationism (putatively) shows that virtue theoretic conditions for knowledge are rarely met, a virtue epistemologist will have to deny non-skepticism. On the other hand, the only way to hang on to both non-skepticism and virtue epistemology is to deny cognitive situationism, but this brings empirical inadequacy to virtue epistemology.

There are many lines of response available. If it turns out that the experimental conditions supporting (c) are often outside of the normal conditions for virtue manifestation in (b), then the philosophical significance of the results is muted, as in cases where a non-culpable mask is present. That would be a largely philosophical response to the empirical challenge. While it is likely that there is some adequate purely philosophical response to epistemic situationism, we focus on a number of empirical lines of response to meet the empirical challenge.

While Alfano restricts his argument to inferential virtue reliabilism rather than perceptual virtue reliabilism, there are Helmholtzian "unconscious inferences" in perception that blur the distinction, so it is important to get clear on what is meant by inference. As Peter Graham (2011) reminds us, association should not be confused with rational inference (discussed further below). The notion of inference should not be restricted to conscious and reflective theoretical judgments because basic inferences that guide action and ordinary speech are implicit. In the case of implicit inference, the rules and heuristics are not introspectively obvious, but they are reliable.

Consider Premack and Premack's research (as cited in Graham, 2011) on inference in apes and chimpanzees. In full view of chimpanzees, researchers took two boxes and placed an apple in one and a banana in the other, and then proceeded to eat the banana out of one box, again in full view. When given the opportunity to pick from the boxes, the chimps went right to the box containing the apple. Their behavior was inferential, the chimps reasoned: "there is an apple in box *A* and a banana in box *B*. But there is no longer a banana in *B*, so there's just an apple in *A*. That's why they went right for *A*. Animals that don't reason like this, but presented with the same information, might still look for a banana in box *B*, or might only slowly make their way to box *A*" (ibid. 136). To show that the chimps were inferring and not just associating, Call and Tomasello's (2008) experiments involved putting two opaque cups in full view of the apes, one full of food, the other being empty, and then shaking both in front of the (primate) subjects. If the cup with food was shaken (making a sound), the apes went right for it. If the cup *without* food was shaken, they went right for the other cup. Call and Tomasello concluded that apes were reasoning something like: "when there's no noise, there's no food in the shaking cup, so grab the other one."

Research on dogs shows that they rely on associative intelligence rather than "logical guidance," reasoning, or inference. Dogs searching for a ball placed behind one of three screens slowed the speed of their search as they went from screen 1 to screen 2, and again from screen 2 to screen 3, whereas children performing a similar task will increase the speed of their search (ibid. 137). This is explained by the fact that reasoning by the child indicates that the failure to find the target in the first attempt makes it more likely that it is behind screen 2 or screen 3, and if not screen 2 then *definitely* screen 3. The dog responds to the failure to find the ball as an "extinction trial" (ibid.) that signals it is *less likely* to be found behind screens 2 and 3. Children exhibit the kind of inferential intelligence attributed to chimps rather than the associative intelligence of dogs.

This brief examination of what inference is (as opposed to associative intelligence) quickly shows us that it is overwhelmingly likely that human beings possess some very reliable inferential dispositions. The best explanation of the above findings is that very robust, stable inferential abilities exist in higher-order animals and children. Graham distinguishes the inferential reasoning of chimps, apes, and children from the full-blown "critical reasoning" exhibited by most adult humans, but the existence of widespread basic and reliable inferential abilities is sufficient for our purposes here. Reliable inferential virtues actually exist.

Returning to Alfano's challenge, which is presented as an inconsistent triad, its first component is non-skepticism: "People know quite a bit through inference" (Alfano, 2013, 141). Alfano here follows Moore in advancing an optimistic intuition about the frequency of knowledge in human life. While we are in broad agreement that "People know quite a bit through inference," it is worth noting that this statement contains an important ambiguity. The expression "quite a bit" requires qualification. Success and function come in degrees. For instance, taking an example from Millikan, the function of the sperm is to reproduce, but it doesn't need to do it very frequently, while the function of the heart, which is to pump blood, needs to occur very frequently. We cannot say that a function fulfills a role "quite a bit" without giving a proper parameter of success. So a single approach to the reliability of epistemic skills will not do. One must look at empirical constraints on frequency as well.

The second element of the triad is the virtue theoretic condition for inferential knowledge, inferential virtue reliabilism, which claims that inferential knowledge is true belief from inferential virtue. It may be true that people know quite a bit through inference all told, but nonetheless perform very poorly within certain domains of inquiry. Cognitively limited creatures using fallible methods of inquiry will be expected to have certain dark areas in their cognitive functioning, even when they are reliable in their actual inferential practices all told. If the research Alfano relies on turns out to expose merely local virtue theoretic failures, then virtue theoretic conditions for knowledge are not problematic, even if certain areas of our cognitive activity turn out to perform poorly.

For the third element of the triad, inferential situationism, Alfano reports psychological research which purportedly shows the reasoning people actually employ typically involve unreliable heuristics rather than optimizing methods of formal logic and probability theory, citing a wide range of studies from Kahneman and Tversky (1979). We shall argue, however, that heuristics as studied in bounded rationality research present a more optimistic story. Simon, Gigerenzer, and others take seriously the fact that rationality theory is the study of a cognitively limited creature. Our understanding of rationality must be "bounded" to reflect the limits inherent in the subjects under evaluation. Bounded rationality currently enjoys flourishing research programs that suggest heuristic reasoning is often *more reliable* for cognitively limited agents than using optimizing rules of rational inference, as might be preferred by Bayesian epistemologists.

Alfano claims that empirical results show that our inferential beliefs are typically formed by heuristics rather than intellectual virtue. At a minimum, it must also be shown that heuristics cannot be virtues, or employed virtuously, otherwise this fact, if it is one, is not a problem for virtue epistemology, but rather supports it. This will be a question of whether or not heuristics are indeed reliable and creditworthy. We argue that, when properly employed, heuristics are often sources of epistemic success. However, reliable heuristic reasoning requires the proper control of the agent, because heuristics easily misbehave and take us in the wrong direction. When heuristic reasoning is properly controlled by an agent, it will not only be reliable, but it will be reliable because of the efficacy of their control. That is a success from ability.

It might be difficult to argue that heuristic reasoning is a form of *responsibilist* epistemic virtue. Heuristics appear to be frugal exactly where responsibilists require high-grade conscious involvement. Perhaps this is so, but we aim only to defend virtue reliabilism here, so this will be left as an independent issue. Frugal virtues satisfy basic needs to represent the environment and succeed at ongoing epistemic tasks *in a timely and assertive fashion*, without spending an unnecessarily long time deliberating among theoretical options. It is beneficial to one's narrowly conceived cognitive success (achieving true belief), as well as overall intellectual flourishing, to utilize efficient methods for acquiring and maintaining true beliefs. There is no reason to think that the proper use of heuristic methods of reasoning could not be included in a virtue responsibilist account of epistemic achievements, although that is not our focus here.[8]

Perhaps the most important point in the bounded rationality research is that limited cognitive agents will often perform *less reliably* when using an ideal or optimizing epistemic rule than when they are properly employing fast and frugal heuristics. Gigerenzer illustrates this with the example of an outfielder tracking a fly ball, who could potentially mathematically calculate the trajectory of the ball, or apply some formal method to determine its future location and a strategy for catching it. Alternatively, the outfielder could just keep the ball held fixed at the center of their visual field and keep running. The latter is a far more reliable way to succeed in catching the ball, even though the former would yield more accurate information if successfully run to completion. Real epistemic agents will rarely if ever be able to complete such a calculation in real time, and when they try they will often make mistakes. In such cases, rational agents *should not* do what ideal epistemic rules prescribe. Theoretically idealized rules are not always epistemically normative for limited cognitive agents, and they are not necessary to succeed in many epistemic tasks.

Consider Gigerenzer's (2011) interpretation of the Linda case from Kahneman and Tversky's research, which is the main example discussed in Alfano (2014).

---

[8] See Fairweather's "Epistemic Situationism" in Fairweather and Alfano (2017) for a discussion using an epistemic form of cognitive-affective personality system (CAPS) traits as a responsibilist answer to epistemic situationism.

To quickly review the case: infamously, when asked whether, given a character description of Linda, it is more probable that she is (a) a bank teller or (b) a bank teller and active in the feminist movement, 85% of the subjects answered (b), clearly committing the "conjunction fallacy" and violating basic theorems of probability calculus. According to orthodoxy, this would entail inconsistency and irrationality. It is impossible for the occurrence of two events (x and y) to be more probable than the occurrence of one of them individually (either only x or only y). This seems to demonstrate that humans have unreliable inferential capacities, because subjects that form beliefs about impossibilities are irrational.

Gigerenzer notes that subjects are here required to use syntactic, content-blind rules of reasoning and do not have access to cues from the environment or a contextually based need to satisfy. Importantly, when asked *how many* out of 100 people who satisfy Linda's description would be bank tellers and *how many* out of 100 would be bank tellers who are also active in the feminist movement, subjects' performance significantly improved and they do not commit the conjunction fallacy as often. Gigerenzer shows that when the same information is presented relative to certain frames, people answer quite rationally, avoiding the skeptical interpretation the situationist favors.

The point here is not that the thresholds used for evaluating actual cognitive agents according to how well they approximate ideal epistemic rules should be informed by facts about cognitive limitations. This is a reasonable enough view, but the stronger implication is that we need to use an entirely different kind of norm, one that builds considerations of cognitive limitations in from the ground level. Adam Morton puts this point very well, "we process only so much information because we get worse results when we process more" (2012, 83). Morton argues that from the fact that we have an ideal epistemic rule, it does not follow that non-ideal epistemic agents should be evaluated in terms of how closely they approximate that ideal epistemic rule. The ability to apply a heuristic in an environment appropriate for its use is a very important virtue for cognitively limited beings. To quickly eliminate alternatives and efficiently solve changing many-many problems requires manifesting abilities with appropriate attentional selectivity and guidance profiles. In many cases, this involves skillfully applying environmentally appropriate heuristics. Selecting environmentally appropriate heuristics is one thing that virtuous selective attention efficiently accomplishes, but consciously applying formal rules of reasoning is not required to do so. The situationist research highlights difficulties we face in the latter.

Gigerenzer (2011) proposes an "ecological definition of terms" according to which elements of an epistemic theory (for our purposes epistemic virtues and vices) will actually represent complex relations between an organism and its environment, rather than properties seated entirely in either. This is a significant move in the ontology of epistemology. The agent is now essentially part of a broader epistemic ecology, and this ecology is the fundamental unit of analysis for evaluating human rationality. This appears to be compatible with a dispositional approach to abilities because dispositional manifestations are only expected relative to certain environments.

However, there may be challenges in reconciling ecological virtues with some aspects of virtue epistemology. Many virtue epistemologists rely on some form of *agent-based credit for success* to answer the value problem and avoid problems related to epistemic luck (Greco, 2010; Sosa, 2007; Turri, 2014; Zagzebski, 1996). Ecological virtues as Gigerenzer defines them appear to be extended features of agents that are coupled with features of environments. It would have to be explained how ecologically individuated virtues are sufficiently person level and sufficiently credit generating for the agent. This can likely be accomplished by incorporating the growing literature on extended knowledge.

If disposition theory can bring virtue epistemology and ecological rationality together in a single account of reliable inferential abilities, virtue epistemologists will have at least the basis of a powerful empirical response to the situationist's empirical challenge. All dispositions, whether of natural substances or epistemic agents, require a network of "causal partners" for their manifestation. The shattering of a fragile glass requires certain properties in the hard surface and gravitational forces, and a courageous person likewise requires danger to be afoot, certain psychophysical regularities to stay put in the environment, and to maintain her basic motor skills. The social dimensions involved in cultivating virtues are also ecological in the relevant sense because institutions can be effective instruments for anchoring and guiding individual and collective attention, and for usefully framing problems for the elimination of irrelevant information in attentional processes. Since virtues most likely have an ecological structure to begin with, accommodating Gigerenzer's research will not require metaphysical revisionism in virtue epistemology.

We shall now give two illustrations of implicit inferential processing at the personal level that satisfies basic epistemic needs concerning human thought and communication, demonstrating the implausibility of the situationist empirical challenge.

1.4   Knowledge of Syntax

This section examines robust, reliable linguistic competences manifested in human knowledge of syntax. We argue that stable epistemic abilities constitutive of knowledge of syntax offer further evidence against the situationist. These reliable inferential abilities also provide evidence in favor of the account of cognitive constitution defended earlier in Section 1.2.

Research on generative grammar, language acquisition, and communication shows that human beings have very stable and robust basic inferential abilities to learn a language. In fact, recent research in neuroscience shows that neural structures track grammatical structures regardless of statistical information, supporting Chomsky's original proposal and confirming an "internal grammar" mechanism (Ding et al., 2015). Given the inferential nature of the abilities underlying knowledge of syntax, this finding by itself counts as a refutation of the situationist challenge against reliabilist virtue theories about inference.

Basic inferential abilities are critically involved in acquiring the lexicon and generative rules of a language. Knowledge of syntax requires the manipulation of information according to strictly formal rules. Children have epistemic skills that allow them to learn any language based on these rules and their robustness is extraordinary. A vast amount of research in neuroscience and linguistics aims at explaining this robustness. Specifically, scientists have tried to understand how it is possible for infants to learn a language given the incredibly diverse contexts they are in, the impoverished stimuli they are exposed to, the complexity of the grammatical rules, and the sense independence of language manifest in deaf children who learn sign language – we expand on this in Chapter 4. Despite there being many open questions, it is clear that some kind of inferential abilities are essential to language acquisition and, like perceptual skills, these epistemic abilities are remarkably stable across different situations and individual differences.

Although knowledge of syntax is highly formal, humans manifest such knowledge at a very early age, and they do so reliably and without conscious effort or monitoring. Infants do not need classes of universal grammar and rules of syntax in order to distinguish the syntactic components of (in many cases, poorly constructed) utterances of a language. Infants do not need classes of how to connect the formal rules of syntax with the specific manifestation of such rules in the spoken language they are being exposed to. They are certainly not introspecting on these rules, or accessing theoretical evidence that could justify them to parse an utterance in terms of subject and predicate. What the infant is doing is highly complex, but the infant performs this remarkable epistemic task in a reliable and unreflective way. Gigerenzer's proposal makes it easy to see this case as inferential but not as an ideal optimization.

The situationist may insist that even the most robust epistemic dispositions can be disturbed by very easy manipulations of the stimuli, the framing effect in the Linda case and other studies on the effect of font size which show precisely how fragile these abilities are. In response, we would like to provide an illustration of why, although information processing may always be disturbed under laboratory settings, this by no means threatens the stability of the actual epistemic dispositions defended above. For instance, in the Stroop task, the interference between inclinations (the automatic inclination to read a word versus identifying a color) does not entail that the capacities involved are unreliable because of alleged context sensitivity. The capacities to read and detect color are incredibly reliable across subjects in many conditions. Interference only shows that having *two* inclinations affects processing. Any virtue conceived as a stable disposition will be disturbed or "masked" under some conditions. But being disturbed in non-standard situations is just part and parcel of being a disposition. What matters for a virtue reliabilist view of abilities is, to restate a point made above, the objective reliability of the ability across situations that are relevant for its manifestation.

It is worth noting that this response to Alfano requires widely individuated abilities for color recognition. It was conceded that in some cases the very narrow disposition to "identify color R in *disturbing conditions* C" may not be reliable, so it is the broad recognitional ability "identifying color R" that allows reliability and susceptibility to disturbing conditions. This appeal to broad abilities is not an *ad hoc* move just to defeat the situationist, but rather is the most natural way of understanding epistemic dispositions in light of the most recent evidence in psychology and linguistics. More important, the environmental conditions and individual motivations needed to satisfy basic epistemic needs, such as the need to communicate and represent the world, specify what is relevant and what is not relevant. In many conditions that are not relevant for the manifestation of linguistic skills, one will find the expected absence of the manifestation.

If Alfano insists that inference must be something rule based, formal, and regimented, then one can hardly think of a type of inferential process that satisfies these constraints better than knowledge of syntax. One constantly uses the rules of syntax to parse words, identify their meanings, and translate from one language to the other. Knowledge of syntax is necessary to understand the meaning of any expression. So, it is not trivial that these robust, widespread, and stable epistemic capacities are performed in a non-reflective fashion. The inferential abilities involved in knowledge of syntax and language acquisition point to a more complex set of implicit inferential abilities involved in communication, such as those involved in paying attention to what is said based on what is salient in a conversation – a topic we focus on in Chapter 5.

What do people know when they communicate, and how are inferential abilities involved? D. H. Mellor's (1990) theory of communication involves a form of indirect inferential knowledge that is analogous to indirect observational knowledge. Communication is "the production in the audience of beliefs about what the speaker believes he believes" (ibid. 92). While successful public assertion requires mastery of linguistic conventions, it is clear that the basic need to communicate can be satisfied and can guide our activity without there being explicit representation of such rules. The cognitive abilities involved in communication are stable, reliable, and inferential, and they manifest in language acquisition and communication for the great majority of human beings.

1.5   Knowledge of Logic

In this section we argue that the knowledge of logic is another stable epistemic ability that situationists are unable to account for. Drawing on work from Paul Boghossian, we force a dilemma on Alfano's situationsim and then turn to normative challenges to the reliabilist element of the epistemic psychology defended here. Consider the basis for any type of formal rule of inference: knowledge of logic. We have, for instance, the capacity to reason according to modus ponens, and this capacity is part of a set of stable dispositions to draw deductive inferences that are truth preserving. One may actually say that these dispositions constitute what we *mean* by deductive inference (see Boghossian, 2000). If this is the case, then one could not know the meaning of what a deductive inference is without having stable epistemic dispositions of this kind. It is a truism that basic deductive reasoning (for example, an application of modus ponens) can be achieved without explicit understanding of such a rule and that these dispositions, like those underlying knowledge of syntax, are remarkably stable. Demanding an explicitly conceptual recognition for satisfying the rules of deductive reasoning problematically increases the cognitive demands of success, and potentially reduces the frequency of success itself. Although we can be trained to have such explicit understanding, this is not a necessary condition for having the stable dispositions that are implicit in our capacity to identify and apply rules of logic.

The situationist seems to face a dilemma: either we possess stable epistemic dispositions that allow us to identify valid rules for deductive inference or we don't. If we do, then situationism is false. If we don't, it is not clear how we are able to understand what we mean when we talk about, for instance, modus ponens. For it is not clear that highly unstable and easily disturbed capacities would help us succeed in specifying what we mean *in every situation* by the inferential practices that satisfy basic truth-preserving moves (modus ponens, modus tollens, etc.). Thus, it would not be entirely clear that we mean the same fundamental rules when we characterize a piece of deductive reasoning as modus ponens or something else. The situationist needs to explain why the psychological evidence would have such a dramatic result. Gigerenzer's interpretation seems much more plausible.

We conclude this chapter by moving away from the situationist's challenge to empirical adequacy to now consider a challenge to the normative structure of the reliabilist account we favor, a challenge to normative adequacy.

1.6   Arguments against Consequentialist Epistemic Norms

This section explains and responds to Selim Berker's challenge to teleological epistemic norms. Relevant work by Selim Berker, Richard Fumerton, Alvin Goldman, and Ernest Sosa is discussed. We argue that Berker's challenge is saddled by serious internal worries and that virtue reliabilism, as understood here, can easily respond to his normative challenge.

In a series of recent papers, Selim Berker (2013a, 2013b) challenges consequentialist normative theories in epistemology. Berker's target appears to be teleological epistemic theories with normative structures analogous to rule consequentialism in ethics, which he believes covers most of them. The clearest and most important instances of teleological normative theories in epistemology would include Goldman's process reliabilism and Sosa's virtue reliabilism. We will take issue with Berker at many points. To the extent that the normative structure employed in this inquiry is teleological, it will not be damaged by his arguments.

Berker argues that teleological normativity, whether in ethics or epistemology, is distinctively "forward looking" because the processes that confer value go from intrinsically valuable effects (pleasure, true beliefs) to valuable causes (actions, belief-forming processes). Berker claims that this involves unacceptable trade-offs in epistemology, so any reliabilist theory with a consequentialist axiology is problematic. We defend a form of virtue reliabilism here, so it is incumbent upon us to address this axiological challenge. This is a very different sort of pressure than the epistemic situationist's empirical challenge above; this is a challenge to the basic normative structure of any reliabilist epistemic theory.

Berker argues that familiar problems that stem from overlooking the separateness of persons in ethical consequentialism apply in devastating ways to epistemic consequentialism as well. The analogous problem in epistemology is overlooking the "separateness of propositions," not the separateness of persons as in ethics. Berker's challenge is roughly as follows:

1. Ethics and epistemology have the same underlying normative structure (normative isomorphism).
2. Because of 1, consequentialism will have analogous trade-offs in ethics and epistemology.
3. Most extant views in epistemology are consequentialist.
4. Consequentialism in ethics is characterized by trade-offs (due to the maximization rule) that are unacceptable in epistemology. These are "Firth style cases" discussed below.
5. Therefore, most extant views in epistemology are theoretically inadequate.

We criticize Berker at a number of points. The normative isomorphism assumption is fundamental to his challenge and is highly problematic. Importantly, there are teleological forms of reliabilist epistemic normativity that are not strictly forward looking and do not have the maximizing structure that leads to the problems in Firth style cases. However, any epistemic theory that endorses DA* will explain the epistemic value of consequences (beliefs) as essentially dependent on the value of their *source* (the epistemic virtues of agents), not the other way around. Our form of reliabilism in particular does not fit the maximizing consequentialism that Berker attacks because epistemic value is grounded in the causal efficacy of appropriate desires, needs, or intentions of the agents to which they apply on our account. The normativity involved in virtue reliabilism is distinctively performance based for Sosa, ability based for Greco, and the view we defend involves the normativity of attention. Since many virtue reliabilists appeal to one or more of these *backward-looking* elements, it can be shown that Berker's argument does not apply to these forms of epistemic teleology. The scope of his argument is significantly limited to begin with.

Nonetheless, since basic reliability is a part of the epistemic value carried by full virtue, we should examine the challenge to epistemic consequentialism itself to secure the viability of utilizing narrow reliability as an element in an overall theory of epistemic virtue. Epistemic consequentialism, according to Berker, is the view that "the epistemic good is prior to what is epistemically right" in the evaluation of beliefs. The determination of whether something is good depends on the prior determination of whether the right consequences obtain. Good actions just are the ones that bring about the right consequences, so determining what is good requires first determining what will count as right. In epistemology, avoiding false beliefs and acquiring true beliefs are strong candidates for right consequences. Things are then good (e.g., belief-forming processes) when they bring about the right outcomes (true beliefs). Reliabilism praises belief-forming processes for this reason.

If normative isomorphism (premise 1) is correct, then epistemology will be stuck with the same kind of unacceptable trade-off seen in ethical consequentialism tolerating, indeed praising, the formation of false beliefs (or intuitively bad actions in ethics) when they bring about more true beliefs downstream than a true belief would in the circumstance. Since consequentialist theories require overall value to depend on realizing final value, there must be aggregation procedures for evaluating conglomerate sums in order to obtain overall value. It is well known that meeting the perhaps laudable end of maximizing utility for the many involves unsavory trade-offs that violate the separateness of persons and their value in ethics: harvesting organs from one person to save five, artfully framing an innocent person to quell unrest in the community, etc. These trade-offs are entailed by essential features of consequentialist axiology.

While the consequentialist trade-offs in ethics might actually be reasonable, Berker claims they are absolutely unacceptable in epistemology and, therefore, epistemologists have a lot of work to do revising the normative dimensions of their favored views. In particular, Berker argues that aggregation processes in epistemology have the unreasonable consequence of ignoring the epistemic "separateness of propositions" (the equivalent of ignoring the separate value of persons), propositions epistemically matter only through the doxastic consequences of their affirmation. If Berker is right, this is indeed a major problem that needs to be addressed by epistemologists.[9]

We propose, however, that Berker is wrong about two key claims he is making, both concerning normative isomorphism. The first concerns the importance of facts as grounds for epistemic norms. The second is that many teleological theories in epistemology are simply not normatively isomorphic with rule utilitarianism, and the ways in which they differ are sufficient to avoid what he calls "Firth style cases." Berker uses an example borrowed from Fumerton (2001, 55)[10] of an atheist scientist that seeks money from a religious organization to conduct important research. A condition for getting the money, however, is that the scientist must genuinely form a belief in the existence of God. Importantly, the scientist will form more true beliefs if she gets the grant, even though she will have to form the (let us grant for argument's sake) false belief in God. Should she form the belief in God? Berker claims that consequentialist epistemic views (to repeat, most epistemic views on offer) are forced to say "yes," because this epistemic sacrifice (accepting a belief one finds objectionable) will increase the overall epistemic achievements brought about compared to not forming the belief in God.

As in any consequentialist view, this is a trade-off one must accept. In the ethical case, this type of trade-off has the unfortunate consequence of eliminating the separateness of persons – persons should have value separately, considered independent of their utility. In ethics, there are circumstances in which these trade-offs are clearly acceptable (otherwise utilitarianism would have no appeal at all). But with epistemic consequentialism, the epistemic value of propositions is pooled like individual pleasures in a utility calculus. The atheist scientist example illustrates, according to Berker, that the justification of a belief depends on an aggregation process and future effects if we are epistemic consequentialists. However, intuitively we should never allow forming a false belief to be the right thing to do simply because so doing would produce a number of true beliefs.

---

[9] Berker cites Firth (1981) for early recognition of this problem. It seems to go unrecognized in the large literature on the "value problem" or the "Meno problem," which began as an attack on the axiology of process reliabilism (see Jones, 1997; Zagzebski, 2000).

[10] It is not clear that Berker uses this as a typical counterexample, the purpose of which is to show the inadequacy of a theory by showing that it entails an unacceptable result (see Goldman, 2015).

One problem with Berker's argument is that in standard conditions one forms beliefs spontaneously. Only very rarely do we find ourselves wondering about whether one should form a belief that one firmly considers as unacceptable in the first place, and it might be impossible to do, despite any avowals we may offer to that effect.

Conversationally, the situation would be quite odd: I ask you, "do you believe in God?" And you respond, "let me see if I can determine how effective that would be in terms of the future benefits to my overall epistemic goals and I will get back to you soon." If this is your response, there is a very important sense in which you did not understand my question. I was not interested in whether or not you believe you would benefit from believing in God. I asked whether you *believe* in God. Firth style cases are unconvincing because belief is pragmatically affirmed, not affirmed with the aim of getting future calculations right. Sosa would presumably claim that the atheist scientist cannot be epistemically virtuous here not only because the belief is false, but also because the act of affirmation is not epistemically motivated (more on this in Chapter 4). Therefore, it cannot be an epistemic success properly understood.

More specifically, a virtuous epistemic agent forms beliefs in ways that manifest cognitive integration. But consider how *poorly integrated* the scientist's atheist belief is with the rest of the beliefs and evidence. To that extent Berker's argument is useful in locating something necessary for full epistemic standing. We have already highlighted the need for cognitive integration and agency and will continue to do so, but it is important to notice its relevance here. While Fumerton's example seems conceivable as a thought experiment, forming such a poorly integrated belief seems normatively impermissible. So long as reliabilism is working with some integration condition that reliable processes must also meet, Berker's criticism can be met.

The fact-involving nature of epistemic normativity manifests in backward-rather than forward-looking epistemic evaluations. According to the virtue reliabilism we defend, the objective success ratio of a given person's epistemic agency will determine the degree to which that agent is epistemically praiseworthy. Epistemic evaluations, therefore, are backward looking because one must consider *how* reliable the source of any objectively successful cognition is, and whether an epistemic success is appropriately connected to a manifestation of agency. But this is not just a question of track record or history; virtuous forms of agency have internal sources of value, the focus of the next chapter. An agential virtue reliabilist axiology will thus include some backward-looking norms, and thus appears to avoid any threat from Berker's challenge.

The only thing virtue reliabilists need to say here is that an essential element of epistemic normativity is constituted by properties of agents (virtues) and these confer a value on their outcomes which those very outcomes would lack absent this causal ground in the agent's abilities. This is backward-looking and agent-based normativity. Berker briefly notes that teleological views such as Sosa's might avoid his criticisms, but only because they depart from the strict rule consequentialism he targets. While his argument against consequentialism is wanting in other respects, we can see that the most plausible form of reliabilism (virtue reliabilism) is not affected, even by his own lights.

In sum, our form of virtue reliabilism is safe from the empirical and normative challenges discussed above. The challenge now is to provide a thorough account of the psychology of epistemic agency as the main source of epistemic value. We proceed to give this account by further developing ACC and the nature of epistemic achievements in our attention-assertion model (AAM), by exploring internal sources of epistemic value and whether epistemically normative attention is self-directed or world-directed. This will bring us to the work of Iris Murdoch, Philippa Foot, Christine Korsgaard, and Imogen Dickie, all of whom are powerful women philosophers that, however, are rarely discussed in virtue epistemology.

2 Meta-epistemology and Epistemic Agency

This chapter examines the nature and role of epistemic motivation, including both the affective category and intentional content of such states, "self-directed" and "other directed" forms of normative attention, internal normative force in epistemology, and assertion as the prime epistemic aim. Relevant work by Iris Murdoch, Philippa Foot, and Christine Korsgaard is discussed. We argue that epistemic motivations aiming at assertion provide a psychologically plausible basis for internal epistemic normativity within a virtue reliabilist framework, and that epistemic motivations have additional epistemic value in the forms of ignorance and inattention they sustain.

2.1 On the Role of Motivational States

In this section we argue that explaining the nature and role of "internal normative force" is necessary for an adequate theory of normativity in epistemology as many have recognized in ethics. We argue that identifying a plausible source of internal normative force in epistemic motives is an attractive move for virtue reliabilists.

In the previous chapter, we defended an epistemic psychology that takes agential cognitive constitutions (ACC) as the primary object of epistemic evaluation, especially for reliabilist virtue epistemology. We also argued that attentional processes are agential and in many cases confer credit to an agent for their success, even for basic epistemic achievements. If this is true, then any virtue epistemology aspiring to an empirically and normatively adequate epistemic psychology will be hard pressed not to endorse this kind of epistemic agency.[1] These psychological points about attentional agency are normatively significant because cognitive constitutions are sources of fundamental epistemic value in premise 2 and direction of analysis (DA*). Cognitive constitutions

---

[1] Of course, alongside other commitments that might remain open, for example, the intentional content of properly epistemic motivations, as opposed to moral or prudential aims one might have for uttering a grammatically assertoric sentence in a conversation (to impress or deceive).

as understood here are essentially agential because epistemic psychology is best understood as essentially attentional.

We further the account of epistemic agency in Chapter 1 by examining issues in epistemic psychology surrounding the role of motivational states in theorizing about epistemic normativity. We consider how to construct "first-person epistemic reasons" from forms of attention, ones which have force over an agent because of their own desires, emotions, goals, and needs.[2] Specifically, we are interested in exploring how the attention-based virtue theoretic epistemic psychology (VTEP) defended here can capture something akin to a reasons-internalist grounding for the authority of epistemic norms, while not requiring reflective endorsement in the process (as both Korsgaard and Sosa do). If attentional agency grounds theorizing about reliable epistemic abilities and internal normative force, this would be particularly attractive to virtue reliabilists. We propose an economical account here as the epistemic motives that make for reliable abilities will also provide a ground for the internal normative force of epistemic norms. Internalism about reasons has a distinguished history in meta-ethics, and some of these figures will be formative in our consideration of their epistemic form, but we do not aim to settle any issues in meta-ethics here. In this chapter, we further examine the types of motivational states relevant to epistemic agency to understand how and if something like internal epistemic reasons are explained in our epistemic psychology thus far. Importantly, in Chapter 4 we argue that the source of internal epistemic normativity defended below does not require consciously represented intentions or reflective endorsement. The work of four important women will be discussed in this chapter, and their work has been formative for the views defended throughout this inquiry. In different ways, Iris Murdoch, Philippa Foot, Christine Korsgaard, and Imogen Dickie all provide insight into motivational states that will benefit epistemic psychology. We will consider ways of utilizing some of their work in normative epistemology in the next two chapters. Murdoch and Dickie both present compelling accounts of non-intellectualized motivational states, but with a focus on moral psychology in the case of Murdoch, and semantics in the case of Dickie. We adjust their insights here for use in epistemology, and enrich our understanding of epistemic motivations.

2.2   The Direction of Attention: Self or World

This section distinguishes between self-directed and world-directed normative attention in ethics and their epistemic analogues. Relevant work by Iris Murdoch, Imogen Dickie, and Christopher Mole is discussed. We argue that

---

[2] A naturalistic nod to the psychology of attention, as we have defended above, will be very fruitful for empirically grounding any account of epistemic virtue, but there are normative issues that must be addressed through independent epistemic theorizing.

world-directed normative attention is best suited for reliabilist accounts of epistemic motivation.

Iris Murdoch (1970), along with her cohorts G. E. M. Anscombe and Foot at Somerville College, Oxford, in the 1950s, helped revive virtue theories in ethics. Murdoch's psychology of the ethically good person, discussed further below, is neither reflective nor self-directed. Murdoch's term "loving attention" describes a motivational state where acquaintance with a person anchors attention toward that person, rather than merely following moral rules. We consider a similar turn to world-directed ("loving") attention in epistemic rather than moral motivation.

Murdoch explains this "loving attention" in terms of attentional anchoring (not deliberate reflection) that provides premises for practical reason (ibid. 35). Moral attention pulls *away* from the self here, according to Murdoch; it "is a kind of intellectual ability to perceive what is true, which is automatically at the same time a suppression of self" (ibid. 64).[3] Appropriate moral attitudes involve a suppression of self which is at once an epistemic attentional ability seeking truth outside of the self. Let's say that virtuous moral attention is world directed for Murdoch, and because of this, the suppression of the self is necessary to perceive what is true. That is one reason why perceiving what is true is difficult in ethics. We will argue that important forms of epistemic attention resemble Murdoch's world-directed moral agency, and that first-person normative grip (of the sort Foot and Korsgaard focus on) can still be accommodated by these non-reflective epistemic motivations.

On Murdoch's view, the motivations of a good person are ways of attending to the specific needs of other people. Reliably directing attention to the appropriate needs of others is a moral-attentional ability whose manifestations are moral-attentional successes from that ability. But this is not a reflective ability. As Lawrence Blum (1986) says, "The moral task is not a matter of finding universalizable reasons or principles of action, but of getting oneself to attend to the reality of individual other persons. Such attention requires not allowing one's own needs, biases and desires regarding the other person to get in the way of appreciating his or her own particular needs and situation" (343). The morally good person must have an attentional ability to "attend to the reality of individual other persons," not to discover universalized principles through reflection. In order to reliably track the needs of others, we must effectively blind ourselves to numerous irrelevant attentional targets, including, according to Murdoch, one's own needs, biases, and desires.

---

[3] In virtue epistemology, manifesting epistemic virtue would then require directing attention toward the world and particular items of concern in the right way: directing attention in this way avoids over-intellectualizing the morally good person. Murdoch's moral psychology is potentially attractive for virtue reliabilism in this respect.

We manage to succeed in blinding ourselves appropriately without reflective attention on the self. This unreflective targeting manifests the important epistemic ability of not letting irrelevant information interfere with the functioning of attentional abilities. Murdoch's view points us to an important epistemic virtue that we call "virtuous insensitivity," discussed later in this chapter and in Chapter 6. The main point for present purposes is that Murdoch's moral psychology provides a clear example of a motivational ability to anchor attention that requires a "blinding" to oneself in order to sustain the appropriate world-directed focus.

The question arises whether epistemic psychology should follow Murdoch in turning away from the self and claim that epistemically successful forms of attention must be world directed as well. In Murdoch's case, she argues that we are far more liable to get things wrong about ourselves than about other people in an external practical environment, so in that sense attention to ourselves is a source of moral failure (1970, 51).[4] On Murdoch's account, a self-directed attentional process is thus not a *reliable* source for good premises in practical reasoning. Self-directed attention does not steer you in the right direction for moral guidance.

Against Murdoch, it may turn out that successful world-directed attention is dependent upon self-directed attentional processes of reflection, for example, the evaluation of one's motivations and abilities. Am I being manipulative or self-serving? Do I have sufficient expertise to provide help in this context? What range of strategies do I have available in the ongoing process of attending to x that will best enable me to continue doing so? It might be irresponsible to attend to the needs of others if you lack the capacity to reflect on potential negative consequences for yourself, or if some other person's needs are weightier. It appears that some self-directed attention is necessary for any responsible world-directed attention of the kind Murdoch describes.

To solve this apparent puzzle, Christopher Mole (2006) proposes to focus carefully on the extended or "stretched" world-involving nature of attention. Mole (2006) says that "Old French: *ad tendere*," the etymological root of the term "attention," literally means "being stretched out." Mole writes:

Really looking does not get its value by revealing purposefulness and pre-existing value out there in the world [...] Nor does it involve an illusory projection of value from the self. Looking at the world is *itself* a bearer of value. Knowledge of the nature of one's character may be indispensable for the more or less reflective thinker's deliberate progressing towards becoming good, but this knowledge of character is not attained through the worthless unstretched-out attention involved in introspection. Even when introspection succeeds in being honed and astute, the features of ourselves that we learn

---

[4] Anscombe (1957, 1962) and Murdoch (1970) both argue that knowledge of one's body and movement does not require reflective attention to its position. Hilary Kornblith (2010) makes similar arguments against the reliability of reflection.

about through introspection are features that are morally salient only on account of their relationship to things outside the self. (2006, 83)

As Mole notes, reflective knowledge about the nature of one's own character may be indispensable for progressing toward the good, but it does not suffice if deliberation is not properly modulated by its "relationship to things outside the self." Reflective attention is not fundamental because it only reveals ourselves as something related to a world outside of the self in a practical context. Things attended to outside of the self provide the relevant subjective saliences for an agent.

We will follow this world-involving aspect of Murdoch's view in our understanding of epistemic agency. Epistemic motivations will typically manifest virtuously insensitive, world-directed, attentional dispositions, the kind of world-directed responses that are insensitive to irrelevant internal desires and properly responsive to others. In epistemology, attention that is properly stretched out is also factive and reliably directs us to the world beyond the self. With this turn in epistemic psychology, we commit to motivations that need not be full-blown intentions and will add detail to this general attentional turn in Chapters 3 and 4.

2.3   Cognitive Needs

This section examines different affective modes that epistemic motivations can take and defends cognitive needs as the best affective category for virtue reliabilist accounts of agency. Relevant work by Imogen Dickie, G. E. M. Anscombe, and Ernest Sosa is discussed. We defend Dickie's account of cognitive needs and propose modifications for a needs-based account of epistemic motivation.

Epistemic attention is constituted in part by a variety of affective or conative states – desires, emotions, needs, inclinations, or intentions. While explicit intentions might be plausible as necessary or sufficient conditions for success in ethics, this is not plausible as a necessary condition for knowledge. Motivational states are effective in part because the cognitive element reliably represents information that can satisfy an interest when acted upon. But as we noted previously, interests and desires are efficient mechanisms for making vast amounts of irrelevant information inaccessible for action, recall, or report. Full-blown intentions are not necessary to accomplish this.

What needs to be spelled out in more detail is what we mean by "explicit intention" and the other psychological state types available to epistemologists. Imogen Dickie (2015), based on the work of Elizabeth Anscombe (1957), defines practical knowledge in terms of the intention to perform an activity, a cognitive commitment to perform that activity, the fulfillment of the activity, and the appropriate luck-eliminating role of such commitments. Dickie describes "cognitive commitment" as a belief-like state to avoid psychologically implausible requirements for explicitly articulated propositional attitudes in order to attain even basic epistemic achievements. This would be to over-intellectualize epistemic success, as Murdoch was concerned to avoid in ethics. With some modification, we endorse and build upon Dickie's view examined below as a further step in the direction Murdoch took us above.

While Dickie steers away from defining motivation in terms of intention, she has an account of justified intention that will be useful for us here. Dickie argues that "an intention justifies behaviours it generates insofar as these behaviours tend towards the intention's non-lucky fulfilment" (2015, 92). If the behavior selected by the intention is a reliable means to its fulfillment, that is most likely because *the intention is luck eliminating*. Following Anscombe, Dickie says intentions constitute a form of knowledge when there is an appropriate luck-eliminating relation between intending to perform an action and successfully performing the action (ibid. 86). Without meeting this reliability requirement, the intention is only weakly justified.[5]

Since the content of any intentional state includes a goal state and a targeted means by which this will be achieved (*S* intends to illuminate the room by turning on the light switch), intentions can be explained in terms of the goal-directed anchoring of attention and the effective guidance process recruited thereby. One might pursue a "justified intention" account of epistemic motivation[6] for belief along the lines Dickie suggests above for action. In a rather specific and limited way, this will be our approach. Neither belief formation nor bodily action will be taken as central here, rather the cognitive, physical, and social act of assertion, and the desire to be in a position to normatively assert will be of interest here. We take normative assertion as the main organizing principle for epistemic evaluation rather than true belief.[7]

Just as cognitive commitments are not fully conscious beliefs but can constitute knowledge for Dickie, we argue that epistemic needs are not fully conscious intentions but nonetheless constitute epistemic motivations. Dickie focuses on the basic *need to represent the environment*. This is a person-level state that guides action but does not have explicitly conceptual content. According to Dickie, basic needs provide reasons for action and can strongly justify a cognitive commitment if and only if a pattern of behavior is guided by

---

[5] See Velleman (2007).

[6] Zagzebski (1996) has a similar division for praiseworthy motivations and virtue. Full virtue requires success in attaining the aim of a praiseworthy motive, while the unsuccessful but praiseworthy motive still carries some basis for praise.

[7] This is a methodological point regarding the derivation of epistemic requirements, not a denial that truth matters. Any principle of normative assertion will endorse some form of that platitude, but grounding epistemic normativity in assertion also allows us to explain how and why truth matters in epistemic evaluation.

the need and is a reliable means to the fulfillment of the need. Both intentions and needs are motivational states, but needs are more cognitively basic.

We argue that needs, but not intentions, are necessary for normative epistemic attention. To appreciate that individuating intentions is highly sensitive to the semantic properties of doxastic states of an agent in ways that individuating needs is not, simply note that two distinct intentions can satisfy the same need. If you have a need to see across a dark room, you can act to satisfy this need by turning the lights on yourself or asking your friend to turn the lights on. The same need is satisfied by either intentional act. Attributing an intention to an agent is to attribute to them the belief that certain means will satisfy a desire, and an explicit commitment to undertake specific behavior that will cause the desire to be satisfied. Rather than desires, we explain basic motivations in terms of needs, where these may simply be defined as drives that seek their own satisfaction. Following Dickie, we will say that *needs provide reasons for action*, they have accuracy conditions (either non-propositional or conceptual), and determine how an agent should guide their actions.

Once a need becomes a reliable guide for action, the skills they guide will rarely be defeated by the peculiarities of situations (they become robust across environments). We call these "reliable needs." Satisfying a cognitive need through an appropriate form of attention is an ability we have reliably and robustly. While Dickie examines the mind's need to represent things outside itself, we turn to *the mind's need to assert* as a core motivating, but non-intentional drive in our cognitive life. Reliably and efficiently satisfying this basic epistemic need is a fundamental epistemic virtue; it helps to meet our general need for reliable communication, understanding, and action. The ability to reliably and normatively assert is a distinctive attentional, motivational success that will require successful communication in varying contexts. This is elaborated in Section 2.4, and Chapter 5 is dedicated to understanding the norms and skills of assertion.

2.4   The Desire to Assert: The Content of Epistemic Motivation

This section identifies the content of epistemic motivation as normative assertion, complementing the account of cognitive needs defended in Section 2.3. Work by Michael Dummett, Wayne Wu, and Imogen Dickie is discussed. We argue that normative assertion is the proper content of epistemic needs.

We have examined how a turn to needs rather than reflection allows for an account of epistemic motivation that accommodates the fact that much in epistemic success is tacit, world directed, and conative (more on this in Chapter 4). As Dickie argues, we have reliable abilities to represent the environment without any overt representation of this as a goal or desire. Here we take this in a slightly different direction (but just slightly). Dickie says the desire to represent the environment is a deep cognitive need, and we are in full agreement. We argue that *the need to affirm a content is a basic epistemic need*. Recall Wu's example in the previous chapter of the species that can represent three objects but which has no capacity to attend to any one of them. This shows us that representation is not the same as attention or selection of a content, so representing and attending will be distinct (though not unrelated) needs. But, while attending is agential in a way that the unusual representations that Wu considers are not, it is not sufficient for affirming. Affirming is a distinct need, and involves a distinct type of agency beyond either representing or attending. This will be discussed at length in the next section.

From this we can see that there is a spectrum of epistemic needs: the need to represent the environment, the need to attend to some particular feature of a represented environment, and the further need to affirm the truth of some content related to a feature of a represented environment. These are all basic needs and presuppose forms of cognitive agency, but they are importantly different kinds of needs. Attending to a feature is agential but not necessarily assertoric. We appeal to assertoric needs to inform our account of the content of epistemic motivation.

The difference between attending to a content and (internally or externally) asserting it reveals much about the essence of epistemic attention. The very essence of linguistic communication depends on reliable needs to assert. As Michael Dummett (1981) says: "That language permits the construction of sentences with determinate truth-conditions, and that these sentences can be uttered assertorically, i.e. understood by the convention that the speaker is aiming at uttering only those the condition for whose truth is fulfilled, appears to belong to the essence of language" (2–3). Surely, the satisfaction conditions underlying assertoric utterances cannot be imposed merely by convention: the speaker *must* desire to commit to such truth conditions for the convention to be meaningful and sincere. There must be an internal judgment or epistemic entitlement that justifies the convention (ibid. 310–312). As we discuss at length in Chapter 5, the skills required to successfully perform the speech acts of assertion and retraction are like those involved in the knowledge of syntax and logic: they are basic inferential skills that satisfy the most crucial communicative goals.

In the next section, we argue that the need to assert confers internal normative force on targeted contents and secures epistemic grip for relevant norms. The normative grip underwritten by epistemic agency is theoretically valuable in a number of ways, especially for virtue reliabilist epistemic psychology.

2.5   Epistemic Needs and the Grip of Epistemic Norms

This section examines how virtue reliabilists can best account for the internal force of epistemic norms. Relevant work by Christine Korsgaard and Philippa

Foot is discussed. We argue that the account of world-directed epistemic needs in Sections 2.3 and 2.4 can be extended to include a ground for internal normative force.

One of the most important issues in recent meta-ethics is locating the source of the authority of ethical norms. What Christine Korsgaard (1996) calls "the normative question" demands an answer to questions about the authority that moral requirements claim over our actions. This problem of normative force demands that the reason-giving force of normative claims must be explained, not just assumed. An epistemic variant of the normative problem will seek the source of the authority of epistemic norms. This will be a problem of epistemic normative force. Where do epistemic norms derive the authority they have over epistemic agents, when in fact they do? Is any belief automatically answerable to standards of rationality, truth conduciveness, etc. just in virtue of being a belief, or must some further condition be satisfied? Does normative authority for an agent have any essential connection to their interests and motivations, such that the former cannot be adequately accounted for without appealing to the latter? These are big questions and our goal is not to ultimately settle debates about internal and external reasons, certainly not in ethics.

In this section, we aim to capture the sort of valuable theoretical resources that internalists in ethics and action theory can claim. Process reliabilism in epistemology is often thought to suffer from cases where beliefs are reliably formed but agents have no reason to think so, or they even have evidence to the contrary, but they reliably accept what comes. We aim to ground epistemic agency in forms of attention that create reliable internal reasons for an agent. This is especially attractive for virtue reliabilism if it does not require reflective endorsement, but rather the thinner needs discussed above.

In *Sources of Normativity*, Christine Korsgaard presents a challenge to any normative theory to explain the source of the authority of its norms. How do the dictates, requirements, or forbiddances of a norm gain purchase on an agent's conduct? Why should I do what moral reasons require me to do? Putting aside for the moment that we reject Korsgaard's (1996, 49–69) solution to the normative problem in terms of reflective endorsement, the normative problem itself places a reasonable demand on a normative epistemic theory.

Let's say the normative problem is to properly locate the basis of normative grip for the norms to which an agent is properly held accountable.

Normative grip: For any norm (*n*) that requires *S* to perform *x* in *C*, *S* is blameworthy for not *x*-ing only if *n* has grip (purchase, authority) on *S* in *C*.

This formulation leaves open what grounds normative grip, and this will be very important for the current inquiry. According to Korsgaard (1996), any norm that demands *S* to *x* has normative grip, only "If we find upon reflecting on the true moral theory that we still are inclined to endorse the claims that morality makes on us ... then morality will be normative" (50). Importantly, this clearly tells us that carrying the status "the true moral theory" is not sufficient to give the norms of that theory grip on individual agents, independent of their endorsement. However, we argue that grounding normative grip does not require any appeal to reflective endorsement, as Korsgaard argues. Affective states in an agent can clearly give grip to a norm, including the world-directed attention emphasized by Murdoch and the cognitive needs emphasized by Dickie.[8] Independent of this important issue, we agree with Korsgaard that an agent cannot be properly evaluated just by citing an external reason that speaks in favor of or against an act they perform, even granting that it is a moral reason or supported by objective rationality.

Korsgaard (1996, 17) says that her argument for a tight connection between reasons, motivation, and grip goes back to Philippa Foot's "Moral Arguments." A clear discussion is also found in "Reasons for Action and Desire," where Foot (1978) argues for a sharp distinction between (true) evaluative judgments and reasons for action. Paraphrasing a convincing example from "Reasons for Action and Desire":

Jones may (correctly) judge that x is a good doctor and that y is a good house by recognizing that they have qualities that are useful to patients and tenants respectively. Yet, even having made such true evaluative judgments about x and y, Jones may quite consistently have no reasons for action or choice with respect to them. (ibid. 151)

A straightforward explanation is that Jones lacks the relevant *interests* of standard patients and tenants, if, for example, she is both very healthy and well housed. Here, Jones has no reason for action, but, ex hypothesi, correctly judges that both x and y are good in their respective ways (as doctors and houses). There is some sense in which moral evaluations have a special connection to reasons for action, but this is only because reasons for action have a special connection to interests and desires (ibid. 150–151).

Foot argues that true evaluative judgments are not reasons for action. As she says, "There is no magic reason giving force in evaluative judgments, and it would be ludicrous carefully to choose a good F or a good G, rather than a bad F or a bad G, if one's own desires and interests were not such as to provide a reason in one's own case" (ibid. 151). Being a good x is one thing, having a reason to choose x is another. What do we make of this for epistemology? Do we want to say that true epistemic normative judgments are not reasons for epistemic action? Do we want to say that being subject to evaluation under an epistemic norm depends on having specific interests? We will defend limited affirmative answers to these questions. These will be limited to norms

---

[8] Functional properties might also ground the authority of norms and criteria of goodness for those things with such functions (see "Goodness and Choice," Foot, 1978, 132–147).

regarding opening and closing inquiry, attending to relevant information, and ignoring irrelevant information. When an agent's interests are not considered, these aspects of epistemic evaluation become disabled in a way that is similar to the point Korsgaard makes – we cannot (internally) fault a person for not doing what they (externally) ought to do. In a particular case, one might cite true normative epistemic judgments ("one ought to proportion credence to evidence") that an agent may fail to comply with, but without specifying some relevant interest that aligns the agent with such demands, we cannot, in that particular case, personally fault them for irrationality when they fail to do what such a principle says they ought to do. When an agent has an interest in proportioning credence to evidence, e.g. in conversational and assertor contexts, internal rationality assessments are viable and the norm can be unproblematically applied without questions about the source of its authority.

Is this a reasonable move for an epistemic theory? One advantage is that, like Foot and Korsgaard can claim for ethics, the source of the normative force of epistemic norms would be overt and clear. However, unless the power of first-person authority is limited in some way, epistemic theorizing becomes far too subjective, and the authority of epistemic norms far too easily slips around. Reminding ourselves about the nature of attention will be helpful here. Because we are constantly solving many-many problems, at any given time, there will always be some norm with first-person grip for any subject of attention. Attention is thus always apt for evaluation under some norm.

The general species of this norm is captured enough by Sosa's performance normativity. Attentional states can be understood as endeavors that select environmental targets and recruit guidance activity relevant to some current aim. Targets for selection might be more or less task appropriate, guidance mechanisms (which are often unconscious) might be more or less efficacious, and output selection may be more or less adequate for completing a given task. Any goal-directed attentional state will thus give grip to some norm with first-person authority, as well as a rationalizing explanation of its motivated activity. The internal normative commitments engendered by attentional states will not always be epistemic, but any form of attending will mobilize norms for internal evaluation. Any cognitive system with selective attention is thereby answerable to an internal norm. Some range of its activities will also be rationally explicable, and this will usually be the same thing, or closely related to what makes them answerable to a norm.

A critic may respond that even if the agential nature of attention suggests that most (and perhaps all) attentional states an agent is in will carry norms with grip, it does not follow that internal reasons must be given weight in epistemic evaluation. These can potentially be ignored in favor of some form of categorical epistemic norm. Against this advice, we gladly take on board the internal normativity generated by attention as an important resource for virtue reliabilist epistemic psychology. This will have to be further developed in the next few chapters, but we can now say that if some state or process is the manifestation of an ACC, some epistemic norm for success is binding on it. The authority of these norms is supported by the agent's own epistemic motivations and thus by their own cognitive constitution.

We now begin developing a sustained defense of epistemic agency in terms of assertion. We examine how basic norms for opening and closing inquiry acquire grip from the motivation to assert, and then examine an associated excellence of "virtuous insensitivity" in the next two sections. We expand on this analysis of assertion in Chapter 5.

2.6   Frege on the Grip of Assertion

This section briefly examines psychological distinctions between assertions and interrogatives noted by Frege, and the unique internal force carried by each. We argue that Frege identifies important aspects of the internal normative grounding of epistemic motivation and pursue this in greater detail throughout Chapters 3, 4, and 5.

Understanding the nature of assertion will help explain how internal normative force enters our epistemic life. Frege (1997, 329) says that interrogative sentences involve grasping a proposition and being motivated to issue a "request," whereas assertoric sentences involve grasping a proposition and being motivated to "lay it down as true." Questions and assertions are clearly distinguished by their respective motivations. An assertoric sentence "lays down as true" a given content p, thereby ending inquiry into p, while the interrogative "whether-p?" does not "lay down as true" any propositional content and keeps inquiry into the truth value of p open. The aim of an assertion is to end inquiry with respect to a certain question and to do so by laying a proposition down as true – it is a factive and epistemically committed speech act. Of particular interest is Frege's (1997, 329) claim that, in assertion, grasping a proposition and laying it down as true are so closely joined that their separability can easily be overlooked. Importantly, their psychology is quite different, asserting (even internally) is not just grasping a proposition, as there are many propositions we grasp but would not assert, e.g., cases where we grasp a proposition but are unsure of its truth value. Assertion is a cognitive performance with a very specific motivation.[9]

In this section, we examine norms evaluating the initiation and termination of inquiry whose binding force is grounded in an agent's need to assert (discussed further in Chapter 5). To avoid any unnecessary confusion over

---

[9] The motivated performance bears similarity to the performance Sosa (2015) dubs "alethic affirmation." We discuss this at length later and in the next chapter.

terminology, let's distinguish between a need (or desire) to assert on the one hand, and a motivation to assert on the other. A need or desire to assert, as we see it here, is a need or desire to be in a position to normatively assert a content. A motivation to assert, on the other hand, will be understood as the occurrent movement toward an act of actually asserting (presumably because one takes oneself to be in a position to do so).

When Frege says assertoric sentences involve a motive to "lay down as true" a propositional content, he is describing what we will call the motivation to assert. When successful, it will satisfy a relevant assertoric need. We follow Murdoch and Dickie in understanding the type of motivational state involved, as a non-reflective and non-intellectual state, such as a need or desire, rather than anything with the cognitive complexity of an intention (though in some cases intentions and reflective deliberation are more important than others).[10]

The difference in motivation between assertions and questions points to a normative difference in the kind of activity that would be (internally) rational for a person who asserts p to perform compared to a person who asks the question whether-p. When an (all out) assertion leads to further inquiry into the truth or falsity of the very proposition asserted with respect to the same question, such inquiry is, ceteris paribus, irrational. This would be analogous to Foot's well-housed tenant who seeks out a good house, just because it was judged to be a good one. Similarly, interrogatives that do not lead to further relevant inquiry are, ceteris paribus, failures of rationality. This would be analogous to a tenant in imminent need of housing who does not actively seek out a good one.

Epistemic evaluations that assess the rationality of opening or closing inquiry, rather than steps in the inquiry itself, cannot be given independent of the motivations of the agent. This is a close epistemic analogue of internal reasons in ethics. The proper evaluation of a stretch of an agent's cognitive activity will require, at a minimum, knowing whether they have asserted a proposition, or whether they simply have taken it as the presupposition of a question, which thereby manifests a curiosity.[11]

---

[10] Regarding worries that such renderings might be insufficiently person-level or insufficiently credit generating, we address these points in subsequent chapters, particularly Chapter 5, in which we examine in detail the motivation to assert through the speech acts of assertion and retraction, and Chapter 6, in which we examine epistemically driven curiosity and its relation to the need or desire to assert. That is a burden we must meet in order to address the fundamental tension facing virtue reliabilism discussed in Introduction. Also, there are many norms governing responsible assertion, and a broader range of them will be under discussion in Chapter 5.

[11] Some epistemic assessments must be sensitive to an agent's motivation, but, of course, this is not to say that all epistemic assessments are motivationally grounded, or that the only aspect of assessment is tied to motivations. Here we point out that the clearest case for the sufficiency of normative authority from agent motives is the requirements to open and close inquiry, but there is much to epistemic success in between.

Here we underscore the fact that important epistemic evaluations depend essentially on the motives of agents, but this does not force us to a reflective epistemic psychology or to account for epistemic agency in terms of attention. In the next section, we examine a very important virtue connected to truth-seeking activity, but it is not a virtue of desiring, loving, or respecting the truth as such.

2.7   The Frame Problem and Virtuous Insensitivity

This section examines the under-appreciated value that normative epistemic motivations carry by keeping us ignorant of vast amounts of contextually irrelevant information, rather than solely because we care for the right thing. Relevant work by Glymour, Fodor, and Greco is discussed. We argue that epistemic motivations carry epistemic value when they support forms of virtuous insensitivity.

Epistemic virtues are often understood as virtues that have something to do with a love or desire for the truth as such. Acting in direct light of this epistemic piety can be problematic for our ability to reliably achieve the aim itself, but it also potentially misses some important points about how truth-seeking cognition works. We approach this first through the familiar issue of "frame problems," and then introduce a reliabilist virtue to join the internal virtue defended above. Epistemic needs are epistemically valuable in part because they help us solve frame problems.

The frame problem is succinctly described by Glymour (1987) as follows: "Instances of the frame problem are all of the form: Given an enormous amount of stuff, and some task to be done using some of the stuff, what is the *relevant stuff* for the task?" (65). Two central aspects of the frame problem, as it is understood in computational approaches to mental states, are the vastness of available deductive and inductive inferences concerning an unbounded number of propositions, on the one hand, and the selective and meager evidence that agents take into consideration when they perform tasks and make decisions, on the other.[12] In this generic form, one can think of many instances of the frame problem, e.g., what is the intended meaning of a sentence uttered by a speaker given all the available options, what evidence should be taken into consideration when one is trying to reach some practical goal? What information and evidence are permissibly ignored? Thus, the frame problem is primarily a problem of relevance, i.e., what information is relevant to complete a specific task given a vast amount of plausible and mutually incompatible

---

[12]   For discussion of these two central aspects of the frame problem, see Fodor (1983, 1987, 2000). Fodor argues that the frame problem is an insurmountable challenge for the computational theory of the mind. For criticism of Fodor's view (in the context of the debate on the modularity of mind), see Carruthers (2006).

alternatives. Competence in this domain is essential for task-oriented success and thus should be part of any epistemic psychology. As Fodor (1987, 140) nicely put it, the frame problem is "Hamlet's problem: when to stop thinking."

Consider this example: if you want to go to a party and don't know how to get there, a good heuristic is to ask someone who is going to the party how to get there and rely on her testimony.[13] Depending on where you live, there might be significant evidence you should ideally take into consideration regarding the probability of events that could interfere with your course of action: accidents, earthquakes, criminals, and traffic. An idealized rational agent will weigh all the evidence concerning these probabilities, but you are actually much better off not thinking about them and just asking a friend how to get there. Action demands that you stop thinking about every possible scenario and the likelihood that it will come to fruition.

The computational problem regarding how to identify relevance in a system with too much information is generally expressed in terms of cognitive architecture and modularity. If the architecture of the mind seems to be such that problems are solved locally by specialized and encapsulated systems, how is it possible to identify relevance in a global, non-encapsulated (personal or agential) way, conducive to action, decision, and performance? The means by which we achieve this (or fail to) are fundamental reliabilist epistemic virtues (or vices). Much of our epistemic success depends on our ability to solve many-many problems of this kind by ignoring or being insensitive to vast amounts of irrelevant information.

We call the capacities through which epistemic agents solve frame problems forms of "virtuous insensitivity," or, collectively, simply "the virtue of epistemic insensitivity." ACCs are essential here because motivation plays a fundamental role in restricting the possibilities of what evidence one should be sensitive to. A properly functioning motivation allows an agent to efficiently and appropriately restrict the information they are sensitive to, and most importantly that which they will not be sensitive to, with respect to some task or goal. In the previous example, you want to go to the party and you also are motivated to get there in the most convenient way. In making such a decision, you should ignore very good inductive inferences to the effect that everything is just a bunch of atoms, and potentially good deductive inferences to the effect that there is no external world, if you want to hold commonsense beliefs that will get you to the party. With respect to different motives, say to engage in a philosophical discussion, an agent might be sensitive to claims about the external world and not to commonsense beliefs,

---

[13] As mentioned in Chapter 1, there is an ongoing debate about the rational adequacy of heuristics in the context of decision-making. While we are not going to settle this debate here, see Morton (2012) and Fairweather and Montemayor (2014b) for a defense of heuristics in epistemology.

but will still need to manifest the general capacity for virtuous insensitivity in either case.

For our purposes, virtuous insensitivity must be explained in terms of epistemic agency with a properly epistemic motivation. Consider the following two cases.

MARIE. Marie is a physicist who constantly worries about the structure of quantum field theory and the vacuum. She also forms an enormous amount of true beliefs about her macroscopic environment. Knowing, however, that most of her beliefs are defeasible, she satisfies the need to accurately represent her environment without ever being motivated to *assert* any content or being epistemically committed to act upon any content. She thus satisfies a basic need to represent without the proper epistemic motivation – she represents her environment in order to systematically withhold judgment.

IRIS. Iris, like Marie, has a need to represent the environment, which she satisfies by using her need as a reliable guide to the world. But Iris is also motivated to endorse these contents and stop inquiry, thereby eliminating other attitudes she could have, such as merely entertaining them. She attends (represents her environment) in *order to be committed* (or to assert). This is her *standard* epistemic motivation. When she withholds judgments, her motivation differs from her standard epistemic motivation, and only does so because in those cases her need to represent accurately may be jeopardized.

Marie exhibits, in essence, an intentional form of Wu's species that can represent objects but cannot attend to any one of them (discussed in Chapter 1), essentially employing a form of *vicious masking*. Representing with no aim to assert is not an epistemic achievement, at any rate it is not a complete one, and may easily be reckoned a vice. It is important to emphasize that Iris' motivation to assert is not just an emotional "push," it is playing the critical role of eliminating attitudes incompatible with commitment, but compatible with the generic category of representing the environment successfully.

Greco (2010, chapter 10) recognizes a form of virtuous insensitivity in an insightful discussion of why epistemic agents should ignore highly theoretical beliefs (and their corresponding web of deductive and inductive inferences) in forming commonsensical beliefs about the world that they can endorse without these theoretical beliefs counting as defeating evidence. Using our vocabulary, norms concerning these theoretical beliefs (such as the belief that everything is merely an arrangement of atoms) have no proper grip on a typical epistemic agent, and rightly so. This is a form of virtuous insensitivity to evidence given the assertions we typically care about. While Greco sees that forms of insensitivity are important, his account of success from ability does not make this condition overt and central, or specify the mechanisms by which the ability would operate successfully. These are essential elements of epistemic psychology and critical functions of motivations.

The above considerations show a few things about epistemic motivations that are often not recognized in epistemology. First, motivations allow us to explain the source of the authority of epistemic norms in ways that are compatible with the most plausible psychological explanations of cognition. Attention is essentially goal directed and agential, and thus easily gives us a basis for epistemic evaluation right in the empirical work itself. Second, when motivations function properly, they create virtuous insensitivity to irrelevant information. This fundamental virtue makes possible most other epistemic virtues, and the motivation involved is to assert (or accomplish some task), not simply to represent a content. Especially in the case of virtuous insensitivity, the epistemic value of motivations is not just in their being praiseworthy ways of valuing what is epistemically good (i.e., truth, etc.). This is a standard reason for praising epistemic motivations. However, the value of the motive to assert is (meta-epistemically) that it gives us a basis for non-categorical epistemic evaluation, subjective rationality assessments, and essential patterns of insensitivity to irrelevant information.

2.8 Some Concerns about Internal Normative Force

This section examines problems raised by "trivial true beliefs" facing any attempt to locate the source of epistemic authority in the desires and motives of agents. Relevant work by Kornblith and Grimm is discussed. We argue that once we take assertion as the internal epistemic aim, there will be far fewer trivial domains of inquiry than required by Grimm's challenge.

A few epistemologists have directly taken up the problem of normative force. Kornblith (1993, 2002) and Grimm (2009) argue that a theory of epistemic norms ought to explain how they get a purchase on us, that is, why we ought to care about or be held accountable to such norms. Kornblith (2002) puts it this way: "If you tell me that a belief of mine is unjustified, this gives me reason to give up that belief. The epistemic claim is something about which I should care, and a theory of epistemic norms must explain why it is that I should care about such things" (145). Without simply pounding our fist on the table, or refusing to address the issue, what is the proper response? Kornblith (1993) offers an interesting instrumentalist solution. Epistemic requirements have authority over any agent that has desires of any kind because desire satisfaction depends on truth. If you have desires that you want satisfied, then you ought to care about norms of truth and rationality. Since all human beings satisfy the antecedent condition, we get a universally applicable epistemic norm, the authority of which is non-problematically grounded in an agent's own desires, though not any one of them or subset of them.[14]

---

[14] Kant discusses a similar possibility for hypothetical imperatives with universal scope when the condition of application is the goal of happiness, which all people seem to hold. Kant notes that this is a merely formal agreement in aims, since people mean such different things by the happy life.

Stephen Grimm (2009) notes a dilemma facing any theory aiming to ground the source of epistemic authority in an agent's desires or interests. Many propositions are utterly trivial, and it would seem that there is no epistemic value in coming to hold true beliefs about them. For example, believing truths about the number of grains of sand on a beach. Since this proposition is trivial, it would seem out of place to epistemically praise agents that believe it. Recalling our discussion of internal normativity above, we see here the lack of agent interests that accounts for the lack of force that norms of achievement exhibit. However, as Grimm argues, once we constrain epistemic evaluation by interests, we now have a problem with the scope of epistemic evaluation. There is an intuition in epistemology that whenever you go so far as to believe, whether the topic is trivial or not, epistemic norms automatically apply. We are not immune from epistemic evaluation simply by noting the triviality or lack of interest we have in beliefs we hold. To form a belief is to commit to being subject to epistemic norms, whether the content is trivial or not. This is a categorical notion of normativity, one that obtains independently of the interests of the agent (e.g., Sosa's AAA account, 2007, especially chapter 3). The source of the authority of such norms would come from the nature of belief itself, that belief aims at truth, and should be evaluated as such. We can see the worry here because the epistemic activity of a person that forms a belief about a trivial subject cannot be blamed for their performance, even if it were clearly irresponsible and shoddy from an epistemic point of view. Say an agent always employed wishful thinking about trivial topics, and predictably does not do so reliably. We seem to be without any basis for negative evaluation of their cognitive performance here, but this is just what we should do. Grimm provides a social solution that extends the interests of an agent beyond that which one individual holds, and into an epistemic community. We will return to this topic in Chapter 7.

This is a very important issue and one which must be addressed by the theory proposed here. Clearly, any agency-based account of abilities and achievements must appeal to interests in some way in order to account for agency. But, given Grimm's worry about the scope of epistemic evaluation, this may come at a great cost, if such a theory is then unable to extend epistemic evaluation to cover unjustified belief in trivial contents. Not forming a belief is easier to excuse, as the Pyrrhonians prefer, but irresponsibly formed belief even about a trivial content should still be negatively evaluated from a strictly epistemic point of view.

A full response to this worry will be discussed in Chapters 5 and 7. To preview, we argue that we have interests in asserting far more than we overtly realize. We want to be in a position to normatively assert quite a bit, independent of whether we follow through with the actual speech act or not. Achieving a robust ability to normatively assert, we argue, is a goal for most epistemic agents and covers a wide range of domains and propositions. As a standing goal or intention, epistemic agents want to be generally competent to assert across a wide range of communicative contexts in order to be flagged as good sources of information. Thus, much less information will be trivial for an agent than would appear at first glance (even to the agent), and this may give us a basis for judging seemingly trivial beliefs. There may well be imaginable cases remaining, but these are outliers. The desire to be a good source of information across a range of contexts is an interest held by epistemic agents.

3 Success Semantics and the Etiology of Success

This chapter examines difficulties faced in explaining the "because of" relation that properly connects an agent to their achievements such that the achievement is due to the abilities of the agent and thus a success credited to the agent. Relevant work by John Greco is the primary focus, but we also introduce work from F. P. Ramsey and C. S. Peirce pointing us in a different direction for understanding etiological requirements for knowledge. We argue against Greco's contextualist analysis of the "because of" relation and motivate a re-direction of analysis toward F. P. Ramsey and C. S. Peirce, developed more completely in Chapter 4.

3.1 The "Because of" Requirement for Knowledge

This section sets out the main difficulties virtue epistemologists face when accounting for the etiology proper to knowledge, or when a belief is properly "due to virtue" as opposed to merely "in accordance with virtue." Metaphysical and normative aspects of etiological requirements are distinguished and we emphasize the importance of the etiological conditions favored by virtue epistemologists in grounding responses to Gettier problems and the Value Problem.

Etiological conditions for knowledge in virtue epistemology seek to connect an agent's abilities to their achievements such that their achievements are sufficiently non-lucky and creditworthy. Gettier cases occur when an agent is epistemically successful, but where success is due to luck rather than their abilities, and a lucky true belief is not knowledge. In short, their success does not count as knowledge because it does not have the right etiology. Etiology also matters in explaining why knowledge is more epistemically valuable than mere true belief. A success that is due to an ability is a more valuable success than one due to luck.[1] Etiological requirements for full normative standing

---

[1] Most virtue epistemologists agree here. Sosa (2007), Greco (2010), and Zagzebski (1996) all endorse some form of this solution to the value problem, although they do not agree on the precise nature of the etiological ground in the agent.

have roots in the Aristotelian tradition. A virtuous action etiologically grounded in a virtuous character is more praiseworthy than the virtuous act alone.[2] Etiology is thus both causal and value conferring.

While the general idea is clear enough, a proper understanding of the "because of" relation has been elusive in virtue epistemology. The standard understanding of "etiology" in medicine, for example, is decidedly causal – we want to know the cause of a disease or condition. It may also be understood more broadly as "giving a reason for." Giving the reason for something and specifying its cause will often coincide, but Anscombe and Davidson have long shown us that understanding action requires keeping this distinction clearly in mind. Greco is especially interested in understanding the etiological conditions for knowledge and we discuss his view in detail below. Greco's work here is important because the primary advantages of virtue reliabilism over process reliabilism include providing a solution to the value problem and ruling out cases of lucky success as cases of knowledge. A virtue-relevant success must have the right causal history to secure both of these advantages and this will come largely through the etiology of success. A clear and plausible account of the "because of" relation is an essential arrow in any virtue epistemologist's quiver.

An etiological condition for knowledge will be both metaphysical and normative, and this is one reason that it is particularly difficult to adequately explain. The direction of analysis (DA*) characteristic of virtue epistemology makes the *cause* of epistemic success (the agent) essential to explaining its value. This is a metaphysical requirement for epistemic achievement not only because we need some account of what an agent is, but also because real causal relations between agents and their achievements are needed. The etiological condition is also normative. When the appropriate causal relation obtains, e.g., epistemic value is generated by an appropriate epistemic motivation, this causal etiology will confer normative standing on any belief with that etiology. Causal dependence explains (epistemic) value dependence in premise 2 and DA* in Chapter 1, and we now have in hand many elements of the explanation for how this is so.

Greco (2010, 71) requires that the abilities of an agent must be explanatorily salient in their success. Sosa (2007, 2015) understands the etiological requirement in terms of the causal/dispositional manifestations that puts an agent's capacities (causally) in touch with the relevant part of the world.[3] Zagzebski (1996) understands the etiological requirement in terms of motivation, where

---

[2] Zagzebski's recent exemplarist virtue theory would appear to be an exception. However, etiological connections between actions and character in exemplars are presumably normative, and so etiology remains a normative variable.

[3] For a clear distinction between a state or an event that is caused by a disposition and a state or a process that manifests the disposition, see also Turri (2011).

an epistemically praiseworthy motivation of the agent must achieve the aim of the motive. We have argued that agency is the etiological origin that matters, and that the form of "success from ability" necessary for epistemic achievement is success from agency. With the discussion of Greco's etiological condition as context, we introduce new perspectives on this important issue from Ramsey, Peirce, and Wittgenstein. We proceed as follows: first, we provide a thorough examination of John Greco's contextualist and virtue reliabilist account of the etiological condition and raise a number of objections. We then proceed to modify Ramsey's "success semantics," originally advanced as a theory of truth, to now provide a theory of success from ability. Ramsey's account is further supported by the seminal work of Peirce, and to an extent Wittgenstein. Collectively, these figures provide the resources for a novel and satisfactory account of an etiological condition for knowledge that comports with the agential VTEP defended thus far.

3.2   Greco's Contextualist Etiology

This section examines Greco's well-developed contextualist account of normative epistemic etiology. We highlight advantages of Greco's account of epistemic etiology in responding to the difficulties raised in the previous section, but we argue that his account faces significant challenges due to his contextualist commitments.

John Greco (2010) provides one of the most thorough virtue theoretic accounts of the semantic and psychological underpinnings of reliabilist virtue epistemology. Greco (2010, 115) construes the "because of" relation in terms of *causal explanatory salience* which he accounts for with a contextualist semantics. In particular, Greco proposes that practical interests, embedded in a socially determined practical environment, will specify which features of a situation are explanatorily salient in the production of true belief. Importantly, such practical environments provide stability to the standards for attributing knowledge, dependent on practical interests, thereby preventing negative contextualist consequences, such as relativism (ibid. 116).

Greco's sophisticated proposal solves difficult problems concerning knowledge attributions by emphasizing the importance of action in relation to knowledge in practical environments. We expand on this relation between action and knowledge in our discussion of assertion in Chapter 5 and our interpretation of Ramsey's success semantics below. Greco's proposal also admirably engages literature in semantics, and brings welcome nuance to the literature on knowledge attribution within a virtue reliabilist framework, which we very much agree with. Thus, we focus on Greco's (2010) account because of its thoroughness as well as its importance for the topics we discuss in this chapter.

Although there is much in common between our account and Greco's, there are crucial differences as well. The main objection we raise with respect to Greco's account concerns the difference between assessing practical relevance and establishing objective reliability. We will focus on some of Greco's main examples of knowledge attribution based on practical salience to illustrate this problem. Practical saliences show a range of agent responsibility, but also worrisome potential departures from the reliability constraint required for abilities, as well as an unstable role for credit-conferring motivations. The essential concern here is whether Greco's commitment to contextualism guarantees sufficient creditability for epistemic success because of the potential difference between practical relevance and objective reliability.

We (like Baehr, 2011; Zagzebski, 1996; and recently Sosa, 2015) have argued that epistemic motivations generate person-level credit. But this might easily be lost on Greco's account, as the factual underpinnings of the contextually *relevant* etiology will shift with practical interests. If the practical interests of the *attributors* that determine explanatory salience do not happen to give priority to the *objective* reliability of a person's abilities, or the objective, causal connection that their motivations have in bringing about success, then their success cannot be knowledge by Greco's own lights, even if there is an objective causal relation between epistemic motivation and epistemic success. Greco says that practical environments, because of their connection with action, are stable and thus prevent problems associated with relativism, but Greco never explicitly addresses the slack between objective reliability and practical salience allowed by his contextualism. If saliency attributions happen to pick out (objectively) non-reliable or non-motivational properties of the etiology of a successful outcome, this success should count as knowledge by Greco's own lights and this seems problematic in ways discussed in detail below. While we raise objections below, Greco's account of the "because of" relation brings many interesting issues together and raises important questions. How is it that context, interests, purposes, and the abilities of agents fit together into an account of success from ability? Greco says that the contexts relevant for the evaluation of causal explanatory salience are practical environments. For instance, to determine that someone is a good baseball player one needs to specify what kind of practical considerations are relevant. Is the player participating in the major leagues or a neighborhood game? Likewise, the causal etiology of belief must be fully specified by the abilities of the agent, but in order to specify such etiology practical considerations must determine whether or not such abilities are salient. Greco (2010) says:

In cases of knowledge, S believes the truth because S believes from intellectual ability – S's believing the truth is explained by S's believing from ability. But the success of this explanation requires more than that ability is involved. It requires that S's ability has an appropriate level of explanatory salience. (75)

Greco admits that his account of explanatory salience in terms of causal *relevance at a context* is far from being a detailed account of the etiological basis of knowledge because it does not offer a theory of causal explanation or the pragmatics of causal explanation language, which he says is poorly understood in general. Nonetheless, he argues that, although provisional, his account can solve a great deal of traditional difficulties in epistemology (e.g., Gettier problems, Barn façade cases, etc.).

One general strategy to answer questions regarding lucky or accidental true belief is to emphasize that the agent's abilities are *not* the direct cause of the belief in such cases (they are not causally and explanatorily salient in the production of such belief). Greco (2010) connects all of these ideas as follows:

What does all this have to do with contextualism? In short, the present thesis is that knowledge attributions are a kind of credit attribution, and that credit attributions in general involve causal explanations: To say that a person S is creditable for some state of affairs A, is to say that S's agency is salient in an explanation regarding how or why A came about. Now add a further, plausible thesis: that the semantics of causal explanation language requires a contextualist treatment. (105–106)

This may be a theoretically plausible account of knowledge attribution, but is it a plausible account of epistemic virtue? What are practical environments and how do they determine objective features of causal explanation, including reliability? As a theory of knowledge attribution it surely has many advantages, as Greco's book makes clear. But one may have concerns about the contextualist commitments of the proposal, particularly with respect to the objective track record required for reliability and the coherence and relevance of the notion of a practical environment. More concretely, the saliencies entailed by practical interests of agents may not match neatly (or at all) with the type of considerations that are usually salient in (objective) causal explanations of reliability. Some practical environments will make the agent's abilities more salient than others, although presumably the causal relevance of such abilities in the actual production of a belief will be an invariant feature of the contexts in which practical interests vary. If this is the case, which of the contexts should we pick, if there are different interests but invariant causally relevant abilities, such as perceptual abilities?

There are two aspects of Greco's account that make it particularly problematic with respect to this issue. One is the role given to the practical environment, which is not how causal explanation is construed in general, at least not in metaphysics, philosophy of science, or even psychology. It seems that Greco's move is justified by the unique type of cause that epistemic virtues require: agents, rather than generic physical events. But, then, why insist that it is the semantics of causal explanation that matters, rather than intention or action attribution?[4] Either it is robust causal explanation (as understood in metaphysics or philosophy of science) that matters or it is a more practically oriented, folk understanding of the salience of an event in producing an effect (a folk theory of causality filtered through action) that matters. We now argue that it cannot be either of these options because both compromise the psychological plausibility of the resulting success attributions. The other problematic aspect of Greco's proposal is that the causal salience of abilities on his account might be entirely unrelated to the *motivational* properties of the agent and thus will not honor any relevant agential conditions for knowledge.

Greco's account appears to be subject to the following counterargument.

1. Knowledge is a creditable success from ability.
2. A success (S) is only from (or due to) ability (A) if A is explanatorily salient in how S came about.
3. An ability (A) is explanatorily salient only if some relevant attributor of knowledge takes A as salient in bringing about S.
4. Therefore, (S) is creditable to an agent only if a relevant attributor takes an A to be salient in bringing about S.

One concern here is that, in some cases, what is salient to one attributor, given a specific set of practical environments and interests, will not match the objective causal salience of an ability. In such a case, contextual salience will not match causal salience, but objective causal salience seems quite important. This is what the manifestation of a disposition essentially involves, the intrinsic causal basis of a virtue brings about a normatively significant categorical state, and this is a matter of brute fact, not of salience to an attributor given a practical environment. We can see the problems contextualism produces by adding a few more premises and witnessing the worrisome conclusions.

5. An attributor may fail to take as salient an ability which is in fact objectively causally salient in bringing about a success (S).
6. A creditable epistemic success must be a success that is objectively due to ability.
7. If a relevant attributor takes a non-motivational ability as salient, then (on Greco's account) some non-motivational causes of success will be creditable successes.
8. Therefore, some cases of 6 will not count as knowledge on Greco's account.
9. Therefore, some cases of 7 will count as knowledge on Greco's account.

We think 8 and 9 are problematic because 7 is problematic. This is why a contextualism that loses its metaphysical mooring is problematic for virtue epistemology. Virtue epistemology requires a stable metaphysics of dispositions,

---

[4] Intentional action in particular is recently claimed to avoid problems of deviant causal chains by Wu (2015) and Sosa (2015).

causes and manifestations to properly explain the generation and transfer of epistemic value.

Greco is well aware that motivation is an important ingredient for any plausible virtue theoretic account of knowledge. For this reason, he suggests that an Aristotelian model may be the best way to understand virtues in general:

> Now it seems to me that the Aristotelian model is the better one for theories of epistemic normativity. This is because, it seems to me, knowledge requires both responsibility in one's cognitive conduct and reliability in achieving epistemic ends. But however this issue is decided, the main point is that virtue theories define the normative properties of beliefs in terms of the normative properties of persons, i.e. the stable dispositions or character traits that constitute their intellectual virtues, however these are to be understood. (Greco, 2010, 43)

Greco emphasizes that full epistemic success requires "responsibility in one's cognitive conduct," a crucial issue concerning the psychological underpinnings of virtues. However, even granting that all the facts about objective reliability have been settled, the contextually shifting saliences on Greco's account leave it unsettled whether or not an agent comports with an etiological requirement for knowledge. This seems counterintuitive.

It is worth noting how explicit Greco is about the importance of motivation and an objective track record for reliabilist accounts of epistemic virtue. He says that an agent S is epistemically responsible "if and only if S's believing that p is properly motivated; if and only if S's believing that p results from intellectual dispositions that S manifests when S is motivated to believe the truth" (ibid. 43). He then defines epistemic virtue as follows: "S's belief that p is epistemically virtuous if and only if both (a) S's belief that p is epistemically responsible; and (b) S is *objectively reliable* in believing that p" (ibid. 43).[5]

Suppose that two agents are identical with respect to the objective reliability of their cognitive processes. Every time they form a belief, they have the same degree of objective reliability (their beliefs have an identical likelihood of being more often true than false).[6] If one of them forms true belief 80 percent of the time with respect to the shape of objects, then the other one will have an identical rate of success. Suppose one wants to attribute knowledge to these epistemic agents. Their being reliable is a big plus in their favor. But this is not enough for a reliabilist virtue epistemology. In assessing their epistemic deliverances and achievements, *their abilities and motivations* must be causally salient (i.e., the agents must arrive at true belief because of *their* abilities). This is why a reliabilist virtue epistemology is much more fine-grained than standard reliabilism. According to standard reliabilism, both agents are equally justified

---

[5] Our emphasis.

[6] For a classic account of the objective or scientifically constrained standards for the reliability of cognitive epistemic processes, see Goldman (1992).

and if their beliefs equally comply with some safety or sensitivity constraint, then they both know. But for a virtue epistemology, one also needs to show that the agent arrived at such beliefs because of the agent's epistemic abilities, which include the *proper motivation* to use those abilities. Thus, it is perfectly plausible to deny knowledge to one of these agents because their abilities did not play the proper role in causing their success, but this should be a matter of objective psychological facts that differentiate the two cases, not differences in attributor interests. Since we see a knowledge-conferring etiology as an objective relation, it is not clear that Greco's contextualism can properly account for the "because of" relation.

3.3   Causality: Folksy, Metaphysical, and Psychologically Constrained

This section examines issues about the nature of causality relevant to a proper understanding of agential success for true belief. We argue that Greco is saddled by a dilemma and propose a way forward that emphasizes motives as causes (as understood in Chapter 2).

Greco utilizes explanatory salience contextualism for the semantic evaluation of knowledge attributions. One worry explored above is that this move marginalizes objective causality in a concerning way. Another concern is that this semantic approach does not properly honor the important role of motivations as objectively reliable causes of success. The examples offered by Greco concerning causal salience illustrate the tension between attributor-based assessments based on interests and practical environments and objective accountings of causal-explanatory salience. Some of Greco's examples are clearly based on practical considerations that the folk use to attribute knowledge based on abilities (such as the example of the gambler, his wife and his friends, who have different standards and practical interests regarding his alleged abilities for choosing winning horses), others emphasize objective causal salience.[7]

More specifically, in the gambler example, Greco (2010, 106–107) illustrates two types of standards for knowledge attribution: one based on the financial interests of the gambler's wife and another based on the desire of other gamblers to acquire knowledge about betting. The result is non-faulty disagreement. The gambler's wife, unsurprisingly, does not attribute knowledge to her husband when he proclaims that he knew the horse he bet on was going to win, based on the horse's past performance. The gamblers, by contrast, attribute

---

[7] One problem with this example is that the ability to succeed in gambling may not be an epistemic virtue at all, especially if one considers what is at stake in gambling (which includes risk and luck as defining features). But we will not focus on this problem here.

knowledge to him. This case presumably captures the kind of folksy causal explanation people generally use in knowledge attributions. Other examples Greco uses, however, seem to rely almost exclusively on causal salience, rather than practical interests and environments. Although they appeal to practical interests, the context is framed in a much more metaphysical setting and they assume causality in the strict metaphysical sense. For instance, Greco's (2010, 106) example of a car accident is also presented in terms of two different standards for salience. In this case, police officers at the scene of the accident determine that speed is the salient feature that caused the crash while, later on, city planners focus on the difficult traffic characteristic of that road. The cops focus on the high speed of the car, while city planners focus their attention on the deficient design of the road. But surely, the relevant standards for what is causally salient in this example are very different from the standards used by the attributors with respect to the gambler's alleged capacities. In the car accident case, the actual speed of the car is a lot more important than the interests of the cops, and the actual design of the road is crucial for anything the planners have to say. Objectively salient causes cannot be explained away by contrary practical interests.

What is causally salient about the accident depends on *objective information that is preserved in the causal chain*.[8] Absent one of the facts concerning road design or speed, the accident would not have happened. This sounds like metaphysical causality, dependent on facts that remain *invariant* across different interpretations and practical interests. For example, at some point, one can imagine a judge asking: "I know that the road in question is in very bad shape and that the speed limit was crossed. But I want to know exactly why the accident happened. Which of these two salient features was *objectively* more relevant?" This is the kind of question that forensic scientists have to answer all the time. Objective causal relations are undeniably significant in the explanation of why any event occurs, including epistemic success.

One may think that forensic scientists bring unique practical interests to the table – a new practical environment, and thus confirm Greco's contextualism. But notice that whatever interests they bring in, their assessment will be fact involving and grounded in objective causal chains. This is in sharp contrast with the gambler example. The attributions of knowledge based on the salience of the abilities of the gambler (or lack thereof) are not constitutive of two different causal chains that preserve objective information about a situation. On the contrary, they depend exclusively on the practical interests of the gambler's wife and his friends. The wife's concern for not having money that month explains her hesitance to attribute the epistemic ability underlying the

---

[8] For discussion on the importance of objective information-preservation in causal chains, see Salmon (1998).

alleged "knowledge that a horse will win" to her husband, while the other gamblers' interests in finding tips for wining bets explain their eagerness to attribute such knowledge. But this seems to be mere hesitance and eagerness, and it is hard to see any reliable causal chain being established by these practical interests such that objective information could be preserved in these two different ways.

In the accident example, there are two alternative causal chains that are ultimately evaluable in terms of facts that should preserve objective information. With the gambler's case there is hardly one (the alleged causal chain seems to be a feature of how different subjects interpret the situation) and it is unclear how one would appeal to facts to solve such a dispute. Thus, this seems to be a folksy understanding of causality that is not really fact involving, at least not in the robust counterfactually supportive way that causality generally requires, e.g., the horse could have won just by pure luck and the gambler just had a lot of consecutive lucky guesses.

Even assuming that these examples are unproblematic, the abilities of *agents as such* need not be targeted as salient by relevant evaluators. This is a problem that is particularly pressing for Greco's virtue reliabilism because even if the notion of a practical environment captures the semantics of causal explanation, it remains to be determined case by case whether such semantics would take into consideration the abilities of agents as such (their agency), rather than other features of the practical environment. We give a more thorough account of epistemic agency in subsequent chapters, but what is crucial to highlight at this point is that what is needed is objectively reliable agency, objectively caused by a proper motivation.

3.4   Success Semantics and the Etiology of Success

In this section, we propose a modified version of F. P. Ramsey's "success semantics" to account for the etiological relation between agents and their achievements. Relevant work by F. P. Ramsey, J. T. Whyte, Peter Smith, and D. H. Mellor is discussed. We argue that an epistemic version of Ramsey success provides the needed etiological condition for knowledge without falling prey to the difficulties facing Greco's contextualist account.

An important difficulty discussed in the section above is Greco's characterization of the "because of" relation, where causal salience does not necessarily preserve objective information in the ways that causal chains do. The worry is that knowledge attribution becomes too dependent on practical considerations to ensure credit for true belief in all cases where credit is actually due. The counterfactual supporting generalizations characteristic of causal relations demand a more direct connection between an agent's success and the causal conditions that promote their success. Practical interests may be relevant for some aspects of knowledge attribution (particularly with respect to how the term "knowledge" is used and conceptualized by the folk), but they do not explain how basic epistemic needs lead to actual success due to objective features of the environments they operate on. Success from the objective causal saliency of agency is more truly a success from ability.

One plausible way to address these problems is by offering a different semantics for knowledge attributions which admits objective causal relevance compatible with naturalistic constraints, and which also requires motivational components and abilities of its agents. Here, we propose a modification of the so-called "success semantics," proposed originally by F. P. Ramsey (1927), as the best candidate to accomplish this. We do not ultimately defend any view on epistemic semantics here, but there are strong similarities between Ramsey's success semantics and the attention-agency view of epistemic achievement defended in the previous chapters, and these resources can be marshaled to provide an attractive understanding of the "because of" relation.

Ramsey (1931) was the first modern reliabilist, he claimed that knowledge is a true belief reliably achieved. Independently of this thesis, he also proposed that the truth condition of a belief is the condition that guarantees the success of *desires* based on that belief (Ramsey, 1927, 144).[9] Together, these theses entail a version of reliabilism that has significant advantages because of the way it incorporates motivational and cognitive factors into reliable epistemic abilities. True beliefs, according to Ramsey's proposal, can be defined as *functions* from desires (or goals) to actions that cause agents to behave in ways that succeed in satisfying their desires or goals.[10] This characterization defines belief-forming processes as functional operations that determine a mapping from an input (i.e., a desire or goal) to an output (i.e., a concrete action or the fulfillment of the goal), and it has the advantage that it does not focus *exclusively* on beliefs and their propositional contents. Success semantics focuses on the agent and her epistemic motivations, and starts the causal order of explanation with the epistemic abilities of agents. This is generally amenable to the virtue theoretic direction of analysis (i.e., DA*).

It is important to emphasize that, as a general theory of content and truth, success semantics is explicitly a *causal theory*. As Peter Smith (2003) says with respect to the content:

For certain beliefs, the content of the belief is that *p* just if, for any appropriate desire, actions caused by that belief combined with a desire will be successful in realizing the desire's object just in case that *p*. And of course, there is no magic about the relation between its being the case that *p* and successful action: it will be a causal condition for success. (49)

---

[9] This formulation of Ramsey's proposal is due to Whyte (1990).

[10] See Bermudez (2003, 66).

While Smith offers this as a theory of content, truth can be defined similarly, by stating that a true belief is one that causes successful actions when combined with appropriate desires.[11] A very important feature of this definition is that it appeals to the objective causal powers of beliefs in conjunction with motivational states of agents. Crucially, the condition that must obtain for the relevant satisfaction of desires is one that must obtain *reliably* when the belief (and desire) is acted upon. A Ramsey success is thus motivated and reliable, and it is reliable *because* (properly) motivated.

The condition that must obtain for the satisfaction of desires or motivations is called the "utility condition" by Mellor (1991). He describes it as follows:

> [We] can't equate a belief's truth conditions with those in which every action it helps to cause succeeds. But we can if we restrict the actions to those caused just by it and some desire. Then its truth conditions are what I shall call its "utility conditions": those in which all such actions would achieve the desired end. (23)

This restriction on beliefs in conjunction with desires is crucial because it shows that motivational components are fundamental to constrain the range of causally relevant doxastic attitudes, as well as the type of cognitive process that leads to relevant success. Zagzebski (1996) has a similar constraint on relevantly reliable processes because a belief has full normative standing for her only if it achieves the aim of a virtuous motivation. She argues that this is a potent resource for resolving the "generality problem." It appears that our account can claim similar advantages in this respect.

Taking stock, we are proposing a modification to Ramsey's success semantics, such that one obtains not a semantics for true belief, but for something approaching a criterion for justified belief. Let's call this an *epistemic Ramsey success* (ERS). This modification of Ramsey's success semantics yields the following straightforward account of epistemic achievements as ERSs:

> ERS: A belief p is justified if and only if acting on p in conjunction with some desire q reliably satisfies q.[12]

We need to make clear the way in which an ERS is epistemic, the way in which it is a success and is a credit-conferring achievement. There is a straightforward sense in which an ERS is a success – a desire of the agent is reliably satisfied. Not all desire satisfaction is to the credit of the agent whose desire is satisfied.

---

[11] See Mellor (1991). See also Blackburn (2010) for some advantages of success semantics as a theory of content.

[12] It is crucial to emphasize the centrality of reliability for ERS. Desires must be *reliably* satisfied, and not merely depend on the connection between desire and successful action at a given time. There is a very important relation between satisfying the utility condition and what we will call (in Chapter 5) "reaching an objective threshold" for assertion. The idea is that a content is assertable when (and only when) one believes that content on the basis of reliable abilities that meet the Ramsey test. We are grateful to Dennis Whitcomb for this insightful clarification.

Our desires might be satisfied because we are lucky, or due to the abilities and actions of others. However, when acting on "p and q" is what causes the satisfaction of q, credit is due to the agent for the satisfied desire.

A more difficult question is in what respect an ERS is an *epistemic* success. As defined above, the desire satisfied will have to be an epistemic desire. Thus, in an ERS, positive epistemic status is conferred on a belief because, in conjunction with certain epistemic desires, it causes successful actions. This is a different kind of normative-etiological explanation than we typically find in virtue epistemology. The typical form is that a normative source in the agent appropriately brings about an epistemically valuable state, and the normative source confers epistemic standing to that epistemically assessable product or outcome. With ERS, the explanatory process is different. We do not begin by assuming a normative etiological source in the belief-desire couplings that produce action, but given that they turn out to be efficacious in causing the satisfaction of the desire due to the presence of the utility condition positive epistemic standing is indirectly conferred upon the belief due to this normative relation between the agent and the environment. This means that what confers positive epistemic standing on a belief is a complex set of relations involving beliefs and desires that are coordinated with actions and facts, all of which bring about the satisfaction of the desire. This is a fact-involving, ecological set of integrated states (including motivations, beliefs, and interests), capacities and relations to the world.

It is reasonable to say that ERS generates positive epistemic standings (other than truth) because it is reasonable to claim that a belief we hold is accurate if we reliably satisfy our desires when acting upon it. This success would be unlikely were our representations quite out of line with the facts. Of course, there is no guarantee here, reliable desire satisfaction can come from acting on a false belief, and thus it is not a proper criterion for truth. Yet, this gives us a plausible basis for defining justification that does not require reflection and deliberation. The abilities involved in ERS will include reliable attentional capacities for belief formation and for cognitively integrating beliefs, desires and mental or bodily action. These abilities will constitute an agent's cognitive constitution. Thus, the success of belief under ERS will be due to a person's *agential* cognitive constitution. Justified belief (or something like it) turns out to be a success from agency on ERS. When belief justified in this way is in fact true, an agent will have knowledge, or something quite close.

We have argued that epistemic psychology should, and most likely must, include causally salient motivational states, and we have proposed a normative structure to accommodate this in ERS. The emerging account of epistemic agency that will receive important additions in Chapters 4 and 5 is also compatible with a plausible account of the function of knowledge attributions. Edward Craig (1990) says that subjects use knowledge attributions to flag good sources of information. Successful navigators of reliable sources need to encode information about the environment that is constantly changing by eliminating cognitive noise and attending to epistemically important environmental variables. The evidence suggests that humans and animals have a large repertoire of these epistemic skills. These can be used to form the basis of a naturalized virtue epistemology, as we seek to accomplish here and will be explored further in the following chapters.[13] We enrich our understanding of ERS above with a turn to Peirce and Wittgenstein, both of whom influenced Ramsey's thinking considerably.

3.5   Peirce, Wittgenstein, and Ramsey: Reliability and Assertion

In this section we examine historical influences on Ramsey and extend the account in Section 3.4 to action and assertion, furthering our account of epistemic motivation in Section 3.4. Relevant work by C. S. Peirce, Ramsey, and Ludwig Wittgenstein is discussed.

We begin the transition to chapters on epistemic agency and the motivation to assert by examining ERS within the historical context in which it developed. However, our aim is not purely expository. We argue that the most natural interpretation of ERS incorporates a deep connection between knowledge, assertion, and action, as this was very much in the minds of philosophers influencing Ramsey, in particular C. S. Peirce and Ludwig Wittgenstein. In the following sections, we expand on Ramsey's ideas by comparing them to the views of these two influential figures, who helped shape his thought during his short life. This historical exegesis will illuminate fundamental aspects of the epistemic psychology defended here.

Ramsey is considered a founding figure of analytic philosophy. Many articles refer to his theories, and there is an edited volume on his work as well as a book devoted to his influential pragmatic view on truth as successful action.[14] The originality and insightfulness of his philosophical proposals are aptly captured by what Donald Davidson (1999, 32) calls the "Ramsey effect," which he describes as the phenomenon that for any theory that a philosopher believes to have discovered, it is likely that it was anticipated somehow by Ramsey. Unsurprisingly, many authors have studied the work of Ramsey very carefully, and a more thorough analysis of his ideas is gaining momentum.[15] Ramsey was influencing and being influenced by the important thinkers

---

[13] See, for instance, Glover and Dixon (2002) for evidence that basic epistemic needs to navigate the environment are more insensitive to irrelevant information than intentional planning. We expand on this type of evidence in subsequent chapters.

[14] See Mellor (1990) and Dokic and Engel (2006).

[15] See Sahlin (1990) and references therein; Nanay (2013). Perhaps the most comprehensive study of Ramsey in a philosophical and historical context is Misak (2016).

Charles S. Peirce and Ludwig Wittgenstein, so we consider them both in the following sections in order to enrich our understanding of ERS above. Ramsey and Peirce both locate agency at the center of their view of truth and epistemic achievements in general – including scientific ones. These associated accounts of epistemic skills appeal to inquirers, their goals and actions. For Ramsey, Peirce, and Wittgenstein, basic, implicit, and immediately guiding normativity is crucial.

We hope to show that Peirce in particular has important insights for epistemic psychology, especially when combined with ERS. Peirce not only identifies the content of essential epistemic motivations, but clearly locates them in the context of inquiry. We follow Peirce in both respects with sustained discussions of assertion and inquiry in Chapters 5 and 6 respectively.

3.6   The Norm of Assertion

In this section we locate important nuances to the account of 3.4 from work on precise assertor-content and the norms of communication. Relevant work from Timothy Williamson and Gottlob Frege is discussed. We emphasize norms of opening and closing inquiry and fixing belief in precise contents found in C. S. Peirce's work that is compatible with ERS defended in 3.4.

Frege, as Timothy Williamson (1994, 46) notes, thought that one could not communicate successfully unless one has a precise language, with no room for either vagueness or ambiguity. In contrast, Peirce thought that vagueness was unavoidable. Precision certainly matters for Peirce, but he thought that the task of developing an abstract framework in which all linguistic expressions are exactly precise is a fantasy. About these contrasting views (in the context of his insightful discussion on vagueness), Williamson (1994) writes:

That successful inquiry involves a movement from vagueness towards precision is a commonplace. Both Frege and Peirce subscribed to it. They differed in this: for Frege, vagueness is to be eliminated at the beginning of inquiry; for Peirce, it is not to be eliminated before its end. On Frege's view, we cannot reason reliably until we have a precise language. On Peirce's, our language will always be vague. Vagueness is harmful only when it leaves the question at hand too unclear to be answered. We can then hope to clarify the question in relevant respects until it can be answered. What we cannot hope is ever to have achieved perfect clarity in all respects. Indeed, unnecessary precision does positive harm, cluttering up our theories with irrelevant complexity and rendering them too rigid to adapt to new evidence. (46)

This rich paragraph exhibits the distinction between propositionally based accounts of epistemic access to consciously represented contents, and action-based accounts with more implicit and non-reflective contents utilized in agency. The language of relevance and proper closure of inquiry resonates with our discussion on idealized versus heuristic rationality presented in Chapter 1. One can think of this difference between Frege and Peirce as a difference in *styles* of closing and opening inquiry. We further explore this difference in our discussion of assertion (Chapter 5) and curiosity (Chapter 6).

Despite this difference regarding the elimination of vagueness at the starting or closing point of inquiry, there is much in common between Frege and Peirce when it comes to the act of *assertion*. For Frege, as well as for Peirce, assertion is a very important epistemic and semantic commitment. Frege (1997) wrote that: "it is possible to express a thought without laying it down as true. The two things are so closely joined in an assertoric sentence that it is easy to overlook their separability" (329). As explained in the previous chapter, one can represent the environment without endorsing these contents as ones that are affirmed, asserted, or attended to. Laying down a content as true is an importantly distinct epistemic act from grasping it.

As the acknowledgment of the truth of a thought, Frege sees the act of "judgment" as a mental action with deep normative implications. Frege calls the manifestation of this judgment its "assertion." Etiologically speaking, then, the mental action Frege calls judgment comes first, before successful communication. Conventional markers specify the force of the speech act of assertion. For instance, one may follow a specific convention governing how to introduce a sentence in order to convey that one is asserting it, rather than sarcastically using it. Such conventions will clearly vary depending on linguistic practices and shifting contexts. What is more controversial is whether conventions are necessary to make assertions. Some authors claim that conventions are necessary (Searle, 1969), while others think they are not (Stainton, 2006; Strawson, 1964).

These are very important issues, but we shall focus here on what Frege considered the fundamental epistemic act of endorsing a proposition – the mental action he called judgment. Although there are many interesting options for thinking about rule following with respect to the speech act of assertion, those rules depend upon, and may radically differ from, the rules governing mental assertion (Frege's judgment). We shall focus on this mental action, associated with the reliable confidence that Peirce says "never disappoints."

In any account of assertion, sincerity and confidence are central. Whatever rule speakers follow to detect assertions and flag good sources of information, as opposed to jokes, lies, ironic statements, and other forms of unreliable speech, they are detecting the sincerity and reliability of the speaker. Peirce, like Frege, also contrasted doubt with the reliable and guiding confidence associated with belief and assertion. Peirce wrote in "The Fixation of Belief,"

We generally know when we wish to ask a question and when we wish to pronounce a judgment, for there is a dissimilarity between the sensation of doubting and that of believing. But this is not all which distinguishes doubt from belief. There is a practical difference. Our beliefs guide our desires and shape our actions. [...] The feeling of believing is a more or less sure indication of there being established in our nature some habit which will determine our actions. Doubt never has such an effect. (1992, 114)

Note the distinctly psychological language that Peirce is using to refer to the mental action of assertion. Is belief, understood as a propositional attitude, such a mental act? We may have imprecise or vague beliefs, and those would not lead to action (e.g., I believe this guy could be either bald or not bald, this might be or might not be a heap, etc.). One could also believe a proposition exclusively for the purposes of identifying its implications, without endorsing it. For Peirce, therefore, such mental states would not be paradigmatic cases of epistemic endorsements, because they would lack the characteristic "practical difference" that judgments make. According to Peirce, general propositions may differ in this respect as well. Believing that "All men are mortal" or that "The set of the real numbers is larger than the set of the natural numbers" may not be conducive to guiding our actions, although they may nonetheless serve as *abstract guides* for our concrete actions and thoughts.

These are intricate issues, but what is crucial to emphasize is Peirce's (1992) characterization of belief as a *stabilizing*, firm, and determinate epistemic mental action, deeply associated with a natural and simple kind of confidence (as opposed to reflective and inferential forms):

Belief does not make us act at once, but puts us into such a condition that we shall behave in a certain way, when the occasion arises. Doubt has not the least effect of this sort, but stimulates us to action until it is destroyed. [...] The irritation of doubt causes a struggle to attain a state of belief. I shall term this struggle *inquiry*. (114)

This struggle to overcome doubt plays a central role in Peirce's philosophy. It is also essential to understand Peirce's influence on Ramsey. The connection between their pragmatic view of truth and belief can be succinctly described as follows: what we believe to be true must be precise in the sense that it must be associated with a set of concrete actions that we should perform under those conditions in which the belief is true – *non-accidentally* true given ERS.

Both Peirce and Ramsey emphasize the activity of *inquirers* in their work, and avoid talking about inquiry as an abstract notion. The end of inquiry is not abstract perennial truth, but the precision and stability of the mental states capable of impelling us to act reliably based on our conception of them. But, how should we then characterize the norm of assertion and the mental act that Frege calls judgment? There are at least two different versions of the norm of assertion, even at this foundational psychological level, that need to be distinguished here. One of them is Williamson's (2000): one must assert that p only if one knows that p. This account may be considered too strong because in some instances rational belief seems to be a better norm of assertion (i.e., what one rationally believes entitles the inquirer to assert such beliefs). Notice, however, that Williamson's account is compatible with ERS because if one should assert only what one knows then such a condition guarantees the success of a belief and epistemic desire pair when acted upon in virtue of having met assertive standards. An alternative proposal requires reflective thought, and seems to be biased toward a substantial version of internalism. Donald Davidson (1979) seems to have proposed this view and Unger (1975) requires that the proposition asserted must not only be known but also be represented to oneself as known. These reflective accounts allow for the possibility that representing oneself as knowing or believing that p is compatible with p being false.[16] We expand on the norms of action and assertion in Chapter 5, but it should be clear by now that we disagree with reflective or metacognitive requirements and find Williamson's notion more plausible.

Although Ramsey is a lot more explicit than Peirce on this issue, both of them seem to defend a knowledge account of the norm of assertion without requiring metacognition, inference, self-knowledge, or reflection. But there is much nuance in their accounts of knowledge. Peirce, for instance, proposed that beliefs have a unique stabilizing epistemic effect because they are *points of convergence* in which reliable habits of thought indicate that there is enough stability to guide action. This point of Peirce's has a fundamental connection with Ramsey's success semantics because the essence of fixed belief is to reliably guide action. The habits of thought that lead to successful action are essential to understanding what Dokic and Engel (2006) call "Ramsey's principle": "True beliefs are those that lead to successful actions whatever the underlying motivating desires" (46). Our account is more nuanced than this: for us a Ramsey success satisfies a specific need or desire, not any desire whatever. This is important because it makes the actual content of desires more salient in explaining detailed features of epistemic motivations.

We form habits for stable beliefs in order to eradicate doubt and act upon the world. Our desires, according to Ramsey, are critical in fine-tuning the contents of beliefs (of *content*, in general). One of these implicit desires is to achieve immediate confidence and ignore irrelevant information incompatible with such confidence, or what Peirce calls the stability of belief which brings an end to constant doubt and uncertainty. These are crucial habits of thought that are constitutive of knowledge, and they are intrinsically related to virtuous insensitivity (see 2.7). These skills are robust, stable, and immediately connected to action. We would not be able to function in the world without these skills.

Recently, philosophers working on the semantics of knowledge attributions have taken the proposal that action and knowledge are intimately related very

---

[16] For other disambiguations of the norm of assertion, see Engel (2008).

seriously. For example, Jason Stanley (2005) points out that: "It is immensely plausible to take knowledge to be constitutively connected to action, in the sense that one should act only on what one knows" (9).[17] The normativity of action and assertion depend on the confidence that builds on reliability: not only in successfully representing the environment through attention, but by endorsing the representation as impervious to subsequent inquiry. Peirce and Ramsey were certainly interested in this constitutive connection between knowledge and action.

3.7   Assertion and Action

This section examines detailed historical and philosophical connections between C. S. Peirce, F. P. Ramsey, and Ludwig Wittgenstein, with an eye toward tying Chapters 1–3 together in the account of epistemic agency defended in Chapter 4 to follow. We defend a close analysis of precise content and habits of thought in Peirce's work that is useful for extending the account of epistemic agency defended thus far and to epistemic psychology more generally.

An obvious worry with such action-driven epistemology is how to account for a priori knowledge of the reflective-deductive kind. Both Peirce and Ramsey were acutely aware of this difficulty, and had a very interesting proposal to solve it. Precision in thinking is a central goal in inquiry, and philosophy must facilitate this goal by not making it implausibly dependent on action. Peirce and Ramsey were original and skillful mathematicians. Both of them cared deeply about the foundations of mathematics, epistemic justification, and above all, precise content that produces tangible consequences and reliably leads to success.

Truth requires precise content, and any content can be decomposed into three components: (1) a level of thought, in which a mental action endorses a specific proposition; (2) a level of action, in which contents are assumed in practical inferences; and (3) a level of determinacy and precision, according to which the only beliefs that are relevant for action and assertion are full beliefs, as opposed to *general* beliefs (such as mathematical beliefs), vague beliefs, or degrees of belief (associated with doubt and uncertainty). A venerable tradition has focused on the a priori nature of mathematical truth and its independence from experience. Surely, an a priori truth cannot depend on an action set for the precision of its content. So why believe the approaches by Ramsey and Peirce are plausible in general?

We are not going to provide an account of mathematical truth, but it is important to appreciate how Ramsey and Peirce addressed this problem. Being a priori is not the only characteristic of mathematics. Besides being

---

[17] See also Hawthorne (2004).

necessary and a priori, mathematical knowledge is also graded: some propositions in mathematics are a lot more general than others. According to the pragmatist, mathematical reasoning depends on concrete and specific contents that are *somehow* linked to action: contents about navigation, spatial relations, numbers one can count and calculations for rate one needs to do routinely, and which many animals also need to calculate in order to survive. These clearly qualify as precise contents that lead to successful action.

Foundational contents, what Ramsey calls "real" contents, are always action driven. General propositions, on the other hand, are mostly normative, in the sense that they guide *reliable precisifications*: ways to better understand contents that guide reliable action. The same is true about vague and not fully endorsed belief – they qualify as standards to assess how committed we are to action and assertion. We do not strictly need this aspect of Peirce and Ramsey's work for our account of epistemic agency. But there are useful resources to be gleaned with respect to how attention and assertion operate in the pursuit of knowledge.

One of these important lessons is that the complexities of general, vague, and scalar (degreed) belief require a fundamental motivation to end inquiry. Higher level normativity does not really have content because content and knowledge bottom out in action. Action is the most fundamental, first-order, normative realm (the realm where reliability and dispositions manifest). Attention and assertion guarantee that this first-level normativity is not susceptible to doubts, or misguided and corrupted by irrelevant information – this is partly why, as Williamson notes in the quote above, Peirce thought that excessive precision is actually epistemically *detrimental* and potentially paralyzing. General propositions and degrees of belief are a second realm of normativity in which one is reliably assessing concrete contents for action, not to exacerbate doubt, but to increase reliable guidance.

One might object that one should assert *p* only if one has a high degree of justification that *p*, based on evidence, and this seems to go in the opposite direction, namely into general and degreed belief. But as Greco (2010) says, there are many theoretical beliefs that would epistemically cripple the common folk. The notion of knowledge required for the norm of assertion needs to be less theoretical, less general, less abstract, and much more linked to immediate and reliable action, both personal and collective.

One should believe with a high degree of justification only those contents that one can assert, and one should assert only those contents that reliably lead to successful action. Ramsey's view seems to be adequately characterized by the following biconditional: if a content leads to successful action, then it can be asserted, and if a content can be asserted, then it is a content that guarantees successful action. The norm of action is knowledge, and so is the norm of assertion.

Peirce also (and previous to Ramsey) thought of beliefs as guides to action based on habit.[18] Deduction, induction, abduction, and analogy are central topics in Peirce, and he thinks of these norms for thought as *habits* that need to be put to use in action. There is, however, a topic in Peirce that seems to be particularly pertinent to mathematical knowledge and explanatory (as well as analogical) general belief, which is his notion of "hypostatization," or counting abstractions as real. Ian Hacking (2014) quotes the following remarkable passage from Peirce:

> It may be said that mathematical reasoning (which is the only deductive reasoning, if not absolutely, at least eminently) almost entirely turns on the consideration of abstractions as if they were objects. The protest of nominalism against such hypostatization . . . as it was and is formulated, is simply a protest against the only kind of thinking that has ever advanced human culture. (255)

There are clear epistemic risks in reifying abstractions without justification, which is why Peirce says that hypostatization must be done intelligently. But the notion of hypostatization provides a different route to the problem of general belief because one could guide thought and action as if these abstractions were concrete entities, in order to solve concrete problems. Thus, there might not be a need to even draw a distinction between deduction and induction in mathematics, as some empiricists have suggested. In any case, the emphasis on assertion and action is clear. Attention, in the case of mathematics, is directed toward abstractions, but with the goal to assert and solve concrete problems: a reliable habit with the same structure as the reliable habits that guide perception.

Wittgenstein, it seems, was also deeply influenced by these ideas. Wittgenstein thought that language should be understood in terms of patterns of use one could and should follow. The influence of Ramsey on Wittgenstein may have led Wittgenstein in the direction of identifying limits of inquiry, as his notion of "bedrock" in *On Certainty* aims at capturing the commonsense end of inquiry. Truth is not only a value that epistemology pursues but also the aim of a stable cluster of integrated habits that frame action and assertion.

Consider the following passages from *On Certainty*:

> 58. If "I know etc." is conceived as a grammatical proposition, of course the "I" cannot be important. And it properly means "There is no such thing as doubt in this case" or "The expression 'I do not know' makes no sense in this case."
> 61. A meaning of a word is a kind of employment of it. For it is what we learn when the word is incorporated into our language. (ibid. 10)

The limits of inquiry here are related to skills for communication and these skills, which determine the use of contents in communication, specify when

---

[18] For Peirce's influence on Ramsey, and Ramsey's influence on Wittgenstein, see Misak (2016). We are grateful to Cheryl Misak for sharing her manuscript with us.

one should assert or retract (much more on this in Chapter 5). The limits of inquiry are also the basis of commonsense or "bedrock." Relevant inquires demand virtuous insensitivity to inadequate doubts. Wittgenstein relates these broadly pragmatic considerations to Moore's solution to the problem of the external world.

115. If you tried to doubt everything you would not get as far as doubting anything. The game of doubting itself presupposes certainty.
116. Instead of "I know," couldn't Moore have said: "It stands fast for me that . . . "? And further: "It stands fast for me and many others . . . " (ibid. 18)
204. Giving grounds, however, justifying the evidence, comes to an end; – but the end is not certain propositions' striking us immediately as true, i.e. it is not a kind of *seeing* on our part; it is our *acting*, which lies at the bottom of the language-game. (ibid. 28)
445. But if I say "I have two hands," what can I add to indicate reliability? At the most that the circumstances are the ordinary ones. (ibid. 58)

Moore's "Proof of the External World" seems to make exactly the point Wittgenstein is interested in making in these and other passages of *On Certainty.*[19] If one were asked how to rigorously prove there is an external world, one could only point at the standard skills we use in interacting with the world – here is a hand, here is another hand, conclusion. This is not meant as a joke, but rather as an expression of bewilderment at the type of doubt being posed. What could help us prove that there is an external world other than the ordinary exercise of our reliable epistemic skills? What could we attend to in order to guide such an inquiry? As Peirce would say, this inquiry is not adequate because it does not have a proper way of reaching an ending point and guiding our actions. We are virtuous by ignoring such conundrums when, as Wittgenstein says, "the circumstances are the ordinary ones."

In the next chapter, we will expand on the psychology of epistemic action and the norms of assertion in Chapter 5.

---

[19] See also Greco (2010) on why Thomas Reid's notion of commonsense and insensitivity to highly abstract or theoretical belief is of a piece with Moore's "proof" of the external world.

4   Epistemic Agency

This chapter examines fundamental tensions between agency, credit, and automaticity, with specific emphasis on Sosa's recent *Judgment & Agency* (2015). Relevant work from Ernest Sosa, Imogen Dickie, and Wayne Wu is discussed. We argue that the attentional model of epistemic agency defended in Chapters 1–3 adequately resolves the tension above through forms of integration rather than second-order affirmation as in Sosa's account.

4.1   Tensions between Credit, Agency, and Automaticity

We present a fundamental tension between epistemic credit and the ubiquity of automaticity in reliable cognition, in particular for virtue reliabilist accounts of epistemic agency. Relevant work by Ernest Sosa, Wayne Wu, Imogen Dickie, and G. E. M. Anscombe is discussed. We argue that mixed attentional processes are both sufficiently agential and credit conferring, despite being largely automatic, and defend this thesis throughout the chapter.

As we have argued, some of the epistemic value generated by agents in the direction of analysis thesis (DA*) comes from the proper exercise of agency. However, any psychologically informed account of epistemic agency must account for the ubiquity of automatic cognitive processes clearly demonstrated by empirical research in psychology, discussed below. Common ways of thinking have it that automatic processes are not agential, so if automaticity is indeed ubiquitous, then epistemic agency will be presumably rare. However, if epistemic agency is rare, then so too is the sort of credit necessary to account for the full value of knowledge. An agential virtue theoretic epistemic psychology (VTEP) would thus not be an adequate psychology of knowledge.

In Introduction, we examined Imogen Dickie's account of perceptual demonstrative reference as a luck-eliminating success and argued for a motivationally grounded safety condition. Here we argue for an account of epistemic agency that is both luck eliminating and which tolerates a good bit of automaticity. This will provide a solution to the tension above because the automatic processes raising concerns will be explained as parts of agential processes, and, since these successful agential processes will be luck eliminating, they are also credit conferring. Agential epistemic success is credit conferring because it is luck eliminating. We extend our earlier examination of Dickie's view below and then devote our attention to Ernest Sosa's recent account of epistemic agency in *Judgment & Agency* (2015). We argue for a slight modification of Dickie's account to connect motivation and luck-reduction, and will focus on agency, credit, and automaticity for the remainder of the chapter.

Imogen Dickie (2011, 2015) persuasively explains various forms of reference (perceptual demonstrative reference in particular) and justification in terms of the operation of luck-eliminating cognitive abilities. We make a similar argument here, but we explain epistemic *credit* in terms of luck-eliminating *agency* in a way that is fully compatible with the ubiquity of automaticity. On luck-eliminating justification, Dickie says "S's justification for the belief that p is 'luck eliminating' if it excludes all relevant not-p situations" (2011, 292). Requiring the elimination of *all* relevant not-p situations may appear too demanding and will depend on how one answers complicated questions about human cognitive limitations. Dickie restricts relevant alternatives to "those the subject knows to be commonplace" (ibid.) and this is sensible enough, but we will define relevant conditions as those in which *a motivation is reliably successful*. Recalling our discussion of Ramsey and Mellor in Chapter 3, the success conditions for motivations are given by the utility condition of belief-desire pairs (or clusters). Acting on an appropriate motivation when the utility condition for that motivation obtains is a luck-eliminating achievement where the luck elimination can be credited to the agent.

Before presenting the main difficulty raised by automaticity research, we will clarify a few fundamental links between motivation and luck-reduction on our account that will be important for the argument to follow. Effective motivations reduce luck in desire satisfaction, and this tells us one reason why acting on a motivation is a generally rational thing to do. Luck elimination is secured in part by the accuracy of the belief element in relation to a specific goal, but an accurate belief is only luck-eliminating for action in relation to specific certain desires, as it may reduce success with respect to others. Desires also play a role in luck elimination because they partition vast amounts of information into relevant and irrelevant categories quickly and efficiently. A motivation that does not reduce luck in these ways is unlikely to be reliably successful.

The luck-eliminating properties of motivations constitute an elegant and potent basis for an account of epistemic virtue, particularly for explaining epistemic credit for true belief. As Dickie puts it, considering the skilled and successful archer Robin Hood: "Because Robin is a skilled archer, his intention selects (causes in the appropriate way) activation of a means of its fulfillment" (2011, 308). His shot is a "non-luckily selected non-lucky generator of fulfillment of his intention (so he will be unlucky to fail and not merely lucky to succeed" (ibid.). A belief that is a non-luckily selected non-lucky generator of the fulfillment of an assertoric intention is plausibly taken as a justified belief. We emphasize here that such a belief or motivation also speaks to the credit of the agent that holds it. Effective agency secures agent-level credit through luck elimination.

We now examine a fundamental challenge to any reliabilist theory of knowledge that requires credit for knowledge. Wu (2013) aptly describes this as the challenge of squaring agency and automaticity such that one can simultaneously hold "that automaticity implies the absence of control and that agency, as an agent's exemplification of control, involves, and often requires, much automaticity" (245). John Bargh and Tanya Chartrand's (1999) research shows that "most of a person's everyday life is determined not by their conscious intentions and deliberate choices but by mental processes that are put into motion by features of the environment that operate outside of conscious awareness and guidance" (citation from Wu, 2013, 245). Koch and Crick (2001) have developed a theory of "zombie agents" (agents that reliably accomplish tasks without any conscious awareness in the process) around automaticity results. Wu (2013, 245–247) argues that the recent history of automaticity and control in recent cognitive science shows a consistent move away from the *"simple connection* between automaticity and control" (245) and actually asserts that *control requires automaticity.*[1] While many of the details are still being worked out, it is reasonable to say that the ubiquity of automaticity is a clear result in the recent history of cognitive science and neurology.

In light of this research, the argument against any epistemic theory that requires agential success for credit will get off the ground as follows:

1. Virtue theoretic success requires credit for an agent-level success.
2. Many epistemic successes are psychologically explained in terms of automatic processing.
3. Thus, many epistemic successes are not agent-level successes.
4. Thus, many epistemic successes are not virtue theoretic epistemic successes.

The final conclusion (4) might not worry a virtue epistemologist if the "many" non-virtue theoretic successes do not constitute an overwhelming plurality, or if they all fall into a couple expected categories (e.g., a priori knowledge, knowledge of time). However, the arc of the research in neurology suggests that automaticity is ubiquitous and widely distributed in our cognitive life, so the "many" non-epistemic successes in the conclusion

---

[1] Automaticity on most views in the psychological literature describes a process that regularly initiates in the presence of a standard trigger (and thus has a reliability component), and that the activation of a sequence of nodes in a process (e.g., nodes in a neural network) does not require active control or attention by the subject.

(4) might be a worrisome lot after all. Recognizing the ubiquity of automaticty in knowledge is potentially problematic because it is difficult to reconcile with any requirement that epistemic virtue requires person-level success. An automatic success does not appear to be a person-level success. Virtue epistemologists have good reason to define knowledge as an agent-level success because knowledge is something we attribute to a *person* (see especially Greco, 2010), not their eyes or ears, so credit attributions should be person level as well, but it is unclear how this will be reconciled with the ubiquity of automaticity.

Clearly, the conclusion only follows if we include another premise linking automatic success (AS) and agent-level success in the right way.

AS: If an epistemic success S is caused by an automatic process, then (a) S is not an agent-level success and (b) S is not a success for which agent-level credit is due.

AS sharply separates automatic processes and person-level processes, and this will be sufficient to show why premise 2 is worrisome. It will be necessary to explain what a "non-automatic process" amounts to here. This will be examined closely in the following sections, but we make a small start by stating the relation between agency and automaticity in terms of *control*.[2]

(C) A process p is agential for S at t if and only if p is controlled by S at t; if p is *automatic* for S at t, then S is not controlled for S at t.

The recent history of cognitive science shows that most of our cognitive states will not be controlled under (C), and in conjunction with (AS), it entails that vast portions of our epistemic life will not generate agent-level credit. To avoid this, we do not need to abandon the spirit of (C), we just need a better understanding of what a "process being controlled by a subject" amounts to, and to leave room for automaticity in that process. Wu has recently argued that (C), when re-conceptualized to accommodate the right way of understanding control and automaticity, is actually true. Once re-conceptualized, the worrisome cases of mental and bodily agency that are significantly automatic can be explained, thus removing any threat automaticity seemed to pose to agency. The additional boon for our account is that we can now explain how manifesting epistemic agency generates epistemic credit for largely automatic epistemic achievements.

If we are successful here, we will have an account of epistemic agency that incorporates the ubiquity of implicit processing but still provides a sufficient basis for crediting an agent for any success that is properly "from agency."

---

[2] Psychologists often prefer "controlled" to the terms most often found in philosophical writing, at least historically, such as "free," "agent," and "will."

4.2   Sosa's Judgments and Functionings: Personal and Sub-personal Success

This section presents aspects of Sosa's thorough account of epistemic agency as manifest in second-order "alethic affirmation." While there is considerable common ground between Sosa's account and the view we defend, we appeal to insights from Anscombe favoring integration over reflection as the basis of epistemic agency.

In his recent book *Judgment & Agency* (2015), Ernest Sosa develops a thorough account of epistemic agency. In broad outline, agency consists in a subject "endeavoring" to perform an action in order to achieve an aim for Sosa. He remains neutral on what freely choosing a performance amounts to, but he is clear that endeavors require a kind of choice that, for example, hearts do not engage in when they pump blood. Endeavors, epistemic or otherwise, are freely chosen performances. Distinctively epistemic agency comes in the form of "alethic endeavors." An alethic endeavor is an (public or private) affirmation of a content, and is thus properly seen as a truth-directed performance, one which aims at getting things right. Affirmations can have moral or prudential aims, but these are not exercises of *epistemic* agency because this requires endeavoring for an alethic end.

However, not all alethic affirmations are expressions of epistemic agency. Sosa distinguishes between "functionings" and "judgments." Sosa says that functionings are entirely below the level of personhood, and thus do not involve choice in the way needed for an endeavor (and thus for any manifestation of epistemic agency). Functionings are sub-personal teleologically guided capacities for information processing. When a function succeeds, its success is like a properly functioning heart or retina because choice plays no role in explaining its success. Successful functionings are wholly sub-personal on Sosa's account.

Judgments, on the other hand, are chosen endeavors to believe aptly in order to get things right. Epistemic agency is thus manifested by, in some sense, freely choosing a second-order alethic affirmation.

> With judgment one aims for more than just getting it right. One aims not just for success but for reliable enough, even apt success [...] The judgmental knower must have a second order grasp—a belief or presupposition—that her first-order affirmation would then be apt. (Sosa, 2015, 151)

Epistemic choosing on this account is a second-order affirmation.[3] Judgments are epistemic choices to affirm that not only aim to get things right, but to get

---

[3] Sosa (2015, 193) has an interesting intermediate region we will discuss further below "which admits a kind of agency, even if performances in that region are not freely determined endeavors, which constitute or derive from choices or judgments." Our proposal later in this chapter might provide an explanation of this intermediate region between freedom and passivity, but it is hard to

them right *aptly*. Apt alethic affirmation requires a very specific (and often burdensome) second-order representation of how likely it is that a first-order affirmation is apt, and that we choose to affirm this second-order representation. The typical objects of our second-order affirmations will include first-order affirmations, the condition of the cognitive mechanisms that produce them, and information about the environment they are operating in. Only judgment manifests epistemic agency for Sosa.

Here we find Sosa caught in the tension noted above. On the one hand, credit for epistemic success and non-lucky success requires the manifestation of agency for Sosa. On the other hand, the ubiquity of automaticity in human cognition appears to entail that a good bit of our intuitively successful epistemic performances will not have the kind of credit and non-luckiness that judgments do. Non-lucky, sufficiently creditworthy epistemic endeavors must be intentional, chosen, person-level tryings for Sosa, but how can all, or even most, cases of knowledge plausibly be seen as involving anything like Sosa's intentions when the psychological literature is clear on the ubiquity of automatic processes? Sosa recognizes an important range of non-intentional epistemic successes, functionings (e.g., basic perception), but these are defined as non-agential successes.

Perhaps Sosa resolves this by recognizing an intermediate category of affirmations which are not "freely determined endeavors," but which "constitute or derive from choices or judgments" and thus "admit of a kind of agency" (ibid. 193). This might avoid overly restrictive conditions for ("a kind of") agency because they do not have to be chosen in the way judgments are, and they will still sufficiently manifest a kind of agency because they derive from relevant choices. If the kind of agency these intermediate affirmations possess is sufficient to earn epistemic credit and sufficiently preclude lucky success and deviant causal chains, then Sosa's theory will satisfactorily explain a wide range of our successful, but largely automatic epistemic performances.

However, this looks like a problematic move. Sosa says these intermediate affirmations either are or derive from choices and judgments. That means they either are or derive from second-order affirmation. If intermediate affirmations "derive from" choices or judgments, the only instance of this kind of affirmation will have a special relation to a very specific type of second-order affirmation (an affirmation about the aptness of a first-order affirmation). We are still saddled with a necessary appeal to second-order affirmations with this move to intermediate affirmations. Where this seems to go wrong is not in requiring that a first-order affirmation be integrated in some way with another cognitive state, but in the specific demand that the other state must be a second-order

be sure because Sosa does not further develop this point in the way he does with the category of judgment.

affirmation. A more psychologically plausible account will say that intermediate affirmations must be robustly integrated, but with no requirement that second-order affirmation plays any significant role in the integrated state or process. Rather than reflection, we have emphasized the integration between fitting attentional states modulated for action, choice, and speech to explain epistemic agency. This form of integration is a kind of agency, but it does not require second-order affirmation. In many cases, second-order cognition would be unwanted, especially if success can be had in its absence or if it disturbs the reliability of stable first-order processes.

There is no need to deny that some affirmations fall into the category of what Sosa calls judgments. However, for his credit and anti-luck conditions for knowledge to accommodate the ubiquity of automaticity, Sosa will need to account for agency in a different way, one that does not tie agency necessarily to judgment. We now defend an alternative understanding of epistemic agency that will make it clear where and how sub-personal and person-level states interact in sufficiently agential competences. This will not require a grounding in any second-order affirmation, as on Sosa's account.

4.3   Mental and Epistemic Action

This section presents accounts of mental and epistemic action emphasizing specific forms of integration. Relevant work by Wayne Wu, Chris Lepock, Susan Mantel, and Imogen Dickie is discussed. We argue that attentional states manifest integration sufficient for epistemic agency, and show Sosa's second-order affirmations to be unnecessary for a theory of epistemic agency.

Both Sosa and Wu present their account of intentional activity as an advancement over the standard causal theory of action, but in importantly different ways. As we have seen, Sosa requires a second-order affirmation of a particular kind. Wu (2013) argues that intentions are quite different psychological states than those proposed by most philosophers (this appears to include Sosa, but Wu does not directly consider him). The best available accounts of mental and bodily action in psychology show that all successfully controlled behaviors require automaticity. Manifestations of agential competences do not require second-order representations, they require *integrated representations*. Second-order representations accomplish a kind of integration, but this is not the kind that is necessary for epistemic agency (though it might be sufficient when second-order activity does not disrupt first-order activity, e.g., if second-order affirmation drains cognitive resources or inappropriately directs attention). The kind of integration necessary for epistemic agency is a special case of the kind involved in attentional states generally.

Let's first pin down an understanding of mental action that allows us to explain epistemic actions as a special case, and ultimately epistemic agency as that process which manifests epistemic actions. Joelle Proust (2012) accounts for mental actions in terms of meta-cognitive processes, such as monitoring and control that "results from the sudden realization that one of the epistemic preconditions for a developing action is not met." While Proust recognizes the ubiquity of automatic processes in mental action, her account requires meta-representations and to this extent exemplifies the aspect of Sosa's account we find problematic. However, Chris Lepock (2014) argues that meta-cognition can occur without meta-representation. Since conscious representation is cognitively costly, this would be an advantage for any theory that explains mental action in terms of meta-cognition. Lepock gives the example of a "regulator" in a train which models and responds to the activities in the engine, but it does not represent those activities. In a similar fashion, we might have "epistemic feelings" (doubt, certainty, curiosity, the "tip of the tongue" feeling) that monitor and control cognitive processes without representing them.

The reality of meta-cognition is well established empirically, and there is no reason to deny that it is sufficient for a kind of mental action. The emphasis, however, is still on second-order states, whether representational or not, and this seems to miss the most essential feature of mental action, namely *integration*. Two states or processes can be cognitively integrated without one of them being *about* the other. For example, the dual process theory of cognition defended in some form by many psychologists (including Stanovich, 2011; Kahneman, 2011) claims that there is integration between system 1 (fast, implicit, automatic cognition) and system 2 (explicit, controlled, conscious cognition), but neither of these is *about* the other in the way that a second-order affirmation is about a first-order affirmation. There are relations of influence and control between them, but not meta-representation, at least not necessarily so. In some cases, system 2 might take a system 1 process as an intentional object, but that is not the standard way they are integrated throughout most of our cognitive life. It may be sufficient for being cognitively integrated that one state (or process) of a system is about another state (or process) of the system, but this is not essential for integration as such.

Susanne Mantel (2013) presents an interesting case for taking Sosa's "accuracy, adroitness and aptness" (AAA) model of performance normativity as a model for acting on normative reasons. She argues that an adequate account of acting on a normative reason can be understood through a "competence to act with normative reasons" as described in Sosa's AAA theory. An important modification she makes is to add sub-competences to Sosa's account. Appealing to sub-competences might allow Sosa to better accommodate automatic processing in agency. Mantel canvasses a number of subjective and objective senses in which an agent can be said to act on a normative reason, and defends the following admittedly strong requirement:

The fact that there is a normative reason from the agent's point of view needs to hold *because* there really is a normative reason that favors the action and the agent exercise a disposition when there really is one. I will call such dispositions "dispositions to appropriate belief." (ibid. 3869)

In order to manifest a "disposition to appropriate belief," it must be the case that any subjectively normative reason (normative from the agent's point of view) to favor an action is somehow explained by the fact that there really is one. This is certainly a commendable disposition. In manifesting such a disposition, an agent not only conforms to factive reasons by acting on subjective reasons, but does so because their subjective reasons are appropriately related to the factive reasons their actions conform to. The "because of" clause, a central plank in most virtue epistemology, links subjective and factive reasons in ways that guard against luck in action explanations. According to Mantel, the competence to have true beliefs about factive reasons and the competence to be motivated by these beliefs conjointly comprise the *competence to act in accordance with reasons*, and acting *for* a normative reason is the successful exercise of that competence. This is one way to apply the aptness requirement in Sosa's epistemology to action theory.

The question for current purposes is whether Mantel's "dispositions to appropriate belief" require second-order representations in agency explanations. The performance is agential because the required etiological source (which should be luck avoiding) is a belief's being motivated in the right way. It looks second-order when she says that the relevant true beliefs must be "about factive reasons," but here these are objects and entities, not our beliefs or attitudes toward them. In order for Mantel's account to be essentially second order in the way Sosa's is, a subjective reason would have to be about another subjective reason, or belief. There is no requirement of this sort on her account. Mantel just requires that (true) beliefs that motivate action are about facts that speak in favor of an action (objective reasons). Even if it can be the case that Sosa's second-order affirmations satisfy Mantel's schema, this is not a necessary condition for doing so.

The worries raised about Sosa's account of epistemic agency are therefore not endemic to his AAA account of performance normativity, instead it is Sosa's specific claim that a second-order affirmation is necessary. Mantel's account has many interesting points, some of which are discussed further below, but she does not specify an alternative integration relation, and she must make the case for objective reasons and their appropriate relation to subjective reasons.

Sosa and Wu both distinguish their accounts of intentional action from simple causal theories that claim that a behavior must have an intention as its cause, but Wu does not require second-order representations. Wu says that many causal accounts of action appear to assume that intentional causality involves one event directly causing another. However, this is clearly not true in many, perhaps most, cases of intentional activity. In most cases, behavior is explained by *standing, static intentions*, which nonetheless causally influence current behaviors. Most intentions are enduring structural features of an agent's mind that reliably "bias" the flow of information by automatically weighting the options presented in many-many problems, or by ignoring information altogether. As automaticity research suggests, these are largely non-conscious, sub-personal processes. What is essential for our purposes is that the weighting and biasing of information is a way that one state or process can control, influence, and become integrated with another without being the case that a second-order affirmation is about a first-order affirmation. This is an integrated, non-reflective way of being related.

Is this sufficient for being agential, even granting that it is a form of integration? Consider that, on our account, this weighting and biasing of information occurs because of an agent-level attentional state, typically a *motive* or goal of an agent. Relations of control will obtain between cognitive processes because of some agent-level integration. As Dickie says,

Pre-conceptual processing parses the visual field into units of coherence ("visual objects") that can draw and hold attention without conceptual assistance . . . Detection of the cue recruits extra information-processing resources to the cued element of the visual field. (2011, 303)

Remembering the world-directed attention Murdoch describes, in (2.2), ordinary attentional states about the world require unique forms of integration. Again from Dickie,

Selection recruits extra information processing to attended parts of the visual field (so that we typically have more information from, and are quicker to respond to changes in attended regions). And selection structures the input from an attended region – for example, binding features together as features of a single object. (2011, 301)

Selection (and attentional anchoring) triggers specific forms of feature integration in the attended region, in this case binding features together as features of a single object. A different form of attention could integrate only colors or shapes, rather than binding features together as a single object. In either case, the research on attention clearly shows that (person-level) selection automatically triggers specific feature-integrating processes. The integration achieved is caused by person-level attentional selection, and is therefore integration due to agency even though much of the process is automatic.

We have explained how attentional states bring about cognitive integration sufficient for agency without requiring meta-representation or second-order affirmation. Let's say these attentional processes constitute mental actions, but what, then, are specifically epistemic actions? As Sosa notes, some affirmings are agential but not epistemic and we are in full agreement here. Some affirmings, private or public, are motivated by practical or prudential concerns. We can say that an epistemic action includes any mental action whose intention (in Wu's sense of intention), standing or occurrent, reliably produces biasing and weighting for solving *epistemic many-many problems*. On our account, epistemic many-many problems are those related to the task of successful assertion. These attentional processes are epistemic actions that can be epistemically evaluated for reliability and internal norms (as per our argument in Section 2.5). This will be explained in detail in the following chapter. The move from mental action to epistemic action here just involves a specification of the type of attention involved (assertoric). Our view is close to Sosa's on this score. For him, properly epistemic agency is that which aims to affirm in order to get things right; we say it aims to solve many-many problems related to assertion.

4.4   Resolving the Tension

In this section, we aim to resolve the tension presented in Section 4.1 without falling prey to the pitfalls of Sosa's second-order affirmations. Relevant work by Wayne Wu, Ernest Sosa, and G. E. M. Anscombe is discussed. We argue that mixed personal/sub-personal attentional processes are sufficiently agential and credit conferring for epistemic evaluation and allow a resolution of the tensions created by the ubiquity of automaticity.

We began this chapter by considering a potentially worrisome tension between the kind of credit we give to agential success and the ubiquity of automaticity in such processes. If automaticity is a threat to agency, then automatic successful performances would seem to inevitably fall short of the kind of credit necessary for knowledge. We now have a way to resolve this. We can say that if a person-level state or process (e.g., a motive or attentional process) controls and integrates an automatic process in ways described in the previous section, then that automatic process will be part of (because it is integrated with) a larger "mixed" process. We say that mixed processes are sufficiently agential to ground agent-level epistemic credit attributions. A mixed process integrates sub-personal processes with some person-level process (e.g., selection from a restaurant menu, intending to kick a ball, answering a question), but the person-level process is not about the sub-personal process. Any such process will be a sufficient manifestation of agency, epistemic or otherwise. Likewise, no process that is *entirely automatic* will count as agential. Mixed and wholly occurrent attentional processes are agential, wholly automatic processes are not agential.

We can now say that any process p is controlled so long as any automatic part of p is either caused by or causes a controlled part of p (or both), where any part of p is controlled so long as it manifests agency as described above. Any mixed process is thus a controlled process, and is thus an agential process. Recalling (AS) above:

AS: If an epistemic success is caused by an automatic process, then (a) it cannot be an agent-level success and (b) is not a success for which agent-level credit is due.

We can see now that it is actually true when properly understood. A process will not be controlled when no part of it is controlled, and this will indeed be incompatible with attributing agent-level credit for success. The argument we began this chapter with is only worrisome if we believe that a process with any automatic element is an uncontrolled and non-agential process. Our reading of mixed processes accommodates the ubiquity of automaticity, but shows this to be compatible with agency and agent-level credit because of the integration achieved by motivational elements of attentional processes. Manifesting this kind of agency does not require any second-order affirmations as Sosa's account does, and it provides an improved account of cognitive integration.

It is reasonable to press the account of mixed processes above for some specification of which aspects of a process must be consciously accessible and which do not in order for such a process to count as agential. This is a difficult point to make. On the one hand, if all members of a set of cognitive processes are deemed agential, it is reasonable to think that there will be pronounced regularities in which elements of these processes involve attention to consciously accessible contents and which do not. On the other hand, the diversity and flexibility of cognition makes it reasonable to think that conscious accessibility might be found anywhere in a particular agential process in a particular person at any particular time. The basic structure of attentional processes that we have been using throughout might locate conscious accessibility in selection of an anchor for input, the recruited guidance processes or selection of output for task completion.

Here is a suggestion from G. E. M. Anscombe that at least points to an answer. In her classic work *Intention* (1957), she writes:

What distinguishes actions which are intentional from those which are not? The answer that I shall suggest is that they are the actions to which a certain sense of the question "Why?" is given application; the sense is of course that in which the answer, if positive, gives a reason for acting. But this is not a sufficient statement, because the question "What is the relevant sense of the question 'Why?'" and "What is meant by 'reason for acting'?" are one and the same. (9)

Anscombe carefully distinguishes different senses of "why" a bodily movement might occur; "consider the question, 'Why did you knock the cup off the table?' answered by 'I thought I saw a face at the window and it made me jump'" (ibid. 9). This kind of answer to "why?" gives a causal reason for action, but does not thereby make the action intentional as in the case where "you ask

'Why did you kill him?' the answer 'He killed my father' is surely a reason rather than a cause" (ibid. 10). Anscombe shows us that we must be very careful in our understanding of reasons and causes in order to properly understand intentional action.

Anscombe also distinguishes "practical knowledge" from "speculative knowledge," the former being of interest here. Practical knowledge is the non-observational and non-inferential understanding one has of "ones limbs and certain movements, such as the muscular spasm in falling asleep" (ibid. 49), and the knowledge of what one is presently doing (e.g., pumping water from the well, going to the store). Anscombe says that knowledge of the position of our body and what we are currently doing are not based on any observations or inferences we make: "a man usually knows the position of his limbs without observation. It is without observation, because nothing *shews* him the position of his limbs; it is not as if he were going by a tingle in his knee, which is a sign that it is bent and not straight" (ibid. 13).

More specifically about practical knowledge, Anscombe writes: "what can opening the window be except making such-and-such movements with such-and-such a result? And in that case what can *knowing* one is opening the window be except knowing that that is taking place? Now if there are two *ways* of knowing here, one of which I call knowledge of one's intentional action and the other of which I call knowledge by observation of what takes place, then must there not be two *objects* of knowledge? How can one speak of two different knowledges of *exactly* the same thing? It is not that there are two descriptions of the same thing, both of which are known, as when one knows that something is red and that it is coloured; no, here the description, opening the window, is identical, whether it is known by observation or by its being one's intentional action" (51).

Even though these states and processes lack observational content (according to Anscombe), practical knowledge is constituted by facts that are consciously accessible, facts that are ready at hand, and facts that we properly count as knowing. We propose a similar understanding of the person-level element of mixed processes in epistemic agency as defined above. For any attentional state, a subject should be able to explain what they are attending to and what task their attentional state is involved in. Facts about what a person is doing (under an intentional description) are generally consciously accessible to them while they are doing it. Call this access to an individual's "current behavioral context," which, according to Allport, "generally includes his or her physical location in relation to physical objects, but also his or her social (and emotional) context in relation to present (or indeed thought about), any ongoing linguistic context" (2011, 36). To claim that agents regularly have access to this type of changing information about themselves is empirically supported because the prefrontal cortex serves a specific function: "the active maintenance of patterns of activity that represent *current goals and the means to achieve them*" (ibid. 39, emphasis ours). Clearly, we could not get along very well without easy access to our current goals and the means we are currently taking to achieve them. These will then be the aspects of mixed agential processes that are consciously accessible in typical cases, and these will typically recruit the automatic processes which now become part of our agency.

Importantly, accessibility does not require constant conscious representation, it would be burdensome and counterproductive to constantly remind ourselves of what we are doing at the moment we are doing it. As Anscombe puts it, "Generally speaking, it would be very rare for a person to go through all the steps of a piece of practical reasoning as set out in conformity with Aristotle's models, saying e.g., 'I am human', and 'Lying on a bed is a good way of resting'" (1957, 79). Pieces of practical knowledge can influence and integrate other cognitive processes by automatically ruling out irrelevant information and weighting relevant information even without being consciously attended to at the moment and without being a second-order state (as Sosa has it).

Putting these points from Anscombe and recent psychological work on attention together with our attempt to resolve the tension between agency and automaticity, we can now say that any mixed process will include causally efficacious forms of practical knowledge (in Anscombe's sense), and the processes relevant to epistemic agency will usually be a subset of these.[4] Practical knowledge is person-level knowledge (knowing what you are doing), so every mixed process will include easily accessible person-level knowledge. When automatic processes are appropriately integrated with person-level knowledge (e.g., by recruiting other relevant information and readying action relevant processing) they become parts of a mixed process. The person-level part is the practical knowledge that integrates the automatic parts, and this can be explained in terms of the neural underpinnings of practical knowledge in contemporary psychology of attention (as noted above). The contribution from Anscombe is essential here because by requiring that agential states include practical knowledge we do not thereby require that any person-level state must be consciously represented, and the contents of practical knowledge will recruit the right forms of automatic processing to create cognitive integration sufficient for epistemic agency. Anscombe reinforces our claim against Sosa that integration rather than reflection is what matters, and

---

[4] It is unlikely that all instances of practical knowledge in Anscombe's sense will be causally efficacious elements of agency, since much of this can be trivial information about the position of our body that is not mobilized in any current action. Our claim is just that any agential process will include states of practical knowledge in Anscombe's sense, not that all practical knowledge is agential. At a minimum, the information relevant to action will usually include self-locating information that guides motor activity.

there appears to be solid research on attention from important psychologists like Allport (above) that supports her view.

Practical knowledge integrates the self, it does not observe the self, and this should be our perspective in epistemic psychology as well. We have many of the resources to incorporate these points from Anscombe into our attention-based epistemic psychology in the current work, but will not aim to develop a full Anscombian epistemic psychology here. We should expect considerable coherence between our account and Anscombe in this respect not only because of the symmetry with Allport's work on an agent's knowledge of the "current behavioral context," but also because our account has been shaped by Ramsey, who is of course no stranger to Anscombe. The modification of Ramsey's success semantics we proposed in our discussion (Section 3.4) of epistemic Ramsey successes (ERS) appears to be satisfied by items of Anscombian practical knowledge. Acting on practical knowledge in Anscombe's sense will typically lead to the satisfaction of a relevant desire. This is not surprising because practical knowledge is typically included in, and often flat out constitutes, a reason for action, and reasons for action aim to satisfy desires. Knowledge of what Allport calls our "current behavioral context," subserved by the active maintenance of the prefrontal cortex, constitutes a form of Anscombian practical knowledge as well (and is thus non-observational), and this knowledge integrates automatic processes in a broader person-level state, a state which also constitutes an ERS.

Returning to the problem of automaticity and credit now, we should have plenty of ground to claim that, according to the epistemic psychology defended here, epistemic achievements that are largely automatic can nonetheless constitute manifestations of epistemic agency, and that agent-level credit is due for successful epistemic agency. What remains to be spelled out are the aims and goals constitutive of epistemic agency. We turn to this in Chapter 5 on assertion and we have already suggested the general view in the discussion of Frege on assertoric and interrogative speech in Chapter 2.

Despite our clear differences with Sosa on the necessity of second-order affirmations for epistemic agency, there appears to be less distance with respect to the intentional contents characteristic of epistemic agency. This will dissipate a bit as we get into the next chapter, but it speaks to an important area of agreement. A necessary feature of the intentional contents of an alethic affirmation on Sosa's account is that the affirmation is performed in order to "get it right" about the relevant part of the world (in order to affirm a content that is true). As noted, we propose that the aim of epistemic agency be characterized in terms of satisfying a need for successful assertion, which also aims at "getting it right." Superficially, these are similar motivational contents. However, the aim to successfully assert does not simply reduce to forming a propositional attitude and endorsing a means for its expression, it requires negotiating a complex array of social-communicative contexts, solving many-many problems, tracking relevant and changing information in the environment, and, importantly, ignoring vast amounts of irrelevant information. This will be detailed in the following chapter in a focused examination of assertion, and this will provide the details of epistemic agency. In the concluding section of this chapter, we examine how complex forms of cognitive integration are involved in animal and infant communication.

4.5   Language and Agency

This section largely serves as a bridge between the account of epistemic agency defended above and the detailed examination of norms governing assertion in the next chapter by way of presenting relevant points from the psychology of communication. We consider research in psychology relevant to epistemic aspects of communication in various animal species and young children.

Agency may be broadly described as the capacity to act in a specific environment for specific goals. In our discussion so far, we have emphasized the importance of cognitive integration for epistemic agency, and the underlying dispositional structure of epistemic agency. Here we briefly consider some implications about agency and linguistic communication to set the stage for closer discussions in Chapters 5 and 7.

Many epistemic achievements depend on a quite minimal and implicit kind of integration. Consider the case of what ethologists call "fixed action patterns," which are specific behaviors that are interpreted in a unique way within a species (for review, see Andrews, 2014). Some action patterns and decision-making strategies, such as tit-for-tat strategies in many species, occur without much integration of information, let alone semantic content. For instance, such strategies can be found in feeding and competition behaviors even at the cellular level. Thus, successful cooperation and communication, for instance, at a strictly metabolic level, does not involve agency or cognitive integration at a personal level. Other fixed action patterns distinctive of a species, however, may involve emotion recognition, social rank, or sexual behavior. Yet others involve the integration of recognitional and motor control skills, as well as knowing how to recognize and access food. Many of these skills are inherited traits that require training in order to improve and develop.

More explicitly semantic aspects of communication that require higher degrees of cognitive integration can be found in the alarm calls of some animals. Many species give specific alarm calls depending on the kind of predator, thereby eliciting different responses. Knowing what kind of predator is approaching is integrated with information about how to respond. For instance, vervet monkeys run into bushes when an eagle alarm is produced, they jump into trees when a leopard alarm is sounded, and they stand bipedally and peer into grass when the alarm is about a snake (Seyfarth et al., 1980) and they can compare these alarms to another species' calls (Seyfarth and Cheney, 1990). Similar behavior has been found in Diana monkeys (Zuberbühler, 2000), meerkats (Manser et al., 2001), and ground squirrels (Owings and Hennessy, 1984).

But nothing compares to the complex form of cognitive integration found in human communication. Because of its importance for human cognition and central role in many epistemic achievements, the skills involved in language acquisition and human linguistic communication are a central example of the kind of cognitive integration constitutive of epistemic agency. Language is claimed to be the basis of abstract thought, and even a necessary condition for self-awareness (Rudder-Baker, 2013). We are not going to assume that language is necessary for consciousness or self-awareness here. It is clear, however, that much of what makes human epistemic agency unique is the way our linguistic abilities integrate diverse bodies of information for action, thought, and decision-making.

Language acquisition not only involves the basic need to accurately represent the environment – i.e., the content of a fragment of vocalization, its reference, the actions they should elicit – but also presupposes knowledge of the abstract structure that frames linguistically well-formed expressions. Language acquisition requires exposure to stimuli, but the skills involved in language learning are remarkably robust, manifesting across cultures, environments, emotional information, and familiar backgrounds. For the vast majority of members of the human species, the reliable and highly integrated skills required for acquiring language will successfully manifest, even in unlikely situations.

Consider, for instance, the case of deaf children's babbling in sign language. Infants around the very early age of 7–10 months start babbling. It was previously assumed that this was a deeply speech-dependent process, based on the motor signals involved in vocalizations. It was also assumed that babbling was an innately specified behavior that facilitated language acquisition and which depended on the anatomy of the vocal tract and the neural mechanisms underlying speech production. Laura Ann Petitto, however, discovered that the cognitive integration required for language learning and production transcends the mechanisms for spoken language because it is found in sign language with the same reliable and predictable features. As Petitto and Marentette (1991) say, the neural basis of babbling in language ontogeny is not specific to the speech modality – speech is not critical for babbling. They conclude that babbling involves the integration of abstract linguistic structures that permit a flexible capacity to express different types of signals, signed or spoken.

These skills are not module dependent, they are highly reliable, manifesting universally with remarkable consistency (Petitto et al., 2012). As with other forms of cognitive integration, the information integrated includes abstract, cross-modal representations which allow humans to assert contents, attend to conceptually structured perceptual stimuli, and communicate with others. Similar to the case of fixed action patterns, linguistic skills are hard wired, and can be improved by dexterity and training. Crucially, the distinctive aspect of the sophisticated cognitive abilities involved in language learning is not willful reflection or the consciously free decision to choose among options.

There is no metaphysical halo separating us from other species. A big part of our epistemic agency is shared with other species. The apparent normative halo of human cognition comes from high levels of cognitive integration, such as those involved in language learning, but this is not a categorical difference. The minimal agency proposed by our AAM is all that is needed to account for such complex epistemic agency. Linguistic skills are dispositional and reliable. They involve implicit knowledge of abstract structures – as we already mentioned, knowledge of syntax is a case of highly integrated epistemic agency without conscious reflection. They also involve motivation, fundamentally, the distinctively epistemic motivation to assert contents in communication.

Cognitive integration for epistemic agency, as the example of language acquisition shows, takes over the whole system at the personal level: it includes the motor basal ganglia, motoric articulatory code for the mouth or hand signs, knowledge of syntax, and the semantically compositional aspects of words and sentences. These skills underlie many other epistemic achievements, and they frame assertions in communication. Thus, there is a crucial link between action and perception (Liberman and Whalen, 2000). Language acquisition and production is a deeply epistemic achievement, requiring the highest degrees of cognitive integration. For this very reason, it does not require constant conscious representation and reflection.

5   Assertion as Epistemic Motivation

In this chapter, we argue that the epistemic capacities for opening and closing inquiry characteristic of attentional routines in perception are also fundamental in linguistic communication, particularly with respect to the speech acts of assertion and retraction. Relevant work by Kent Bach & Robert Harnish, Sanford Goldberg, John MacFarlane, Friederike Moltmann, John Turri, Robert Stalnaker, and Seth Yalcin is discussed. An important goal of this chapter is to highlight the similar cognitive structure between epistemic success in perception and communication and to identify specific epistemic achievements involved in successful communication.

5.1   Attention and Communication

This section examines the analogous structure between perception and linguistic communication, and argues that the success conditions for assertion and retraction require tracking social-factive conditions constitutive of conversational backgrounds. Work by Kent Bach and Robert Harnish is discussed in this context. We argue that successfully producing an assertion is an inferential epistemic achievement that is independent of the truth (in good cases) of the content asserted.

We argued in Section 2.3 that epistemic motivation requires implicit and reliable needs to successfully represent the environment. These needs manifest in virtues that satisfy accuracy conditions without the guidance of explicitly assessed rules or reasons. This chapter details the abilities required for producing an assertive speech act and for successfully communicating reliable information. We argue that both are epistemically significant because they show that, in addition to the value of being true, which an assertion might have in good cases, additional epistemic credit is due because of the abilities manifested in the successful assertion itself. Here we extend and refine the account of epistemic agency defended in Chapter 4 by returning to themes from Chapter 2 concerning assertion and epistemic motivation. We focus on the epistemic accomplishments of asserting (closing inquiry) and retracting (opening or leaving open inquiry). We committed to understanding epistemic motivation in terms of the motive to assert in Section 2.6, but now explain this motivation in greater specificity in terms of abilities to track social-communicative facts in conversational contexts. Successfully identifying conversational backgrounds is an epistemic achievement and is so independent of the truth or falsity of the content asserted.

We defend two theses in this chapter. The first is that the epistemic capacities for opening and closing inquiry characteristic of attentional routines that guide perception are also fundamental in linguistic communication. In the context of communication, these capacities manifest in the speech acts of assertion and retraction. Knowing how to speak requires attending to the right contextual cues to identify specific speech acts, and assertion and retraction are paradigmatically epistemic acts because of their facticity. In addition, these speech acts include felicity conditions concerning social knowledge, which must also be reliably satisfied. Two different types of attention, one to facts and the other to social expectations and mutually held beliefs, satisfy these two conditions.

Just as attention may operate in contexts where facts are not tracked – as in cases of attending to imagery – language can also operate in contexts in which facts are not being tracked. But the paradigmatic cases of successful linguistic communication are like the paradigmatic cases of successful perception: they are cases in which epistemic capacities, based on epistemic motivations, are tracking facts and solving problems concerning which information is relevant. The facts here are not merely cats on mats, but facts about interlocutors, relevant information, and communicative contexts. We explain the attentional processes underlying assertion and retraction with the notions of backgrounding and foregrounding conversational information. We argue that these are basic and important epistemic achievements.

The second thesis we defend is that reliable needs to satisfy social-factive conditions give stability to the intuitions guiding contextually appropriate assertion and retraction. The speech acts of assertion and retraction are performances and as such are evaluated by other speakers. These speech acts have satisfaction conditions that are objective (they entail truth or the possibility of doubt) and felicity conditions, primarily concerning sincerity and mutually held belief. Successful communication would be impossible without the epistemic abilities we have discussed in previous chapters, and in this chapter, we elaborate on how these constraints relate to the acceptance of assertions and retractions in conversational contexts. This second thesis, therefore, concerns the relation between assertion and reliable needs (discussed in Section 2.3).

The robustness and stability of these linguistic and inferential capacities is not epistemically trivial (Bach and Harnish [1979, 92] characterize these inferences as abductive, or inferences to the most plausible explanation). As such, successfully producing an assertion is an inferential epistemic achievement that is independent of the truth (in good cases) of the content asserted. Clearly, making a *true* assertion is a veritic epistemic success, and merely making an assertion does not entail success of this kind. However, if one overlooks the complex, inferential abilities required for producing a normatively appropriate assertion itself, it may appear that we need to find additional sources of epistemic value for a true assertion, beyond having said something true, in order to yield an epistemic standing like knowledge from a true assertion. We argue that this value is sufficiently located in the epistemic achievements of skillful assertion itself.

5.2   Dispositions to Assert and Successful Communication

This section introduces the notion of a "Ramsey assertable" content and emphasizes the importance of reliable inferential capacities. Work by Bach and Harnish is used to support some of these claims. We articulate epistemic virtues involved in normative assertion, which will be extended in Chapter 6.

The robust skills involved in making and detecting assertions express themselves very early on in language acquisition and they frame the speaker's intuitions underlying explicit judgments concerning the normative aspects of assertions. At the implicit need-based level, one finds the basic needs to represent the world and to communicate truthfully that we have been describing. To appreciate the importance of these basic needs, it is useful to reflect on a linguistic skill that plays a fundamental role in social game theory, decision-making, coordinated action and communication: the capacity to lie. Humans lie in all sorts of situations and settings. Good lies are prudentially guided by norms of etiquette and décor – you don't tell someone you just met at a party that something they said is incredibly stupid, even if you think or even know it is. We do not challenge each other all the time, the way it happens in the eavesdropping cases analyzed in recent philosophy of language. We challenge each other's veracity in rare situations, when the stakes are high (Stanley, 2005). In these cases, we are motivated to assert or affirm, rather than just communicate prudentially and cordially. We lie, in other words, not because we are unreliable at detecting good sources of information or incapable of making assertions, but because we are *good* at doing it, and we mask these dispositions to assert a truth for social and practical purposes – *many assertions would be unacceptable given non-epistemic values (such as moral values) or infelicitous because they are simply irrelevant*. Social intelligence is critical for successful communication.

We also lie in commercial settings by manipulating customers, pretending that something is the case which both customer and seller know is not true (or not entirely true). We tolerate and even encourage this deceitful behavior for the purpose of entertainment and also to satisfy practical needs. But when the stakes are high, we are all relatively good at telling who is lying and at flagging good sources of information. The flexibility of language allows us to pretend, be allegoric, poetic, creative, and to use language metaphorically. But the most fundamental role of language, at least for epistemic purposes, is to assert veridical information and the most fundamental epistemic motivation in linguistic exchanges is to lay down a proposition as true. This is the basic case in which language is being used in a way in which one must assume factivity, which grounds the assumptions and expectations concerning the perceived reliability of the speaker (Schlenker, 2010).

The speech acts of assertion and retraction comply with the triggering factors for initiating and closing inquiry characteristic of attention, and with the principles of acquiring information and halting search routines. Such abilities may be modeled computationally and be understood propositionally as practical modes of presentation (see Pavese, 2015), although this is not crucial for our purposes. What is critical is that the inferential skills underlying linguistic communication are implicit in the same way that the epistemic needs to represent the environment successfully are implicit. One may consider the inferential skills underlying communication as members of the set that Kent Bach (1984) characterizes as the repertoire of *snap judgments* that are crucial to successfully perform pressing tasks, such as the epistemic task of reliably recognizing assertions and retractions.

Being disposed to assert and being disposed to accept an assertion are two sides of the same epistemic success: factive and reliable communication. But, some distinctions are important here. One may satisfy the felicity conditions of a sincere assertion by identifying the relevance of an assertion and the mutually held beliefs that justify it, but not satisfy the factive accuracy conditions, thus asserting something false, and vice versa. In either case, one would fail to successfully assert but for very different reasons. In either case, however, one succeeds by reliably satisfying epistemic needs to communicate information.

Flagging reliable sources of information is essential for language users, and it has long been recognized as a fundamental epistemic goal (see Craig, 1990). The abilities required for producing and accepting assertions are foundational for successful communication, and other less factive and more indirect forms of communication depend on them. Authors disagree about the content of the norm of assertion. Some think that the norm of assertion is knowledge (DeRose, 2002; Turri, 2010; Williamson, 1996), others that it is truth (Weiner, 2005), justified belief (Douven, 2006; Kvanvig, 2009, 2011) or sincere belief (Bach, 2008; Grice, 1989). Some authors think that assertion is an unnecessary category (Cappelen, 2011). It has also been claimed that social norms for assertion may include exclusively practical or prudential norms. Clearly, a cognitive state related to success and reliably representing facts must be at stake in all accounts of the norm of assertion, but there is much controversy about the exact content of the norm.

Fortunately, we now have more than just intuitions to guide us in this quest. As we explain below, it seems that the norm of assertion may invariantly be knowledge. In any case, our interest here is not in giving the ultimate account of the norm of assertion. Rather, we argue that regardless of what cognitive state one favors, attention and reliable needs are fundamental to understand successful assertion.[1] These reliable needs are part of the repertoire of stable and cognitively integrated dispositions that we constantly use to accurately represent the world. We argue that these epistemic abilities are essential features of a virtuous cognitive constitution and examine their structure in this chapter.

The speech acts of assertion and retraction have received substantial treatment in the recent literature on contextualism and the semantics of epistemic modals. We analyze this literature in the concluding section of this chapter. We first focus on assertion and its epistemic underpinnings to illustrate the epistemic capacities for opening and closing inquiries in linguistic communication. This more detailed and focused discussion on assertion and retraction provides further support to the attention-assertion model (AAM).

Most accounts agree that assertion is both factive and normative, as well as being, in many ways, fundamental to our epistemic (individual and social) lives. Our aim is to investigate the psychological processes in play when a person correctly asserts or retracts a propositional content. Specifically, by looking at the psychology of "assertoric force," we aim to show that the psychology underlying cognitive factive expressions in language (assertions) must be very similar to the epistemic psychology defended here. Sincerity conditions for assertions, for example, can be explained in terms of the alethic grip provided by attentional anchoring and halting conditions. This points to a certain constitutive relation between assertion and cognition that we appeal to for purposes of epistemic evaluation. This can be explained as "having a proposition (or content) assertively," as opposed to actually asserting it, which requires an explicit performance. What we are interested in are the reliable communicative dispositions – without appeal to explicit rules – that help speakers to identify assertions and halt inquiries for assertable contents.

In this chapter, we show how assertion requires halting thresholds. In Chapter 6, we explore the possibility of describing epistemically constrained curiosity in terms of similar thresholds for opening and terminating inquiry – although we discuss important differences between halting thresholds for assertion and curiosity in Section 5.3. The main idea is that inquiry into p terminates at the normatively correct epistemic threshold if p is assertable for S. A major question for us then is: what, then, is this normatively correct

---

[1] This term comes from Dickie (2015). It means that a need (like the need to communicate) is satisfied reliably by being produced by stable dispositions properly integrated with motivations to successfully communicate and distinguish between factive speech and other varieties of communication.

epistemic threshold? We will argue for a practical answer and have already laid our cards on the table in Chapter 3. The correct norm of assertion, whatever that turns out to be, will provide the right halting condition for inquiry. Whether this norm is determined by justified belief, knowledge, or action is a matter of debate. It is important to note that interpreting assertion in terms of an "action norm" has a clear advantage: it would constitutively relate assertion to contents that are epistemically normative because of their adequacy for successful action and their satisfaction of the right epistemic threshold. Ramsey's principle captures this structure: S's inquiry into p terminates at a threshold if acting on p in conjunction with some desire D leads to the satisfaction of D. P would be "Ramsey assertable" for S in such a case.

Characterizing epistemic skills for assertion in terms of thresholds is also attractive because it fits nicely with reliabilism. If attention and assertion solve many-many problems by implementing a halting function that reliably satisfies basic needs to represent the environment, then there will be purely objective standards for halting that will be reliable and mechanical (such as computational processes). However, these will not suffice for *virtuous halting* or even for epistemic agency in cases that lack proper motivation (i.e., the motivation to satisfy felicity and factive conditions). Objectively reliable halting is necessary but not sufficient for virtuous halting. Virtuous halting requires, in addition, proper motivation and cognitive capacities integrated at the agential level, as we have argued in previous chapters. This is explored in detail in the next chapter as well.

The virtue theoretic direction of analysis requires that features of agents generate or transfer epistemic value. Thus, an assertion-based virtue theory would have to provide the relevant features of *asserting agents*. If a virtue theoretic norm is useful here, there must be some agent-level, value-generating, or transferring abilities to be described in an adequate epistemic psychology of reliably successful assertion.

The reliable needs that underlie the speech act of assertion require reliable inferences concerning the mutual recognition and identification of analogous inferences in other speakers. This inferential reliability is central in the contemporary literature on assertion and retraction, and it has been fundamental since the analysis of speech acts became central in linguistics and the philosophy of language. This speech act is a complex performance because it involves not only saying something, doing something by saying it and by affecting the hearer, but also attending to what is salient in the context of the conversation in order to specify mutual assumptions about what speech act is being intended.

As Bach and Harnish (1979) say: "In general, the inference the hearer makes and takes himself to be intended to make is based not just on what the speaker says but also on *mutual contextual beliefs* (MCBs), as we call such salient contextual information" (5). They explain that for the speech act performance it is not necessary for the beliefs to be true in order to figure in the speaker's intention and the hearer's inference, but this capacity to attend to the intentions of speakers and the expectation of hearers must be highly reliable across subjects in order for communication to be possible. There are presumptions concerning shared language and communication that ground how we attend to a speaker's intentions. These assumptions are common knowledge, necessary for communication.

The AAM has important implications for the normativity of assertion and speech acts once attention and epistemic needs are seen as essential to reliably detect salient features of a conversation. Consider the *Communicative Presumption* (CP), which is the mutual belief in a linguistic community that "whenever a member *S* says something in *L* to another member *H*, he is doing so with some recognizable illocutionary intent" (1979, 7), namely, the speaker intends to do something by uttering the sentence, rather than merely producing some sounds. This assumption licenses what Bach and Harnish call "R-intentions," which are reflexive intentions in the sense that their execution seeks simultaneously their recognition. In contrast to John Searle's (1969) view that communication is based on constitutive rules – a norm-based account – Bach and Harnish (1979) propose: "In our view an utterance counts as a communicative illocutionary act of a certain sort as a matter of R-intention not convention. Successful communication consists in the hearer's recognition of that intention by way of an inference" (127). The AAM, with its emphasis on attention for salience, is fully compatible with a need-based account (intentions that are not explicitly represented) that tracks what Bach and Harnish call R-intentions.

Speech act theory demonstrates that the set of assumptions, reliable dispositions to attend to the goals of speakers, and the mutually held implicit beliefs in reliable communication require cognitively integrated capacities that are stable and ubiquitous. We shall now examine the speech act of assertion in more detail. We argue that important elements of the AAM are present in the different forms of assertoric force discussed by Goldberg (2015) and Turri (2013). This gives support to the model of attention introduced earlier, but will also enhance it because agent-level epistemic virtues are now clustering around assertion and social communication. Assertion, we shall conclude, is a paradigm form of epistemic agency.

5.3   Forms of Assertoric Force and Forms of Epistemic Attention

This section discusses different accounts of the epistemic status of assertoric force, based on the work of Sanford Goldberg. We argue that assertoric force depends on epistemic skills that are best understood in terms of epistemic attention. Special emphasis is given to an asymmetry between assertion and other forms of communication, showing that assertion is the standard for epistemic communication.

Sanford Goldberg (2015) distinguishes four forms of "assertoric force." It is useful to distinguish and focus on the force of assertion rather than its content, as this is where many interesting epistemic processes are in play. The four accounts he canvasses are the attitudinal account, the common ground account, the commitment account, and the constitutive rule account. Most of these rely on something like the model of attention and epistemic agency we have been defending. Seeing this will not only support our model but will also help us extend the model to the paradigmatic epistemic action – assertion – and precisely explain the sense in which it is an epistemic achievement. We will highlight how all accounts require some type of threshold to accept an assertion, which if not satisfied, results in a request to open inquiry or to retract the assertion.

We first have Bach and Harnish's (1979) account.

Attitudinal Account: To assert is to express a certain attitude.

Bach and Harnish (1979, 15) defend this view, which consists in expressing an R-intention while uttering a sentence. In their terminology: "For S to express an attitude is for S to R-intend the hearer to take S's utterance as a reason to think that S has that attitude."

Bach and Harnish focus specifically on intentions as an important type of psychological state. As discussed in the previous chapter, Ernest Sosa (2015) has recently argued that intentions to affirm are essential for explaining fully apt epistemic performances within a reliabilist virtue epistemology. We agree that assertion is a paradigmatically epistemic mental act, but defend a more minimalist account of assertoric intentions as implicitly articulated needs to communicate and represent the environment. Importantly, this account is compatible with Bach and Harnish's.

Sosa focuses less on the underlying psychology and more on the work that intentional epistemic success does in addressing "problem cases" such as Truetemp, safety concerns, and rebutting skepticism. For us, like for Sosa, performances are the central object of epistemic evaluation, but we provide a different account of the psychological structure of those performances. Attention and assertion are intrinsically related to action, and we agree with Sosa that suspending judgment and opening inquiry are as fundamental as the activity of endorsing or asserting. But we disagree with Sosa that these capacities need to be reflectively explicit – although of course we do not deny that they *can* be. In the typical speech act, these capacities are automatic and implicit, and they include the act of retraction, as we will explain below. In fact, one may go further and affirm that in any typical conversation these capacities must be implicit and automatic. So, the attitudinal account clarifies and explains the linguistic manifestations of epistemic achievements according to AAM.

A second account in the literature comes from Robert Stalnaker.

The *Common Ground Account* is based on the "essential effect" an assertion has on the background of propositions taken for granted in a conversational context. (Stalnaker, 2002)

Assertion is based on a selective process to make some conversationally relevant propositions salient, similar to the processes we discussed in the context of attention. When a new assertion is made and not challenged, this changes and enriches the conversational context. Opening and closing inquiry will depend on this *salience function*. Assertive force, as opposed to content, is specifically the force to change the conversational score by mutual acceptance and consensus. Although this approach is neutral with respect to the type of psychological processes underlying such saliency functions, it is clearly compatible with AAM and may actually necessitate the AAM, as we proceed to explain.

In linguistics, it is standard to distinguish information that is assumed and information that is highlighted as salient for conversational purposes. This structure requires attention to background information that is mutually shared and also to what is salient in a conversation concerning how the background information shifts. These aspects of attention to communicative intentions are best understood in terms of solutions to many-many problems with halting thresholds that trigger specific speech acts. Psychological states associated with assertable contents are paradigmatically epistemic for two reasons. First, they involve capacities to accept information as veridical. According to Stalnaker (1984), attitudes of acceptance are correct if and only if the complement is true, expressing an implicit judgment of truth – as opposed to attitudes that do not entail such judgment, such as desires. The need to assert and communicate a content as involving truth, therefore, assumes a common ground for the evaluation of such truth and makes salient the commitment that one has accepted the information as veridical. Second, attitudes of acceptance license epistemic modals (Anand and Hacquard, 2013), which in the case of assertable contents is part of the foregrounding and backgrounding of information. In assertion acceptance of veridicality is backgrounded and assumed as unchallenged, while in retraction a lack of commitment to mutually accepted information is made salient or foregrounded. This is an epistemic process of *shared evidence updating* that occurs in virtue of the basic and reliable epistemic capacities constitutive of linguistic communication.

Thus, the complex speech act of assertion involves at least three distinct epistemic abilities: (a) an ability to grasp the literal meaning of an expression, (b) an ability to complement literal meaning with background assumptions, and

(c) an ability to detect shifts in background assumptions when new information becomes salient. Consider the intricate communicative needs a child must reliably satisfy in order to learn a language. The child needs to learn the meaning of words and then how they are used in a context (i.e., is mom joking, or is she serious? Was that a sarcastic remark or an observation?). Then the child needs to learn how different attitudes not only reflect reliably the mental states and intentions of speakers but also how they are used to background or foreground information. When mom says "I think the cat is in that room" she is foregrounding her commitment to veridicality, but she could easily retract with "but I am not sure." By contrast, when she says "I know the cat is in that room" or simply "The cat is in that room" her commitment to veridicality is the background of what she means. Language learning requires complex attention routines.

This process of backgrounding the acceptance of veridicality distinguishes assertion from other speech acts, making it the most distinctively epistemic attitude. The epistemic abilities to assert establish an asymmetry between halting thresholds for assertion and other epistemic achievements associated with closing inquiry. Assertion is the *standard* by which other processes of closing inquiry are evaluated. In particular, in assertion there is acceptance of veridicality and committed-communicable content – one may consider this acceptance as the basis for the reliability of testimonial evidence. This is not the case with other epistemic virtues, such as properly constrained curiosity. There is a similar structure for halting thresholds, but an important asymmetry.

In assertion, thresholds license acceptance, in curiosity only probable acceptance and no committed-communicable content. In curiosity, attention is directed to a salient interest and it functions by virtuously opening inquiry, while in assertion attention is directed at closing inquiry. This is an important result of a threshold norm based on AAM.

Asymmetry: Assertion is the default epistemic standard for communicable contents and serves as an evaluative constraint on virtuous halting thresholds. Assertion does not depend on other speech acts or communicable contents to reach an epistemic standard. Therefore, other speech acts asymmetrically depend on assertion for reaching epistemically virtuous halting thresholds.

Curiosity makes salient a halting threshold for assertion, as we explain in Chapter 6, but it has the opposite background structure – instead of accepting information as true, the epistemic act of opening inquiry in order to reach an assertion threshold explicitly denies commitment until the threshold is reached, if at all. Curiosity, by its very definition, assumes a state of indecision. Assertion, on the contrary, assumes a state of epistemic satisfaction and acceptance.

There is an important difference, therefore, between retractions and processes of initiating inquiry. Retractions assume assertions, while curiosity seeks to arrive at an assertion by assuming indecision or bewilderment. The mental actions underlying both assertion and retraction are attention dependent with respect to backgrounding and foregrounding, and both seek to admit or reject the highest standard of epistemic acceptance in communication.

The final account we discuss is

Constitutive Rule Account: To assert is to make a move defined by the constitutive rules of assertion.

The constitutive rule could be the knowledge norm: assert p only if you know that p. There are many variants or departures from the knowledge norm for assertion: justified belief, rational, and prudential norms (see Rescorla, 2009). As stated above, we will not argue for a specific norm of assertion. We believe the action norm can provide a way for the AAM to non-circularly explain why achievements that comply with AAM are typically knowledge – in fact, we think this is an important implication of the AAM. But what is important to emphasize now is that the norm of assertion needs to be dependent on *abilities of agents*, and in this sense, we favor Bach and Harnish's attitudinal account. The AAM is an agent-centered account, rather than a norm-centered account, so the norm of assertion needs to be constitutively dependent on the achievements of epistemic agents that are explained because of their epistemic abilities.

Similar to our account of the epistemic aspects of attention, AAM would have to explain assertion in terms of anchoring, integration, guidance, and output selection. Goal-relevant guidance and integration triggers subsequent cognitive activity appropriate to evaluations of both achievement and ability (for assertion). Anchoring abilities will require reliability in selecting adequate contents, where often there will be many propositions that could be adequate, but far more that could not. As part of being a competent speaker, abilities for adequately responding to possible error should lead to retraction, and attention to such possibilities must be integral to the abilities to assert. This requires both insensitivity to irrelevant information and "grasping abilities," *but selecting the content that one wants to bring about in the hearer is a different mental act than either of these*. Agential processes of assertion will allow for a good bit of automaticity, and although they need not be consciously represented, some of them will typically be conscious, as in the case of retraction. Selection success is straightforwardly constrained by the goal of communicating the right information and also by being able to communicate it from one source to another (speaker to hearer). These will be guidance successes up to the point of utterance itself. Guidance successes will be largely implicit in cases of common assertions.

The essential conclusion from the previous discussion is that, according to the AAM, attention and assertion are *basic epistemic abilities* that ground a variety of epistemic achievements. In the standard or "good" case of perceptual belief, there is an intrinsic and automatic connection between attention and assertion: attention is allocated to features of the environment licensing, for example, the belief that there is a book in front of you, and the entitlement that this perceptual information is safe, which you could assert if the context required it. If distractors or potential falsifiers emerge, then attention will bring them to the foreground and you may come to doubt whether the lighting conditions are ideal and whether or not you should assert the proposition that there is a book in front of you. Alternatively, you could assert that there is a book in front of you, and someone could point out you are in fake-book country, requiring you to retract your assertion. All of this epistemic updating requires that there is a baseline of certainty and safety, provided by the basic needs to attend to features of the environment and to assert such contents. *The foregrounding and backgrounding of information, implicit in the structure of attention, provides the type of epistemic entitlement that prevents us from thinking we are in the matrix or that we are in an evil demon scenario.*

5.4 Factivity, Credit, and Social Environments

A central goal of this section is to distinguish two senses of "factivity" in linguistic communication, one concerning the veridicality conditions typically associated with semantic content and the other concerning the shared assumptions and cognitive states of other speakers. We explore a public kind of "mask" on the disposition to assert, the distinction between unasserted but assertable contents and successful public assertions. The previous discussion on virtuous halting thresholds is enriched and enhanced.

While attention operates analogously to assertion and has similar epistemic constraints, assertion brings in an important social commitment. One unique feature of assertion will be that attentional anchoring will select for a public performance (a speech act), whether or not the utterance is actually performed. The forward-looking aspect of selection is very important here. Utterances are public deeds; they are actions in the world. The forms of attention we find in assertion would then be world involving because the act is motivated by an intention to change things in the world by so acting. Things are more complicated, however, than with simple actions, such as grabbing a hammer. Assertions aim to make the social and informational environment different by publicly asserting a content. Attention that represents the environment is not inherently world involving in this social way. Let's say that assertion therefore carries a kind of socially committed factivity that attention need not. We now examine this factive aspect of assertion and how it bears on another important issue: epistemic credit. A central question we want to consider is: does asserting p in a context confer any fundamental epistemic credit to a person that unasserted knowledge that p does not confer to that person in that context?

It is important to disambiguate two senses of "factivity." One question raised in this line of inquiry is: what kinds of social facts will be relevant in explaining the act of intending to change the social and informational world? Here felicity conditions are important: the hearer of an assertive utterance must recognize the sincerity and seriousness of the speaker. To the extent that there are facts about the socially determined conditions for a successful assertion, a reliable way of tracking or attending to social facts is required for being able to reliably assert a content. Reliably tracking social facts is one way that assertoric attention is world involving, and this is a factive attentional competence that an assertor must possess. This world-involving competence is an essential element of any cognitive constitution that reliably manifests assertions. We examine the dynamics of these specific abilities in much greater detail in the following section.

A successful assertion is factive in a second way. A successful assertion must usually get things right about the non-human world, or at least be non-culpably close to doing so. The first form of factivity will be *social-communicative factivity*, the second is *non-social factivity*. In the first sense, a speech act that succeeds in being an assertion requires getting things right about the human environment (about social facts). But there is a difference that matters to how attention is allocated and which inferences it licenses – some will concern facts about the environment, while others will concern facts about which inferences and beliefs the hearer shares with the speaker.

The social-communicative factivity involved in assertion is connected to familiar issues about epistemic credit for true beliefs formed through communication (see especially Greco, 2010; Lackey, 2007). The most widely discussed example in virtue epistemology is Lackey's case of Morris who forms a true belief by asking the first passerby how to get to the Sears Tower. Upon receiving a correct answer, Morris automatically forms a true belief and seems to have knowledge. Quite a bit of our knowledge seems to be of this sort, but yet the hearer, in this case Morris, does not seem to deserve credit for the true belief he forms, rather it is the speaker who communicates the true belief that deserves credit.

We now examine a number of connections between the overt act of assertion, the epistemic relation of assertability that holds between agents and contents, the attentional state of being disposed to assert, and epistemic credit. Since Bach and Harnish appeal to intention, a successful assertion will generate credit for the speaker, but so too does a successful question seeking an assertion. Because intentions by nature are successful only if they actually cause the intended outcome (as opposed to desires), there is a clear path from the agent to the public act of questioning that is causal and (socially) factive. But, is this enough for the kind of credit we need to give epistemic agents when they have knowledge? In this case, Morris' question is successful in that he receives the information he wants from the target he chooses, and this manifests social-communicative competence. But, as we are about to illustrate, even crediting the *speaker* for the assertion is complicated.

Consider the cases of Shy Sean and Chatty Cathy. Sean cannot bring himself to assert anything when asked a question, even when he is in an epistemic position to do so, because he is so painfully shy. Cathy cannot help but assert what she is in an epistemic position to assert, even when she is not asked a question. Say Sean knows that p and is in some environment E where he can authoritatively assert p in E, and Sean has been asked whether p (or can otherwise helpfully volunteer that p). Assume further that, simply because he is so shy, Sean remains silent and does not assert p in E, but this in no way changes his knowing that p. The content p is thus normatively *assertable* for Sean because it is known, but p is not asserted. We might say that the disposition to assert is here "masked" by shyness. Is Sean epistemically blameworthy? What kind of epistemic credit does Sean deserve? In some broad sense of "epistemic," clearly he is blameworthy. But, in a narrower sense, an actual avowal or withholding is a pragmatic issue, one that neither generates nor decreases epistemic value: Sean knows that p. In other words, Sean is culpable of infelicitously masking an adequate assertion, perhaps because of extreme caution in public speech, but he is not culpable of not complying with the objective and subjective halting conditions for assertable contents – he is properly motivated to assert and cognitively integrates reliable and veridical information.

This raises the following question: in virtue of what, if anything, does *asserted* knowledge that p have greater epistemic value than unasserted but *assertable* knowledge that p? Shy Sean arguably presents a case where assertion itself (the speech act) does not generate purely epistemic credit beyond that which knowing that p generates (although it would be transferring it). Transferring knowledge is valuable, so an assertion that p has transference value that mere (unasserted) knowledge that p does not. But transference value is axiologically *instrumental*. An ability to transfer knowledge would be valuable just in case it reliably takes some fundamental epistemically valuable state (e.g., a true belief) and confers an epistemic status or standing on some other state or process, either of one's own (as in inference) or to a mental state of another person (as in testimony). Lacking *fundamental* epistemic value is a big price to pay for the transfer of knowledge. If assertion is merely instrumentally valuable for transferring epistemic value, it may well be epistemically valuable in a narrow sense of epistemic credit, but much less than we are interested in here, because "transfer" may not require epistemic constitution for agency. Moreover, the transfer value of an assertion depends on the hearers of the assertion and is thus beyond the control and responsibility of the speaker. Just like recognizing good sources of testimony is an epistemic virtue, transmitting assertions that increase social knowledge is a virtue. But the capacities in place are socially shared: successful transfer depends on the adequate recognition of the assertion.

If an epistemic theory is substantively assertion based, some fundamental epistemic value or epistemic achievement must be recognized where, under that theory, knowing without asserting would lack that specific value or fall short of that achievement. If Sean's failures are merely practical and non-epistemic for some epistemic theory, then that theory would not be essentially assertion based. There are a number of responses to this challenge, some of which will be pursued further below. One response is that asserting p inevitably involves more epistemic achievements than merely knowing p simply because assertion requires the reliable capacities necessary for communication and the successful use of language, which are non-trivial epistemic achievements. No matter how much epistemic value we attribute to an unasserted but asser-table content, asserting that content raises the overall epistemic value mani-fested in the target of evaluation. If Shy Sean were to assert, he would add to the overall epistemic achievements attributable to him at that time.

This still leaves us with questions and concerns. In many cases, we actually want to accomplish a goal by manifesting fewer abilities rather than more, so there is no reason to think that epistemic assessment should evaluate subjects by simply aggregating basic epistemic achievements. Also, if we go so far as to require actual assertion for sufficient epistemic success (knowledge), we face a different problem. If (normative) assertion generates the credit that turns true belief into knowledge, and we grant that people generally know a good amount, the world would have to be a very, very chatty place. Perhaps the actual world is a chatty world, depending on how one sees the impact of media, information, and technology. But this is a descriptive issue about our contemporary world, and we are seeking to defend a normative account.

Generally, people do not feel a need to assert everything they know. We can, however, imagine such a person, Chatty Cathy, who asserts everything she takes herself to know. Does she improve her epistemic situation just by virtue of asserting normatively assertable contents? Clearly not. However, substantive points can be marshaled in favor of a robust and purely epistemic value for assertion itself. *The capacities that generate epistemic value for belief in the agent are not distinct from the capacities manifested in assertion*, and assertion also has content transference value. Both Shy Sean and Chatty Cathy would *have p assertively*, even though only Cathy asserts. We argue that *having p assertively* generates epistemic credit for an agent when p is (normatively) assertable for that agent, and this is different from simply knowing p. Psychologically, having p assertively engages the guidance and outcome processes that an actual assertion that p would, but assertion is masked (virtuously or viciously), or otherwise prevented. Psychologically speaking, then, Sean has what Cathy has, and both are in a mental state essentially modulated by assertoric forms of attention and by properly integrated abilities.

The psychological state of having p assertively will then give the agent quite a bit, and we can explain this without extending the boundaries of epistemology too far. But there are important issues in philosophy of mind. Since p will be assertable and we grant that p engages many of the psychological mechanisms of assertion, Shy Sean will have access to reasons that will be adequate for meeting challenges to his assertion. This is a justificatory state that merely requires access to responses to reasonable challenges. One may understand this as an issue in favor of internalism, but it is more accurate to understand it as an issue of properly integrated motivation. Shy Sean and Chatty Cathy are opposites in a spectrum of knowledge transfer.

We can state the upshot of the examples of Shy Sean and Chatty Cathy in slogan form: *Motivation modulates by cognitive integration.* On the one hand, Shy Sean has the right Ramsey-assertable content: he is properly motivated and meets the satisfaction condition. But by constantly preventing himself from asserting adequate contents he suffers from a form of epistemic *akrasia*: he should assert, but refrains from asserting for no good reason.[2] His motivations are epistemically correct, but they are not powerful enough. On the other hand, Chatty Cathy is epistemically intemperate: she is *not* properly motivated, even though she satisfies veridicality conditions about trivial assertions. This kind of information is not worth transmission. If Chatty Cathy says: "Now I am here and you are there, and there are stars and there are cars" her assertions would be accurate but there is no value in their utterance. Attention to salient conversational cues is not driving motivation.

There is a clear issue of a subject's social epistemic contribution when comparing belief and assertion. Assuming that p is assertable for S at t, not asserting p will often deprive the shared epistemic environment of an available improvement. If asserting p would "change the score" in a Stalnakerian sense, assertion arguably has epistemic value that belief does not. But is this pure (or narrow) epistemic value? Would allowing this as a general epistemic requirement lead to some form of pragmatism or pragmatic encroachment? We will look further into the social dimensions of epistemic achievement and assertion at length in Chapter 7, but those will not be essential to the points defended here.

Now we examine how some of the issues above illuminate or are illuminated by a contemporary debate between John MacFarlane and Seth Yalcin involving epistemic modals and the norm assertion. The social-communicative factive

---

[2] For an excellent discussion of epistemic akrasia, see Hookway (2001).

abilities required for reliably asserting will be understood in much greater detail, and hopefully address some of the worries regarding pragmatic encroachment. This will add essential elements to a virtuous cognitive constitution as we understand it here.

5.5   Epistemically Virtuous Halting Thresholds and Assertable Contents: The Case of Epistemic Modals

This section examines the problem of specifying the standards of evaluation that should be at play in accepting the veracity of an assertion, focusing on the work of John MacFarlane and Seth Yalcin on epistemic modals. We argue that, independent of the particular standard one settles on, epistemic modals reveal patterns of attentive commitment that are *virtuously sensitive* to options for ending inquiry and *virtuously insensitive* to irrelevant information.

Frege thought of assertion as a way of laying a proposition down as true by not only grasping its content, but also by being committed to its veracity. This motivation is implicit in perceptual states.[3] Communicating knowledge about the world is a fundamental epistemic need, as is representing the world itself (see Dickie, 2015). The need to communicate, and thus to assert, is cognitively fundamental in the sense that a human being cannot have a rational perspective on the world without reliably satisfying that need. This would seem to show that Shy Sean and Chatty Cathy are (near) epistemic equivalents. This general direction would support our requirement that a person must have "*p* assertorically" in order to receive a certain form of fundamental epistemic credit.

But there is a speech act dependent on assertion that requires not only overt communication but also constant assessment of salient evidence: the act of *retraction*. Speech act theory has produced sophisticated accounts of the epistemology of utterance assessment – is this utterance an expression of humor, pretense or an assertion? Inference and other cognitive capacities are certainly involved in this process on both sides. Speakers and hearers must rely on mutually shared contextual cues for detecting the use of factive expressions. In the specific case of assertion, success conditions involve shared evidence and knowledge of facts, but also shared normative commitments, interests, and mutually accepted stakes of the truth or falsehood of an assertion (Stanley, 2005), as well as what would count as a potential defeater – if I am talking about the bank being open, its being Sunday may count as a potential defeater, but the possibility of being a brain in a vat will not. Assuming motivation is adequately working (unlike the cases of Sean and Cathy) the public commitment of an

---

[3] For an argument that perceptual states manifest "selection for action" (work based in neurology), see Wu (2013).

assertion to the veracity of its content entails that should a defeater become salient, the responsible epistemic act is retraction.

This generates the problem of specifying what standards of evaluation should be at play in accepting the veracity of an assertion. The semantics of expressions involving epistemic modals has been notoriously difficult to explain (Yalcin, 2007, 2011). We argue that, independent of the particular standard one settles on, epistemic modals reveal patterns of attentive commitment that are *virtuously sensitive* to options for ending inquiry and *virtuously insensitive* to irrelevant information. These abilities are essential components of successful cognitive constitutions because they manifest as factive social-communicative states. The forms of social knowledge and the abilities by which this knowledge is had are both very important credit-generating achievements. However, there are many subtleties surrounding the extant accounts of the semantics of epistemic modals. We will focus on how experts on this issue present the differences between their views, particularly relativism and expressivism. Epistemic modals express uncertainty, and to that extent, they are expressions of open inquiry of a very specific kind. They are not expressions of open inquiry for the sake of open inquiry – they are motivated by a rejection of the veracity of an assertion and could be understood as expressions of holding accountable the speaker to an unreliable assertion. Retraction is, therefore, a mechanism for the control of reliable communication.

There are interesting aspects of what one is epistemically and semantically *committed to* in uttering an expression containing an epistemic modal. Consider how such claims are retracted and rejected. Suppose you hear the following conversation between Mary and Monica, based on an example by John MacFarlane (2014):

MARY: *John might be in China. I didn't see him today.*
MONICA: *No, he can't be in China. He doesn't have his visa yet.*
MARY: *Oh really? Then I guess I was wrong.* (240)

This is a typical conversation, and there are several questions about what Mary and Monica are epistemically entitled to. First, as MacFarlane notes, Mary's retraction does not entail an admission that she *should not have made* her original assertion. She realizes that she had inadequate evidence, which is why she now retracts the statement. Unlike a typical *disagreement* about assertions, such as "John is here," "No, he is not," Mary and Monica agree about the fact that John cannot be in China. Mary and Monica don't seem to be mistaken about what standards of evidence apply to their conversation and they both seem to agree on such standards. Thus, there is common ground with respect to the content of the retraction, the adequacy of the original assertion, and the standards of evidence: these three aspects determine a virtuous halting threshold for Mary and Monica, and both of them are satisfied with the retraction.

Normatively speaking, Monica is epistemically warranted to reject, not the claim that John is in China, but the claim that he might be. And Mary is epistemically warranted to retract her original assertion. Mary correctly accepts Monica's rejection, and Monica correctly rejects Mary's assertion. Reliable communication depends on all of these "shoulds" having a grip on speakers as they transmit information. How to make sense of all the normative aspects of their conversation?

In terms of the AAM, a critical issue is that virtuous sensitivity is present in all types of conversational skills. Mary is originally sensitive and attentive to the fact that John was absent today. Given the context that John will be traveling to China, his absence is a fact that warrants an assertion to the effect that it is possible that John is in China. Monica is sensitive to both Mary's ignorance of the visa situation, and to the now salient fact that John's absence remains unexplained. Attention to these facts is quite selective and the right halting thresholds for assertion, rejection, and retraction depend fundamentally on the aboutness of the contents expressed. In perception, this occurs automatically and through the causal interaction between specific features and perceptual attention routines. In linguistic communication, attention is also allocated automatically to relevant contents, but assertions and other speech acts depend fundamentally on the context of conversation and the background of beliefs that are assumed. The possibility that needs to be eliminated is that John might be in China, not that he might be in North Dakota. What is salient is that it is not possible for John to be in China. The fact that he might be in many other places is not salient or relevant. Like the foregrounding and backgrounding of information in speech acts, evidence assessment in assertion and retraction is fully dependent on the salience of evidence and on background information about mutually held assumptions.

Thus, Monica rejects and Mary retracts, manifesting both virtuous sensitivity to information about John's visa and China's immigration requirements and virtuous *insensitivity* to information about all the possible whereabouts concerning John and about the immigration requirements of all the other countries in the world. We propose that this combination of virtuous (normative) sensitivity and insensitivity is constitutive of the practices of assertion and retraction and that these forms of sensitivity and insensitivity are factive manifestations of virtuous cognitive constitutions. Stephen Yablo (2014) nicely describes the conversational specificity regarding aboutness and sensitivity to information in the following passage:

The standard analysis of *It might be that* Φ has it expressing something in the neighborhood of *I don't know that not-Φ*. But that cannot be right. Suppose Mary asks Jen where Bob is, and receives the answer, *He might be in his office.* This statement Mary receives in reply is directed at the very same issue as her question: Bob and his location. It is *not* about the extent of Jen's knowledge. There is a concern aspect here, too. Imagine that the building has caught fire and we are out on the sidewalk looking around for colleagues. Bob is nowhere to be seen. I am worried that he might be still in his office. The limited extent of my information does not worry me in the slightest; it plays a role in *why* I am worried, perhaps, but it is not what I am worried *about*. (18–19)

Epistemic modals reveal patterns of commitment that are virtuously sensitive to options for ending inquiry and virtuously insensitive to irrelevant information. The importance of assertions in communication is that they help end inquiry collectively and that they are subject to contextual forms of salience that respond to motivations and specific contents. The commitments underlying epistemic modals demonstrate the importance of attentional abilities to the relevance of very specific information. As Yablo's example shows, it is the specificity of the content of these states that makes them naturally related to motivations and action – being worried about the whereabouts of Bob and taking measures about securing his safety. In the context of an emergency, one says "*Bob might be in his office,*" in a serious and sincere way, not just to start a conversation about Bob's punctuality, for example. So there is also specificity in shared motivation. Moreover, the purpose of such assertion is not to show that we lack enough evidence to settle the issue one way or another. Rather, the purpose is to act and help Bob.

A critical issue is how much of the relevant information is beyond the subject's evidence. This is a very central and controversial topic in semantics. Views differ on whose evidence counts, depending on the role of practical interests or stakes in the attribution, the subject of evaluation, or the attributor.[4] But regardless of who ends up with the most explanatorily powerful semantics for epistemic modals and knowledge attributions, cognitively integrated and attention-guided mental states of epistemic agents must play a fundamental role. In fact, the recent literature on epistemic modals exemplifies a tendency in semantics that resembles the agency turn in epistemology: to move away from invariant and rigid relations between propositions and subjects, in order to place the capacities of agents and their mental states, including the need to represent information reliably and be sensitive only to the relevant information, at the center of analysis.[5]

---

[4] Stanley and Hawthorne focus on the subject of evaluation's evidence, while Lewis, Cohen, and DeRose focus on the attributor. See Greco (2010, 111) for discussion and explanation of the relevance of this issue in epistemology.

[5] For some discussions of agency and motivation, see Broncano (2014), Sosa (2013), Mitova (2011), and Mantel (2013). Responsibilists have long required agency for epistemic success in virtue epistemology. For an interesting debate between Jason Baehr and Linda Zagzebski on the question of whether knowledge requires virtuous motivation see Chapter 6 of Steup et al. (2013).

5.6   Retraction and Virtuous Sensitivity

This section examines a debate between MacFarlane and Yalcin concerning how to best characterize epistemic modals. We argue that the debate is furthered by introducing halting thresholds and attentional capacities for salience. Different types of halting thresholds are defined and summarized.

Epistemology has moved toward agency-based accounts, and something similar has occurred in semantics. Truth evaluation in contemporary versions of contextualism has taken agents as central contributors to the specification of meaning. Critically, the recent literature on contextualist semantics shows that successful communication depends fundamentally on the *capacities* of epistemic agents to attend to the satisfaction and felicity conditions of assertions that lead to factual information and reliable testimony, differentiating them from those that lead to weaker commitments and open inquiry. Commitments concerning when and how to retract, when and how to reject, and when and how to disagree are very much part of being a virtuous epistemic agent. Successful communication would be seriously threatened for any agent that makes too many mistakes because of a lack of virtuous sensitivity or insensitivity to the right cues, or who lacks reliable capacities to establish commonly held information.

A crucial issue raised by AAM concerns the extent to which the thresholds underlying capacities for evidence assessment approximate the thresholds for assertable contents. Eavesdropping cases show that this is not a straightforward matter. One can imagine the conversation between Monica and Mary involving four more friends, all of whom ignore that John has not gotten the visa, and then an eavesdropper reveals this information, forcing all of them to retract. One can also imagine the precision of the information increasing. For instance, relevant information may require details about when exactly John will have to leave and when he should get his visa. The thresholds for asserting and rejecting seem to go in the direction of more and better evidence. But there will clearly be a limit. In a standard conversation, the limits of how much information is relevant implicitly follow the rules of immediate interests and specific goals, rather than overall and idealized evidence assessment. Thus, it is clear that a central feature of any solution to eavesdropping scenarios will be the reliable and *sensitive* capacities of agents in a conversation to open and close inquiry, based on shared motivations rather than idealized standards for evidence gathering and updating.

We shall now briefly focus on relativist and expressivist accounts to illustrate an important epistemic point. MacFarlane's (2014) relativist account rejects the contextualist view that the context of use suffices to assign truth-values to utterances involving epistemic modals. Yalcin (2007, 2011) also rejects contextualism. However, MacFarlane proposes that the context of use plays an important role and argues that truth-values should be assigned to a context of use and a context of assessment. MacFarlane relies on cases of assertion and retraction to explain these assignments of truth-values. Yalcin rejects context-relative values for epistemic modals entirely, favoring an expressivist, non-factualist view. MacFarlane (2014) describes their disagreement as follows:

Yalcin's account cannot appeal to a generic story about assertion to explain the special features of epistemic modal assertions. Instead, Yalcin tells a special story tailored to the case: whereas assertions of straightforward factual propositions express full beliefs, assertions of "It is possible that *p*" express a special cognitive state we might call *leaving-open*, and have the communicative function of achieving coordination on a set of open possibilities. (One *leaves-open* that *p* just in case one is sensitive to the question whether *p* and does not believe that not-*p*.) (277)

The disagreement between MacFarlane and Yalcin concerns the nature of epistemic agency in assertive communication. Both of them agree that assertion is the typical cognitive state in which full belief is fact involving, in a reliable manner. This is, presumably, a shared assumption of speakers. The disagreement seems to be about cases of assertion in which commitment is weak. This illustrates the distinction we made before between objective satisfaction conditions and subjective felicity conditions, including cognitive integration and motivation. Sensitivity to eavesdroppers with better evidence goes up when the reliability of an assertion goes down. But this could also occur because of objective or subjective conditions. If a speaker can decisively settle the evidence, the conversation will go in the direction of satisfying an objective halting threshold – a threshold that, in the ideal situation, would halt a program that seeks to satisfy a function or complete a search. But if the situation concerns uncertainty on the part of the speaker, manifest in a lack of commitment, then the threshold will be about reaching the right motivation, and potentially conflicting interests will become much more salient. The questions in these cases would be "is it relevant for me to say this now?" or "how confident am I in this information?" Here one finds oneself on the Shy Sean and Chatty Cathy spectrum.

For Ramsey, truth requires precise content, in the sense that only precise contents can lead to reliable action, as explained in Chapter 3. Assertions can be decomposed into three components: a level of thought in which a mental action endorses a specific proposition; a level of action in which the content is used in practical inferences; and a level of determinacy and precision according to which the only beliefs that are relevant for action and assertion are full beliefs, as opposed to *general* beliefs (such as mathematical beliefs), vague beliefs, or partial beliefs associated with doubt, possibility, and uncertainty. Yalcin's view resonates with Ramsey's approach because determinate content is associated with action and full belief, which satisfy the threshold for assertion. A different story is needed for general and partially endorsed belief. According to Ramsey, the cognitive state of *leaving-open* cannot be described as assertion because of the commitment to full belief and action. The asymmetry between assertion and other speech acts, as well as between the need to assert and the motivation to start inquiry, is manifest in such commitments.

As we have argued, the right cues that trigger reliable dispositions to assert or leave inquiry open are dependent on environments and conversational backgrounds, but our abilities to reliably and automatically detect those cues are robust across environments. Evidence in linguistics from languages around the world demonstrates remarkable regularities in structure and semantics, including semantic primes (or primitive concepts) for: (a) mental distinctions, such as "thinking" and cognitive factives such as "knowing"; (b) assertive communicative acts such as "say"; and (c) strictly epistemic notions such as "true" (Goddard, 2002). Like other robust epistemic skills, such as those involving perception, linguistic skills successfully articulate epistemic distinctions across a wide variety of environments, educational practices, and cultural contexts. Linguistic skills are largely constitutive of human cognition, and they are among the most robust epistemic abilities. In fact, these skills are distinctive of our species.

This emphasis on agency – the cognitively integrated interests, motivations and goals of linguistic agents – is fully compatible with virtue reliabilism. Actually, if the AAM is correct, virtue reliabilism is needed to explain how agents succeed at these communicative tasks. The targets of evaluation according to the AAM are not on the static relations between contents and bodies of evidence, propositions, or collections of facts. This resembles the contemporary emphasis on practical goals, skills, motivations, and attention to what information is foregrounded or backgrounded that one finds in contemporary linguistics. An integrated mental state with the right sensitivity to information about which inquiries are properly kept open and which are not *can only be the result of robust abilities for communication*. These, in turn, require a cognitive constitution that reliably manifests in factive social-communicative states.

Given AAM's assumptions about the importance of action, an interesting issue for future research is the role of action in assessing motivations to assert. According to the pragmatist account of Peirce and Ramsey, the norms of action and assertion are indistinguishable in the sense that one should only act and assert based on what one knows. While there is obviously need for more evidence, we believe that this pragmatist approach is roughly correct about the basic and foundational epistemic abilities we are focusing on: attention and assertion. Some authors seem to be leaning in this direction. For instance, Friederike Moltmann (2014) argues that understanding propositions as mind-independent abstract objects is inadequate because of complications concerning accessibility. This is a general contemporary concern. Moltmann's own account is to model propositions in terms of what she calls "attitudinal objects" which include entities like judgments and beliefs. She argues that they are *products* of agency-based processes, and analogizes this distinction with the distinction between the action of *passing* a law and the law itself.

The emphasis on products illustrates what Ramsey had in mind with his distinction between full beliefs and other kinds of beliefs, which, as mentioned, resonates with Yalcin's distinction between asserting and "leaving-open." Products are successes reliably achieved by actions based on needs and motivations. Timothy Williamson (2000) has emphasized deep analogies between knowledge and action as part of his *knowledge-first* program. Although a critical part of his analogy is to highlight the difference in direction of fit (which we think need not be juxtaposed in such a way, but rather make room for the cognitive integration between both motivations and beliefs), both involve success conditions, and there is much in common between Williamson's account and the virtue reliabilist *agency-based* account we propose.

The dynamics of linguistic communication, therefore, seem to necessitate an agential framework in which communicative needs are reliably satisfied. An essential aspect of this framework is how speakers expect each other to provide reliable information. One can construe assertion as a kind of *request* to assume a background of propositions in which the proposition asserted is true. These propositions are mutually believed and accepted by those who partake in the conversation, and the abilities to accept such a background must be very reliable for communication to take place. Robert Stalnaker (1978, 2002) proposes that assertion could be modeled as a request in which the context of the conversation is not only one in which a proposition is compatible with the set of possible worlds constitutive of the conversational context (which would be simply grasping or understanding the proposition), but one in which such a proposition is accepted as true in all the worlds of the context set. At first glance, the inferential skills required to have access to this information, reliably and in a mutual way, may seem daunting. One would think they demand enormous cognitive effort and resources. But as the research by Goddard (2002) shows, they are part of the repertoire of implicit, incredibly reliable, attention-driven, action-oriented, and virtuously sensitive epistemic abilities that are the foundation of our earliest and most fundamental access to the world.

Just like we need to distinguish jokes from insults, deeply offensive language from tolerable generalizations about human traits, one also needs to distinguish assertions from speculations. In Chapter 7, we explore more implications of the AAM for social epistemology in detail. We shall now summarize the main halting thresholds that we analyzed in the context of how AAM applies to communication in this chapter, which can be defined in three ways. AAM requires the *cognitive integration* of these three thresholds, which should also be linked to action (either mental or overt).

Halting-Computational: Selecting an assertable content requires some kind of informational program that operationalizes semantic values and stops when the relevant epistemic threshold is reached. This kind of halting is susceptible to computational analysis.

Halting-Factive: Selecting an assertable content requires the specification of communicational relevance and the accurate representation of facts. Such a process of selection should stop only when a safety epistemic threshold is reached so that a satisfaction condition is met.

Halting-Subjective: Selecting an assertable content requires the specification of communicational relevance based partly on the shared motivations and interests of speakers, determined by a common background of information. Such a process of selection should stop only when those motivations and interests are properly satisfied by the assertable content.

These halting thresholds guide reliable communication. The dynamic character of communication (e.g., how evidence, interests, and conversational backgrounds are updated) depends on reliable skills to satisfy these thresholds. Agents have those skills because of their virtuous epistemic constitution.

As we explain in the next chapter, the type of curiosity that is epistemically virtuous aims at reaching an assertive threshold. The threshold for assertion, however, as illustrated by the epistemic asymmetry between assertion and other speech acts, is unique because it is basic and not reducible to other communicative epistemic achievements. Like perception, it satisfies a basic need: to reliably communicate factive information. Curiosity, by contrast, explicitly depends on assertion as a goal and originates from open inquiry.

5.7   Conclusion

This concluding section shows the importance of discussing halting thresholds and cognitive integration more explicitly in epistemology, including debates regarding contextualism. Focusing on an example from the literature on contextualism and skepticism, we can see that authors appeal to some version of these thresholds without contemplating the possibility that they need to be integrated. Some authors, for instance Sosa (2000) and Kornblith (2000), have argued that contextualism is not really relevant for addressing traditional skeptic problems in epistemology. Kornblith (2000), in particular, raises the worry that the type of "high standards" skeptic is not using the term "knowledge" in an epistemically *relevant* way. He uses the example of an eccentric Vermonter who refuses to say it is cold outside unless it is 25° below 0° F. The intuition is that the Vermonter's standards surely should not settle matters concerning knowledge of the external world, at least with regard to cold temperature. This criticism resonates with our criticism of Greco in Chapter 3. Surely, the standards of an attributor or the interests of a community of speakers should not determine what counts as objectively reliable. But, how is the relevance of an assertion going to be determined by strictly objective standards? There must be some interests that determine the *relevance of an assertion* – relevance is different from reliability because determining relevance is not the same as determining the *objective cause* of a success, which is a distinction that is not addressed in Greco's treatment of this issue.

DeRose's (2009) contextualist solution to skepticism may be more nuanced than a simple "standards" version of epistemic commitment, particularly if interpreted along the AAM we propose. DeRose uses sensitivity to account for the fact that we are attentive to claims about hands and external objects, but insensitive to and uninterested about claims concerning brains in vats. This type of virtuous sensitivity and insensitivity must be grounded in *psychological processes*, and the AAM is a natural candidate for explaining virtuous sensitivity in terms of the halting functions described above. Agents utter relevant assertions because attention is reliably sensitive to only a subset of information, and insensitive to a vast body of irrelevant theoretical and hypothetical information, even if the information is veridical (e.g., information about the quantum nature of the universe). A diagnosis of the impasse between contextualists and their opponents suggests itself: DeRose seems to be interested in a more subjective form of halting, while Kornblith is clearly interested in a purely objective or factive one. We are not claiming that the AAM entails DeRose's contextualist solution, or that we favor such a solution over its criticism concerning epistemic irrelevance. We only want to illustrate how the AAM is useful in reinterpreting debates in terms of the underlying psychological processes and *agency*, rather than rules one must reflectively endorse in counterfactually complex ways, or the reflective endorsement of principles based on the assessment of epistemic and metaphysical possibilities. In particular, *cognitive integration matters for epistemic agency* and it should, therefore, be discussed more prominently in epistemology.

6   Curiosity and Epistemic Achievement

This chapter presents a theory of epistemic achievements grounded in the normative epistemic properties of agents that reliably and responsibly satisfy their curiosities. Virtuously sated curiosities have a unique and important epistemic standing we explore at length. The work of Ilhan Inan is prominently discussed. Assertable contents are used to specify the normative epistemic thresholds for satisfying curiosity in ways that extend Ramsey-assertable contents as discussed in Chapters 3 and 4.

6.1   Epistemically Virtuous Curiosity

We introduce the virtue of "epistemically virtuous halting" in the context of sating a curiosity. The importance of providing a normative threshold for terminating inquiry is emphasized, and epistemically virtuous agents are characterized as agents that reliably and responsibly sate their curiosities by satisfying the relevant epistemic thresholds.

We examine the criteria and psychology of virtuously satisfying a curiosity and argue that a belief has positive epistemic standing if it results from the virtuous sating of a curiosity. This will be an *epistemic* theory of curiosity because our analysans will be strictly epistemic achievements, rather than any practical concepts that curiosity might also illuminate. We will not, however, propose necessary and sufficient conditions for knowledge here. Although we believe the achievements of virtuously curious agents will be close approximations to knowledge or justified belief as traditionally conceived, curiosity is fundamental to our intellectual lives and clearly supports a number of important epistemic achievements, wherever these might fall on a given analysis of knowledge. We must provide an account of achievements, abilities, and virtues that is epistemic and grounded in virtuously sating human curiosity. Given the ubiquity and motivational significance of curiosity in our epistemic life, articulating the virtues of successfully curious agents should be useful for a number of epistemic perspectives.[1]

---

[1] Virtue epistemology is perhaps the most directly relevant epistemic perspective. Curiosity is often listed as an intellectual virtue by theorists in this field (Baehr, 2011; Montmarquet, 1993; Zagzebski, 1996). While we do not deny this by any means, we argue that curiosity can be a vice.

Since we seek to illuminate *normative* concepts in epistemology – epistemic achievements – we cannot simply describe the process by which agents typically sate their curiosities. We can imagine, and perhaps are all too familiar with, cases where a person feels that they have satisfied their curiosity through an inquiry that clearly fails to meet any interesting standard of epistemic achievement. From an epistemic point of view, such a curiosity is not virtuously sated. Any epistemic theory of curiosity must explain when curiosity is virtuously (or otherwise normatively) sated.

Where will this normative element be found? What makes the sating of a curiosity responsible, virtuous, or otherwise normatively appropriate in an epistemic sense? As mentioned in Chapter 5, some of the normative dimensions of curiosity will be taken from the normative dimensions of assertion.[2] However, this presents an immediate worry. Most norms for assertion are epistemic norms. The "knowledge norm" is arguably the most common norm of assertion (Williamson, 1996), and it counsels that one should only assert what one knows. We seek to illuminate epistemic achievements that are at least close approximations to knowledge and justification, so a norm of assertion that relies on such concepts will not be especially useful. We address this in Section 6.3.

In addition to assertion, our account appeals to another fundamental feature of our intellectual life, namely attention. Most (if not all) epistemically interesting cognitive processes involve attention.[3] We argue that the forms of attention required for virtuously satisfying curiosity constitute epistemic virtues and achievements. The assertoric forms of attention we appeal to may or may not involve the public act of asserting. A person can have psychological access to a content as something *assertable* for them, but have clear reasons not to assert that content, no particular reason to do so, or pragmatic reasons that are based on conversational norms and goals to withhold the act of assertion. An agent may nonetheless manifest the same attentional state when they possess an assertable but unasserted content as when they actually assert that content. Psychologically, they have what a person would have were they to assert that content.[4] Here we consider what an agent has psychologically when their assertion closes an inquiry that satisfies a curiosity.

---

[2] The philosophical literature on assertion has grown tremendously over the past decade or so. Some recent examples include MacFarlane (2011), Littlejohn and Turri (2014), Goldberg (2015), and Lackey (2008). As we explain below, this is not the case with respect to curiosity, in spite of its importance and ubiquity.

[3] With some disruption in the heyday of behaviorism, attention is and continues to be the central cognitive phenomenon studied by psychologists, and has recently sparked interesting investigations into essential connections between attention and philosophical questions about the nature of consciousness. For a fine collection of essays, see Mole et al. (2011) and a sustained investigation by Montemayor and Haladjian (2015).

[4] Thanks to Dennis Whitcomb for helpful suggestions on how to put this point.

One potential objection to our approach is that epistemic norms appear to be hypothetical imperatives.[5] If a subject S is curious about some question Q, principles of epistemic evaluation will be relevant to their inquiries and epistemic activities relevant to Q. However, as with hypothetical imperatives generally, principles of evaluation carry no authority over agents that do not hold the relevant interest. (Otherwise, we have categorical epistemic standings that are independent of the properties of curious agents.) Any authoritative evaluation of the epistemic status of an agent's inquiry that is derived from the curiosities attributable to the agent will be contingent upon their actually having *interest* in the relevant topics. On a pure curiosity-based epistemology, there is no obligation to inquire into a topic where there is no interest. Even worse, if one happens to engage in inquiry despite not being interested in the issue, there are no grounds for criticizing irresponsible inquiry. Stephen Grimm (2009) has nicely described this as a problem about the narrow scope that epistemic evaluation takes when limited to issues that matter to the agent being evaluated. This is a difficult problem, and we will not aim to settle it decisively here. The upside is that basing epistemic normativity on how well epistemic agents perform in pursuing important truths is promising and has advantages in characterizing a common and important epistemic achievement.

One line of response to the worry of limited normative scope is that a person might be curious about much more than they realize, or would directly report being curious about. All people have an interest in being seen as a reliable source of testimony (not just in being able to flag *others* as reliable sources) by their fellows.[6] As such, we want to be in a position to (responsibly) assert a wide range of propositions on a wide range of topics and for others to believe most of what we genuinely assert. This will presumably require some level of curiosity in a wide range of domains, more than one might claim when queried about their interests in ordinary contexts and conversations. We may find that we are generally curious about most propositions in a given field to which we give scant explicit attention because we want to be generally competent in giving testimony, and there may be many such fields for which we want to possess this testimonial competence that would not be reported as direct interests. If extended in this way, we can cast a broader net for epistemic norms whose authority is grounded in the actual curiosities of epistemic agents. This is not a complete answer to the concern about limited scope, but it may take us some of the way to answering it.

---

[5] For a very interesting account of epistemic norms as hypothetical imperatives, see Kornblith (1993).

[6] Craig (1990) provides an insightful account of the origin of the concept of knowledge in terms of the desire to flag reliable informants. The point here simply shifts that emphasis to a desire to be flagged as a useful informant.

6.2   Basic Principles of Curiosity

Here, we present basic commitments for any understanding of curiosity, not just the epistemic form of interest, in terms of interest and uncertainty. The work of Ilhan Inan is discussed. We argue that Inan's principles do not provide a sufficient basis for epistemic evaluation because he does not provide a normative threshold for terminating curiosity-based inquiry. We examine some basic principles of curiosity and why some additional work will be necessary for an adequate account of epistemically virtuous curiosity.

The two main forms of curiosity discussed by Ilhan Inan in his excellent monograph, *The Philosophy of Curiosity* (2012), are propositional curiosity and objectual curiosity (also in Inan, 2014). These are distinguished according to the kind of question each seeks to answer. Propositional curiosity aims to answer questions about whether some proposition is true or false, a "whether question" (2012, 50), whereas objectual curiosity seeks to answer "wh-questions" – who, what, where, or why questions (ibid. 50). In both cases, a curious agent desires knowledge, but the content is significantly different. In the case of whether-questions, we want to know the truth value of a certain proposition (whether it will rain today, whether an invitation to the party will be offered, whether we will live past 80). Propositional curiosity thus seeks to answer questions that have "yes or no" answers and takes as its object the truth values of propositions. Objectual curiosity, according to Inan's usage, seeks to answer questions such as, "what was Plato's father's name?", "when will Sue arrive?", and "who will John marry?" These are not answered by finding the truth value of a proposition, but rather by finding the referent of a definite description, name, or other referring expression. A detective, for example, wants to know which individual, if any, is picked out by the referring phrase "the murderer of Smith" and this requires knowing what item in the world satisfies a definite description.

Inan insightfully argues that degrees of curiosity are negatively correlated with degrees of certainty, but positively correlated with degrees of interest (2014). The more certain we become that we possess the answer to a question of either type above, the *less curious* we are (although we enjoy the greater assurance of truth). The more interested we are in the answer to a question, the more curious we become. An individual's overall degree of curiosity will be a function of at least these two variables (and, for Inan, a third one he calls "acquaintance"). Inan (2014, 146–147) is led to the following principles as part of the core of curiosity:

CU: S's degree of curiosity with respect to a proposition (p) or a wh-referent (r) is inversely correlated with the degree of subjective *certainty* assigned to p or r by S.
CI: S's degree of curiosity with respect to a proposition (p) or a wh-referent (r) is positively correlated with S's level of *interest* in p or r.

What does this tell us about epistemic abilities and achievements? Assuming that CU and CI do in fact tell us something essential about curiosity, any curious agent must have a complex attentional ability to form and track subjective probability assessments during an ongoing inquiry, and to psychologically integrate this information with interest-directed forms of attention.[7] The basic process of opening and closing inquiry requires at least this basic toolkit of cognitive and interest-directed attentional abilities, and, importantly, their integration.

Given this cursory characterization of some essential features of curiosity, we suggest three principles to which any theory of epistemic curiosity will be committed.

(1) Curious agents initiate and close inquiry because they are interested in some "whether" or "wh" question, and their inquiry is motivated by the aim of reducing uncertainty.

(2) A curious agent is minimally successful when inquiry leads them either to understand a content that provides an adequate answer to a question of interest, or to drop their interest in the question itself. A curious agent is successful when their curiosity is extinguished.

(3) Epistemic abilities will be those person-level dispositions required for success as a curious agent as defined in (2).

This is a beginning, but only that. We will now argue that extinguishing curiosity *per se* is indeed a virtue of sorts even when it falls well short of the epistemic achievement we demand for (fully) virtuous sating of curiosity. (2) might be satisfied by any agent that holds very low standards for acceptable answers to their questions (e.g., wishful thinking, or the first thing that comes to mind). Such a sating would not be a full epistemic achievement, but we argue that even this non-responsible sating of curiosity is nonetheless a virtue of a sort. This is easily appreciated when we consider the unenviable position of an agent that is not able to sate any of their open, ongoing curiosities.

A different problem arises if the standards for an adequate answer in (2) are set too high. Inan rightly states that it is impossible to be certain and curious about the same content at the same time (2014, 145). More problematically, he also says that any credence below 1 allows for continued curiosity (ibid. 154–155). A potential worry here is that, outside of curiosity about mathematical or logical questions, holding an overly stringent standard for answers to

---

[7] Interest-directed attention is also an ability to track and update of sorts, since we might become less interested in a topic precisely by inquiring into it further. For instance, we might find that a question has less bearing on things that we are truly interested in than we initially thought, or we might find that our lack of success in reducing uncertainty leads us to drop or reduce our interest. A curious agent should be attending to these variables in the process of inquiry in addition to probability assessments.

our questions can make curiosity a vice.[8] Very few inquiries could responsibly come to an end if certainty were required to do so, and this (or any unattainable threshold) would have disastrous consequences for our intellectual life. Curiosity will be a very dangerous vice if this is where it leads us for too many of the questions that really matter to us. The general worry here is that (2) does not provide a *normative halting threshold* for inquiry. This will have to be a point at which inquiry has reduced uncertainty enough that fixing belief at such a point will give one something approximating justification, but where reaching this point is also feasible for cognitively limited, finite creatures like ourselves. On the one hand, any epistemic theory of curiosity needs halting thresholds that constitute genuine epistemic achievements when inquiry halts at threshold (some epistemic merit or praise is due). On the other hand, what we call *the problem of far too many open inquiries* below must be avoided. An adequate account of epistemic curiosity will require defining the right halting threshold for inquiry.

6.3   Curiosity and Halting Thresholds

This section answers the demand for normative thresholds. Distinct virtues of reliably and responsibly sating curiosity are introduced and their epistemic value is explained. We argue that without virtuous insensitivity it is impossible to virtuously satisfy curiosity.

Thresholds are important in the study of cognition and rationality in a number of ways, only one of which directly concerns us here. Herbert Simon discuss the use of "value thresholds" for acceptable options in reasoning in the place of calculation. For example, Adam Morton describes a case of deciding on an acceptable option for a house in terms of value thresholds for timing (within two months of being on the market) and price (anything above a certain dollar amount).[9] Ernest Sosa (2015) discusses thresholds at which a virtuous agent ought to withhold an attempt, for example, a basketball player standing at various distances from the net. Gigerenzer and Gaissmaier (2011) discuss stopping rules for cognition which permit an inquiry to terminate. Here we are primarily concerned with halting thresholds for curiosity-based inquiry similar to Gigerenzer's stopping rules.

A halting threshold will be a principle that states when a curious agent may terminate an inquiry and fix a belief in an answer to a question. For just a moment, we put aside the important question of when a halting threshold is

---

[8] As a descriptive, psychological claim it may be plausible for some types of curiosity, but one worry is that such a high standard will make it impossible to find a reliable *enough* way to end inquiry. This issue reminds us of the so-called "frame problem."

[9] This example is taken from Morton (2012) who provides an excellent and more extensive account of rational decisions that involve success in setting thresholds.

epistemically praiseworthy, because there is an important virtue that is independent of this. An agent whose inquiries reliably halt at *any threshold* is an agent that possesses a minimal virtue.[10] Assuming that agents reliably halt at some threshold, they will reliably sate or extinguish their curiosities and have information available for further action, either by finding a (subjectively acceptable) answer to their question, or dropping their interest in the question. We call this the *virtue of reliable sating.*

Why is this a virtue, even if a minimal one? First, in a well-functioning cognitive system, any principle whose *function* is to serve as a halting threshold is one that ought to effectively bring about termination of inquires that reach threshold. Internally, the system is functioning properly. Reliable sating is also a virtue because it avoids the problem of "far too many open inquiries." An ideal epistemic agent will have all and only highly justified premises for reasoning for action. However, a limited epistemic agent is clearly better off having a good number of *premises they can use*, irrespective of their ultimate epistemic quality, than having none or very few.[11] At the extreme, lacking any capacity for reliable halting seems incompatible with having a recognizably human epistemic life of any sort. A pervasive lack of answers is especially problematic in the case of curiosity, since the questions are, *ex hypothesi*, important and interesting. We have an epistemic need for some answers to some of the questions that matter to us. We only defend reliable sating as a minimal virtue here, but it is important to note that curiosity can be a vice in any agent that lacks it.[12]

The kind of reliability involved in reliable sating is quite different from familiar forms of process and agent reliabilism, as there need not be a particular process that reliably leads to termination, nor any agent that produces a preponderance of true beliefs simply by reliably halting at threshold (we examine something closer to this next). Inquiries that reliably halt at threshold are valuable because they ward off the problem of far too many open inquiries. The virtue of reliable sating can be explained in terms of reliably successful selective attention and partial solutions to many-many problems. For instance, out of many options for focusing attention, the virtuous agent eliminates many

---

[10] Consider the traditional issues surrounding a Pyrrhonian type of infinitely open inquiry, and the consequences it may have for decision-making and action, as well as more academic-like skeptical worries about being sensitive to possible, but too remote, scenarios. To the extent that resisting skepticism is an epistemic achievement, halting inquiry at some point is a minimal kind of epistemic virtue.

[11] Here, we have a fairly practical view of an epistemic agent, one that can form and revise beliefs in a rational way, enabling the agent to act in the world and to continue an epistemic life. As mentioned, Pyrrhonian skepticism, for example, would not be a reasonable perspective for our purposes. The exigencies of action are epistemic, and one must consider those exigencies in modeling thresholds for closing inquiry.

[12] This may be related to the vice Heather Battaly calls "epistemic immoderateness."

alternatives in favor of the most relevant one given a specific epistemic motivation and a concrete inquiry. It is very important for an epistemic agent to possess this kind of reliability with respect to their curiosities.

We can see the need for reliable halting in basic attentional processes by recalling Wayne Wu's argument that attentional processes are solutions to "many-many problems," discussed in Chapter 1.[13] An agent confronts a many-many problem in any situation where they have some task t in mind, and multiple available options to initiate, guide, and complete activities that are likely to accomplish t. We do this when we focus on part of our visual field to find our keys, search memory for a name, or select an action in order to complete a task (e.g., kicking a ball). In each case, there is a psychological process that requires input selection (anchoring attention on a target), output selection (selecting an action to complete a task), and motivational guidance from input selection to output selection. What we are calling reliable halting is the ability to reliably terminate an inquiry according to a threshold in relation to a particular goal state.

Recall Wu's example of a person that intends to kick a ball, and in front of them is a football and a basketball. The options include at least these four: kicking the football with the left foot, kicking the football with the right foot, kicking the basketball with the right foot, or kicking the basketball with the left foot. One path through this "behavior space" must be selected in order for any action to occur. Action here will require attentional selection and subsequent attentional focus and control. Along the way to, say, kicking the football with the left foot, additional many-many problems will arise while approaching the area encompassing the ball, and even at the very end there are many spatial regions to coordinate with foot and body movements to finalize the kick. A successful kick will arise from this motivationally initiated navigation task within a behavior space, which depends on the reliable solution to a number of many-many problems.[14] Likewise, terminating an inquiry at threshold and extinguishing curiosity is a type of successful navigation of a (mental or physical) behavior space and requires solving many-many problems. Epistemic virtues must be based on these admittedly minimal, but necessary capacities to halt inquiries.

---

[13] Many accounts of attention in psychology see them as person-level states, or "whole organism" states. See especially Alan Allport (2011). Allport specifically says that "*attention* (better still, *attending*) refers to a state or relationship of the *whole organism* or person" (ibid. 2011, 25). Allport (1987) emphasizes that attention is selection for action, an idea that is shared either implicitly or explicitly by many psychologists. While it is more controversial to say that all forms of attention are at the organism level, we shall assume that all forms of attention that are *epistemically relevant* are personal. See Burge (2010) for a similar criterion concerning why mental representation should occur at the personal level. Notice that integration at the personal level does not suffice for integration for action. This is an important insight we take from Wu (2011).

[14] Even in cases where we simply, for no apparent reason, want to maintain attention to a specific feature of an environment, we will instantiate this basic structure.

While reliable halting is a (minimal) success, *fully virtuous curiosity* will require that additional epistemic praise is due to agents that reliably satisfy their curiosities that mere reliable halting does not give us. The additional value of fully virtuous sating over merely reliable sating is found in the additional achievement provided by *responsible* sating. Fully virtuous sating requires at least these forms of reliability and responsibility. As a first approximation, let's say that inquiry terminates *responsibly* if terminating at the relevant threshold connects an agent to a content in a way that gives the agent some epistemically authoritative relation to that content. This is responsible halting, and it is a more strictly epistemic accomplishment than reliable halting, as no authoritative epistemic relation is achieved through its manifestation.[15] Any responsibly sated curiosity should give an agent some form of rational, justified, or otherwise epistemically praiseworthy belief. We are not especially concerned with settling exactly what to call this epistemic accomplishment using the traditional vernacular of contemporary epistemology (knowledge, justification, warrant, rationality, etc.). We want to identify a threshold that clearly points to an epistemic achievement, and to provide a sharp criterion for this, but without settling any questions about strictly necessary and sufficient conditions for knowledge or justification. While we need this to be a substantive achievement if it will accomplish all or some of the work we want from a theory of justified belief, we need to locate the proper halting threshold without raising the bar too high in the process, otherwise we lose reliable halting and take on the problem of far too many open inquiries. Putting reliable and responsible halting conditions together, we will be in a position to say that agents that reliably halt inquiry at a responsible threshold will have an epistemically authoritative relation to a good number of the beliefs that matter to them.

A person that is reliable and responsible in these ways will be a pretty successful epistemic agent. But, where to find the adequate threshold? Unsurprisingly, we look to assertion. As a first approximation, an agent's inquiry into the truth or falsity of a content can responsibly terminate when that content is normatively assertable for them. The answer to their question does not have to be overtly asserted, it must simply be assertable according to an appropriate assertor norm. Assertability is a normative notion as we use it here, and differs from a mere utterance in that way. We thus need to state the norm-regulating assertion in order to use it as a normative threshold for curiosity-based inquiry. This is no easy task, in part because assertion is a subtle issue that is drawing the attention of many philosophers at present. Furthermore, since we here seek to provide an epistemic analysis of curiosity,

---

[15] Think of how halting is a reliable property of a computable function or program. While this is certainly an objective property of a process that yields a systematic output by halting, it is implausible to model any epistemic virtue along these lines.

and most norms of assertion are analyzed in epistemic terms, there is a worry of circularity. As mentioned in the previous chapter, the most common norm for assertion is likely the "knowledge norm," which says "assert only what you know." Other epistemic norms for assertion are "assert only what you rationally believe" or "assert only what you are justified in believing" (for further enumeration, see Rescorla, 2009). Defining responsible halting in terms of an epistemic norm of assertion is potentially problematic for our purposes because we want to define epistemic concepts in terms of responsible halting.

Fortunately, there are other options. We look to action. Some philosophers have appealed to *action* as the norm of assertion (Maitra and Weatherson, 2010). This norm says, roughly, "assert only what you can act on."[16] There is a reading of Ramsey's success semantics (1927) that provides an attractive way to pursue this kind of account (see also Fairweather and Montemayor, 2014b). Modified for assertion rather than truth, a Ramseyian approach would be like this: P is assertable for S at t if and only if, were S to act on P and have some desire D at t, S would satisfy D. This tells us that if an action leads to the satisfaction of a desire, the belief component of the intention of the action is assertable. We can call any such belief "Ramsey-assertable." When having a Ramsey-assertable content coincides with that content having some epistemically significant status, something in the ballpark of justification or warrant, we can say that a belief is (ballpark) justified when it satisfies the action norm understood through Ramsey. Finally, an inquiry that gives us a content that is Ramsey assertable is an inquiry that can responsibly terminate.

This account of virtuous sating is intuitive for a few reasons. A person is a good source of testimony if, when queried, their assertions enable the questioner to get what they want by acting on the information given. It also seems to be no miracle that their desire was satisfied because, were the world quite different than how the communicated information represents it as being, it is unlikely that their desire would be satisfied. It is not impossible for the desire to be satisfied when the belief is false, but we are just looking here for something like justification, not truth or certainty. It is reasonable to believe that the world is roughly as you take it to be if your desires are reliably satisfied when acting on that representation of the world. Assertability so understood seems like a reasonable place to close inquiry, and a responsible way to sate curiosity.

In this section, we have argued that an agent that virtuously sates a curiosity will be credited for the epistemic achievement of possessing Ramsey-assertable contents. Furthermore, we have argued for a specific virtue necessary for

---

[16] It is worth noticing that the literature on the norm of assertion may be interpreted in terms of *epistemically responsible halting thresholds* (i.e., certainty, knowledge, justified belief, and action – all well-known "norms of assertion").

achieving this – virtuous halting. In the next section, we explore an additional virtue necessary for virtuously sated curiosity.

6.4   Curiosity and Virtuous Insensitivity

This section explains virtuous insensitivity in terms of attentional inhibition. Standard versions of the "frame problem" are discussed and assertability is defended as the correct epistemic threshold for closing inquiry. The work of Adam Morton is used to justify the need for such thresholds.

It is intuitive to think that because curiosity brings interests to our intellectual life it functions something like a spotlight that sharpens and makes salient what we care about. This is not entirely incorrect, but much of this occurs indirectly. Having an interest enables us to become sensitive to (attend to) specific features of our environment by enabling us to become *insensitive* to a much greater amount of information that is irrelevant to the interest. In this section, we argue that becoming insensitive to irrelevant information is an important achievement of virtuous curiosity. This achievement requires an epistemically valuable form of *attentional inhibition* that eliminates possibilities relative to a particular interest.[17]

By anchoring attention in line with their interests, a curious agent (whether ultimately virtuous or not) will become insensitive to a huge amount of information. In this way, curiosity helps solve what William James, in the *Principles of Psychology*, calls the fundamental problem of consciousness, namely "What to think next" to avoid the "blooming buzzing chaos" that would otherwise result.[18] Virtuous insensitivity is also an instance of solving what Ronald de Sousa (1987, 192–194) calls "the philosopher's frame problem." He argues that emotions mimic the encapsulation of perception and that they efficiently tell us what we need to ignore. Extreme informational overload prevents any inquiry from opening, progressing, or closing. It is useful here to restate some of the points made in Chapter 2 (Section 2.7). As mentioned, Glymour (1987) describes frame problems as follows: "Instances of the frame problem are all of the form: given an enormous amount of stuff, and some task to be done using some of the stuff, what is the *relevant stuff* for the task?" (Ibid. 65). Understood in computational terms, two salient features of this problem are the vastness of inferences concerning an unbounded number of propositions, on the one hand, and the select and meager

---

[17] Some scientific research (Gruber, 2014) suggests that when subjects are performing cognitive tasks while curious they are more successful at retaining information. However, the test subjects retained information that was of interest as well as information peripheral to their interests. This suggests that some additional virtue, such as insensitivity, is important to reap the benefits that curiosity can bring.

[18] The "blooming, buzzing chaos" is James' description of a baby's first experiences in the world, but it would equally well describe any person lacking the capacity for informational insensitivity.

evidence that agents take into consideration when they perform tasks, on the other.[19]

In this generic form, one can think of many instances of the frame problem, e.g., what is the intended meaning of a sentence uttered by a speaker given all the available options, what evidence should be taken into consideration when one is trying to reach some practical goal? Thus, the frame problem is primordially a problem of relevance and aboutness, i.e., what information is relevant to complete a specific task given a vast amount of plausible and mutually incompatible alternatives. Curiosity provides the essential variable of *relevance* because it always involves an interest, and this typically shields human beings from falling prey to frame type problems.

Referring back to the example used in Section 2.7, consider this ordinary situation. If you want to go to a party and don't know how to get there, a good heuristic is to ask someone who is going to the party how to get there and to rely on her testimony for action.[20] Depending on where you live, there might be significant evidence you should ideally take into consideration regarding the probability of events that could interfere with your course of action: accidents, earthquakes, criminals, and traffic. An idealized rational agent will weigh all of the evidence concerning these probabilities, but you are actually much better off not thinking about *all* of the possible evidence compared to asking a friend how to get there. Action demands that you stop thinking about every possible scenario and the likelihood that it will come to fruition. As Fodor (1987, 140) nicely put it, the frame problem is "Hamlet's problem: when to stop thinking."

The computational problem regarding how to identify relevance in a system with too much information is generally expressed in terms of cognitive architecture and modularity. If the architecture of the mind seems to be such that problems are solved locally by specialized and encapsulated systems, how is it possible to identify relevance in a global, non-encapsulated (personal or agential) way conducive to action, decision, and performance? This problem can also be expressed in terms of relevance understood as epistemic sensitivity: given that there is a torrent of deductive and inductive inferences concerning evidence that can be considered at any given time, how can one be sensitive to only a small amount of such evidence and insensitive to the rest in order to succeed at epistemic tasks?

---

[19] For discussion of these two central aspects of the frame problem, see Fodor (1983, 1987, 2000). Fodor argues that the frame problem is an insurmountable challenge for the computational theory of the mind. For criticism of Fodor's view (in the context of the debate on the modularity of mind), see Carruthers (2006).

[20] There is an ongoing debate about the rational adequacy of heuristics in the context of decision-making. While we are not going to settle this debate here, see Morton (2012) and Fairweather and Montemayor (2014b) for a defense of heuristics in epistemology.

Motivation is playing a fundamental role in restricting the possibilities to which one should be sensitive. In the previous example, you *want* to go to the party and you also are motivated to get there in the most convenient way. As Greco (2010) points out, there are inductive and deductive versions of the problem of epistemic sensitivity reminiscent of the frame problem: one should ignore very good inductive inferences to the effect that everything is just a bunch of atoms and also very good deductive inferences to the effect that we have no certain knowledge of the external world if one wants to be a virtuous epistemic agent that holds common-sense beliefs.

How is virtuous insensitivity, as discussed above, related to virtuous halting, discussed in Section 6.3? The minimal virtue of reliable halting appears to accomplish some of the same functions as insensitivity, but there are subtle and important differences. Here are two important differences between reliable halting and virtuous insensitivity. First, halting can be precisely defined in terms of a computable function, but it is dubious one can model virtuous insensitivity, based on motivation and the specific content of an inquiry, on simply computational rules. Second, computational halting can be identified with the complexity of a function or program, but it is dubious that such a characterization will explain the frame problems mentioned above. Thus, reliable halting and virtuous insensitivity can come apart, even if they seem to overlap systematically.

Cognitive integration also matters. Reliable halting avoids the problem of far too many open inquiries, and virtuous insensitivity avoids the problem of information overload. The former may or may not be a special case of the latter. Reliable halting avoids information overload if the number of "going concerns" one would have by not halting would be overwhelming and incapacitating. However, numerous interrelated open inquiries might simply make our intellectual life disorganized, confusing, and unintegrated rather than informationally overwhelming. We may be unable to get answers to one set of questions because the needed lines of inquiry relevant to another set of questions have not closed.

Furthermore, reliable halting is praiseworthy in a teleological sense because curiosity by its nature aims for its own demise, it aims to be sated like hunger or thirst. Thus, it is roughly analytic that an agent that does not reliably sate their curiosity is not a successful curious agent. Virtuous insensitivity, on the other hand, strictly concerns information overload, and this is a practical barrier due to the cognitive limits of curious agents. It is plausible to see virtuous insensitivity as a necessary condition for reliable halting. We will not provide a full defense of that claim here, but in either case, the interest variable in curiosity produces informational insensitivity, and this is an important cognitive achievement based on the agent's epistemic motivations.

Because insensitivity to irrelevant information is a virtue, curiosity creates *negative epistemic entitlements* – an epistemic right to ignore information. Which information an agent can normatively ignore will depend on their specific curiosities, and, of course, in a given case a person might ignore information that is indeed relevant to their curiosity. Insensitivity will not be virtuous in such a case. We will not aim to answer exactly which and how much information can be ignored in particular cases, but we can offer a few suggestions. We are limited epistemic agents, and virtuous insensitivity should not only be attuned to what we are interested in, but also to our limits and capacities for handling information.[21] This will vary from person to person, so there is no reason to expect a set answer here, save for this general principle.

We have not yet said much about cognitive integration. Virtuously sating curiosity requires virtues of integration as well. We here examine some philosophically well-known instances of integration which essentially involve creativity. The goal of the remainder of this chapter is to illustrate how cognitive integration – of motivations, evidence, and inquiries – may actually account for cases in which epistemically responsible curiosity grounds creativity.

6.5 Attention, Curiosity, and Creativity

In this section we examine creativity as a manifestation of epistemically constrained curiosity. Three examples are given in order to illustrate the range of applications of the theory presented here. We will discuss ways in which curiosity involves creativity and discovery, and how some of the points above are explanatory in cases ranging from Descartes' mathematical curiosity to cases of referential curiosity.[22] In all cases, a proper epistemic motivation to initiate an inquiry and arrive at a responsible answer can be characterized in terms of attentional routines for asserting the appropriate content. In voluntary and involuntary attention, perceptual or intellectual routines predict the saliency of specific features and start inquiries in order to answer questions about these features. All of this happens implicitly, but it can become explicit, as in the case of explicit inference and reasoning. Attention is inquisitive by nature. The distinction between halting and insensitivity plays a role here: creativity is not the result of mere intellectual daring, but also of responsible curiosity. Epistemically responsible curiosity may produce creative results in virtue of being constrained by halting thresholds that nonetheless go beyond available information.

---

[21] Adam Morton (2014) is an excellent treatment of intellectual virtues that takes the limitations of their possessors seriously.

[22] An interesting point made by Inan (2014) is that a curious agent must have the ability to form a definite description, the referent of which is unknown to her. In such cases, Inan says that we must manifest the capacity to imagine the unknown in order to reliably satisfy certain forms of curiosity.

We first consider cases of creativity as the result of intellectual curiosity. Since our account is based on attention and, in many cases, implicit forms of satisfying halting thresholds, there might be a worry that our account cannot generalize beyond perceptual skills and basic linguistic communication. We use the following example of attention and a priori reasoning in order to demonstrate that our model generalizes to other relevant epistemic cases, and that it actually explains how attention guides explicitly conscious reasoning. The emphasis is on how halting thresholds and virtuous insensitivity may interact in creative, yet epistemically responsible ways. A particularly challenging case for an action approach, such as the one we are proposing, is a priori *reasoning*. We first focus on this case and then argue that in spite of the apparent lack of connection with action, the creative achievements of a priori reasoning can be fully explained by the proposal we defend.

One of the remarkable intellectual achievements of René Descartes is that he established an epistemic relation between algebra and geometry such that truths about algebra could be established geometrically and truths about geometry could be established algebraically. This is an impressive epistemic achievement for many reasons. Ian Hacking (2014, 6), for instance, finds it astonishing that "algebra, born of arithmetic, can be applied to geometry," as initially outlined by Descartes. Appearances would indeed militate against the supposition that mathematics obtained from the cognitive framework of geometry can be applied to solve problems in arithmetic and vice versa. Why would knowledge about numbers entail knowledge about geometric figures and vice versa?

Descartes' achievement is the product of an impressive exercise in cognitive integration. The application of arithmetic to geometry and of geometry to arithmetic involves language skills, perceptual representations of shape, inferential reasoning, and conscious visualization or visual imagery. Descartes was guided by attention to contents of a complex kind which required virtues of cognitive integration to generate the type of curiosity that leads to creativity in the field of mathematics. It was a kind of attention that took creative risks and had properly constrained epistemic halting thresholds (e.g., proving truths of arithmetic in terms of proofs of geometry and vice versa). Although mathematics is a priori (or epistemically necessary), there is no reason to think that truths achieved through the framework of perceptual and imaginative visualizations could translate into truths about the symbolic and language-like framework of numbers. Descartes' discovery is indeed astonishing.

Descartes was curious about whether aspects of shapes could be understood without paying any *perceptual* attention to shapes. Why was Descartes curious about such a thing? What kind of inquiry does it open and how can it be sated? In particular, is his curiosity epistemic in nature, rather than the type of curiosity that is not strictly epistemic, such as mere speculation or groundless inquisitiveness? Halting thresholds allow us to explain why Descartes was not just speculating without epistemic guidance from mathematical truth. Rather, he sought to answer concrete inquiries that had specific halting thresholds with an entirely new way of thinking – an entirely new way of being virtuously insensitive to information.

In his inquiry, Descartes displayed an intellectual kind of attention, far removed from its sensorial origins.[23] He shifted attention to his understanding of geometry and its mathematical basis rather than the visual perception of shapes and their features. His curiosity was grounded in this shift of attention, and his sated curiosity about such questions materialized in an expansion of mathematical truth. Descartes' curiosity was epistemically adequate because this attention-based wondering could be answered by satisfying halting thresholds with proper assertions. Had he done this for exclusively aesthetic purposes, for example, then his inquiry would have not been epistemically motivated and would not count as a responsible exercise of epistemic capacities. This kind of curious inquiry can be adequately characterized as aimed toward understanding (Whitcomb, 2010). It does seem, however, that Descartes' investigations were essentially motivated by attention and assertion, and this makes them epistemically adequate according to our account.

The topic of cognitive integration and curiosity, as it relates to creativity in epistemology, is a rich one. It may be the case that the higher the levels of cognitive integration, the richer the possibilities for creative curiosity. There are forms of curiosity, however, that may be crucial for creativity but with implications that may not be entirely epistemic. Consider Frank Jackson's case of Mary, the colorblind neuroscientist. Mary knows all the physical propositions regarding the nature of color experiences: what causes them, which neurons are activated, etc. By assumption, the thought experiment requires that Mary not be curious about the truth of propositions regarding color – she knows all of these truths in so far as they concern facts about color vision. Actually, Mary's assertions about color are epistemically faultless. She is a reliable source of information regarding statements about color. But it is perfectly conceivable that Mary is curious about *how* such color experiences are experienced subjectively by the subjects she studies – what it is like to have those experiences. Mary is not curious about the truth of propositions regarding color perception abstractly considered, but about how it would be to have an experience. As Paul (2014) has argued, cases in which one is curious about an experience that may have transformative repercussions with respect to how one interacts with the world do not fit neatly into standard accounts of evidence updating and rational deliberation. These cases, therefore, may not count as

---

[23] For some interesting points on the difference between "cognitive attention" and "perceptual attention," see Wu (2011). Cognitive attention typically involves selection for items that are not presented simultaneously, whereas perceptual attention requires selection from a range of potential targets present simultaneously, for instance, in the field of vision.

cases of epistemically constrained curiosity. Descartes' inquiry is epistemically constrained but Mary's may not be.[24]

Referential forms of curiosity are the most typically epistemic ones. However, there needs to be clarity with respect to what exactly the psychological underpinnings of referential curiosity are and whether or not referential curiosity relates to creativity and insight. The messy shopper (based on John Perry's famous example) is curious about the identity of the person who is making a mess in the store. At first, she doesn't realize that *she* is the messy shopper. She reasons as follows: someone is creating a mess here. I will follow this trail of sugar to tell that person about this mess. Passing a mirror quickly she points at the shopper without her glasses and says: that person is the messy shopper! She then realizes that she cannot get a good look at the messy shopper and puts on her glasses. She then realizes that she is the messy shopper. The messy shopper goes from *de dicto* to *de re* to *de se* belief as a result of curiosity, all driven by what should be asserted in the right circumstance. She is not only curious about the truth of the proposition "There is a messy shopper in the store" but also about *how* that proposition is true – *what makes it true*. This curiosity of aboutness is what drives her attention. Her curiosity is epistemically adequate because the halting thresholds are different in each case and they all halt with assertable contents.

More precisely, the messy shopper is curious about the inquiry "who is the messy shopper?" and any of the propositions above would halt or stop the inquiry, in general: *a* person in the store, *the* person you are pointing at and *you*. But there has to be a process of becoming insensitive to some of these options and in favor of one of them. This process cannot be merely about halting: it has to be about getting the right content relevantly related to the *motivation* for asking the question concerning the messy shopper in the first place.

The different inquiries the messy shopper initiates can, therefore, be expressed in terms of attention to contents. She is not only curious about the truth of the proposition "There is a messy shopper in the store" but specifically about who exactly this person is. She is not satisfied with just knowing that there is a messy shopper in the store, so she opens an inquiry in search of the shopper and guides her attention accordingly. She then has perceptually anchored referential acquaintance with the messy shopper in the store, so she opens an inquiry in search of the shopper because the halting threshold is not *properly* sated. The messy shopper knows two propositions, the original one – there is a messy shopper in the store – and the more specific proposition – *that* person is the messy shopper. Both propositions are true, but there is still another

[24] One possibility here is to construe curiosity about what it is like as curiosity about knowing how. This is an interesting alternative that could count as epistemically constrained curiosity, but it would take us too far afield to argue for this view and we will leave it as a possible alternative.

inquiry she needs to open to truly know who is the messy shopper. She needs to eliminate the possibility that the person she is now looking at is not herself, and she cannot do that until her visual attention is more reliable and informative. She puts on her glasses and realizes she is the person who is making a mess. Curiosity is now properly sated, constrained by epistemically guided attention and by beliefs that could satisfy a norm of assertion if expressed linguistically by the messy shopper. The content "I am the messy shopper" need not be asserted for the halting threshold to be properly satisfied; it need only be *assertable*. Admittedly, the relation to creativity is thin here, but it is not irrelevant – the messy shopper could stop at finding out that "there is a person who is making the mess" and that proposition would accurately describe her situation. One can see how in cases of scientific investigation one needs to get creative to answer referential questions in a way that is not overly general.

We have argued for a number of claims here. Most important, we argue that epistemic abilities and achievements can be understood in terms of inquiry that virtuously opens, guides, and sates curiosity. Virtuous halting and virtuous insensitivity are two virtues necessary for virtuously sating curiosity, and assertion and attention are the psychologically foundational features of these virtues. These are the normative properties of agents that confer normative status on beliefs.

7   Collective Agency, Assertion, and Information

This chapter extends the attention and assertion account defended throughout this work to issues in social epistemology and collective epistemic agency in particular. The work of Miranda Fricker, Margaret Gilbert, and Philip Pettit & Christian List is discussed. Two central problems are addressed, one concerning reliable communication in economic markets and reliable communication among collective agents in general. Further implications regarding moral masks on collective epistemic goods, the structure of legal systems, and the foundations of democratic discourse in reliable communication are discussed.

7.1   Collective Epistemic Agency and Cognitive Integration

This section defends a distinction between thin and thick cognitive constitutions for collective agency. This account of cognitive collective constitution grounds discussions of the different types of collective epistemic capacities discussed in the remainder of the chapter, with an emphasis on the importance of reliable collective communication.

Increasingly common in recent philosophical literature is the claim that collectives make *judgments* and perform *actions* (see Anderson, 2007; Copp, 2006; Fricker, 2010; Gilbert, 1987; Lahroodi, 2007; List and Pettit, 2011). Furthermore, the beliefs and actions of a collective are often claimed to be irreducible to the beliefs and actions of its individual members. It has also been claimed that wisdom can be had collectively (Gilbert, 2006). In this chapter, we argue that collective agents have epistemic lives that can be understood in terms of the attention-assertion model (AAM). We will argue by analogy: our aim is to demonstrate that processes of attention, virtuous insensitivity, and reliable communication also drive the epistemic lives of collective agents. Our emphasis will be on the type of epistemic constitution required for reliable communication based on collective agency, but we will consider other examples of virtuous collective agency as well.

While a consensus might be emerging that collectives have epistemic lives, they might turn out to be *poorly integrated* epistemic agents. We have emphasized the importance of integrated cognitive constitutions for individual epistemic agency thus far. Here, we argue that collective agents may qualify not only as having a minimal kind of epistemic agency analogous to modularized and integrated individual epistemic abilities, but that in some cases, they may also satisfy the more demanding constraints of virtuous epistemic agency.

Margaret Gilbert, Christian List, and Miranda Fricker have revived the topic of collective epistemic achievement (collective wisdom, in particular), but they emphasize different kinds of cognitive integration for epistemic agency, as well as different consequences of such agency, some more political and ethical than strictly epistemic. Gilbert (2006), for example, raises worries about limitations on individual freedoms engendered by wise joint commitments. Christian List (2012) defends a "thin" conception of collective wisdom that is achieved by solving *correspondence* and *consistency* problems facing collective agents. List notes that the account of wisdom he has in mind is very "thin," whereas wisdom as possessed by individuals typically involves attributes of character, bundles of virtues and vices, appropriate motivations, and tendencies toward actions that promote *important* ends. Miranda Fricker (2010) examines thicker collective states and argues that institutions can be virtuous or vicious. Thus, one can espouse the view that there are collective agents capable of virtuous epistemic performances, but attribute to them different levels of cognitive integration, thereby characterizing some collective agents as more virtuous than others simply based on how well constituted they are. The epistemic constitution of individual human epistemic agents will serve as the standard and collective agents would be compared to such a standard, normally falling short on the cognitive integration score.

List and Pettit (2011, 77) argue that some social groups are "rational agents in their own right." They focus on cases where groups form collective beliefs by *aggregating* the beliefs of the individual members – a case of integration by aggregation! This already requires some significant degree of cognitive integration that a group of people waiting at a bus stop does not possess. Compare a group of individuals that constitute a housing board to a group of individuals that constitute a crowd waiting for a bus, or "redheads" or "volvo owners." The last three groups are *mere* groups, not genuine collectives, and are not capable of producing collective belief or action. A crowd waiting for a bus might all of a sudden come together and form a reliable belief about why the bus has not arrived yet collectively by comparing different schedules and consulting traffic reports, but such a fleeting process hardly counts as epistemic constitution for agency. In contrast, the individual members of the housing board collectively *constitute* an entity capable of forming judgments (Smith must compensate Jones for the damage) and performing actions (sending Smith a formal assessment of charges) due to the constitutive principles of the housing board itself. One difference between a nonintegrated group of epistemic agents and a collective epistemic agent is that we can assign an institutionalized collective motivation to the latter but not the former. A collective epistemic agent integrates beliefs from individual members because of its structural and collective motivations. Collective epistemic agency thus seems to require that we can attribute at least the following to a group collectively:

1. Representational states that should accurately depict states of affairs.
2. Motivational states that specify why an inquiry should be opened, which conditions would satisfy the inquiry, and what course of action should follow if the inquiry is satisfied.
3. The capacity to process representational and motivational states, leading the collective agent to close inquiry, to assert, or to complete an act.

A mere crowd does not possess these features, and genuine collectives will typically manifest them by exhibiting appropriate forms of integration between the cognitive states of its individual members and between other collectively formed beliefs and aims. The constitution of collective agents required for cognitive integration resembles the cognitive architecture of individual cognitive agents. There will be "massively modular" collective agents that do not require much centralized monitoring, and also highly integrated collective agents with several attention-like routines to search for relevant information regarding a task the collective must accomplish as a whole. We illustrate these cases below.

Integration through aggregation can be in part computational or algorithmic, but requires a motivation or aim as well. Aggregation functions take many forms, but they are all reliable ways of integrating collective judgments out of the judgments of individual members of the collective. Aggregation procedures may take the form of "a voting procedure, a deliberation protocol, or any other mechanism by which the group can make joint declarations or deliver a joint report. Such procedures are in operation in expert panels, multi-member courts, policy advisory committees and groups of scientific collaborators" (List, 2012, 207). An aggregation procedure will be any function which assigns to each combination of the group members' individual "acceptance/rejection" judgments on the propositions on the agenda a corresponding set of collective judgments.

List and Pettit have shown, however, that it is surprisingly difficult to aggregate the beliefs of individual group members in rationally coherent ways. For instance, *the discursive dilemma* and similar results show how easily group agents exhibit patently inconsistent judgments in ways that individual agents rarely do. We have defended the view that idealized rationality should not be used as the standard for virtuous (individual) epistemic agents across the board, but perhaps the situation is different for collective epistemic agents (consider also the case of artificially intelligent agents). This is a very important question and formal results about how non-human epistemic agents could comply with different standards for rationality should inform an answer to this question. However, we will not address these issues directly here. Our goal is to discuss how collectives integrate motivation, attention, and assertion in reliable collective communication and thereby manifest a form of epistemic agency analogous to that manifested by individual agents on our account.

A different question, the one we are interested in, is what kind of integration does aggregation provide? Not much, or the right kind, in discursive dilemma cases discussed above. Dietrich and List (2008) show that certain desirable formal properties of aggregation procedures can be achieved if it is a dictatorship or reverse dictatorship (e.g., ruled by a chairperson or in receivership).

More optimistically, List (2012) argues that the worrisome results about collective irrationality only follow if we require that collective agents satisfy rigid forms of the following desiderata on aggregation functions: *Universality* (aggregation functions must take any consistent and complete set of individual judgments), *Decisiveness* (aggregation functions must produce complete judgments on all propositions), and *Systematicity* (collective judgments must depend only on individual judgments and patterns of dependence). List argues that we can attain meaningfully *collective* wisdom (not just dictatorial wisdom) only if we "relax" one or more of the above desiderata, thereby foregoing strict universality, strict decisiveness, or strict systematicity. For us, the important result is that formally idealized aggregation-integration must be relaxed in order to satisfy basic norms of rationality. Thinly wise collectives manifest agency through reliable collective communication, which often serves as an important source of epistemic authority (e.g., through collective testimony) for individuals. Distinguishing (thinly) wise from unwise collectives will be an individual epistemic virtue entailed by List's account.

How about more robust forms of collective "cognitive integration"? Miranda Fricker (2010) distinguishes three ways of relating groups to their constituent members. A group may be any of the following:
1. A number of individuals – the group considered as the sum of its component individuals.
2. A collective – the group considered as non-reducible to its component individuals.
3. An institutional structure – its formal and procedural structure *as such*.

Fricker (2010) distinguishes between properties that an individual might have as *a group member* and properties they have *as a private individual*. Collectives can have properties lacked by each of its members qua private individual. Likewise, every member of a group possessing a feature is insufficient for the group to possess it (e.g., being open minded about gay rights). Fricker concludes that "Some practical identities of individuals are thus intrinsically group-involving, and in such cases there is no lower level of group-independent features to which the higher-level features can be reduced. Any attempted reduction of the group to a sum of uncommitted non-group-identified individuals would literally change the subject, and so fail" (ibid. 238–239). This gives us one important sense of group agency that nonetheless foregrounds the individual.

Such irreducibility signals a much higher level of integration for collective agents that a purely procedural approach, such as List's, might not capture. When an agent performs an action under an essentially group-involving practical identity, *the collective has done something*, but has done so only because a full individual action was performed. Fricker argues that institutional actions of this kind, and the institutions themselves, can instantiate thick collective properties such as virtues and vices. According to Fricker, the institutional racism of the police force, the open mindedness of the jury, or the tenaciousness of the research team are proper virtues of collectives. Moreover, she argues that collectives can have these virtues *both* in a "motivationally demanding way" (Aristotelian virtues) or as a sheer excellence or skill (Stoic virtues). This is potentially attractive here because List was able to provide only a thin conception of collective motivation (perhaps closer to a "sheer excellence" or skill of the collective). If we use Fricker's account of individual actions under a practical identity and we agree that these actions (a) are sufficiently actions *of the collective*, (b) promote important aims of the collective, and (c) can be acted upon or give the collective a compelling reason for action, then we can clearly see how an individual action under a practical identity can constitute virtuous collective action. These are critical issues for the integration of courts of law, democratic governments, and the scientific community at large.

Exactly which collective epistemic virtues should be promoted will be an important and perhaps vexing question for social and educational policy. Education, learning and communication at the collective level depend on reliable skills for asserting relevant information and attending to the right features of a problem or task. In addition to the role of integration in collective agency, we will emphasize the role of reliable collective communication as the manifestation of collective epistemic agency. We proceed to review evidence in support of collective reliable communication, including instances of such communication in the animal kingdom. Although the issues just examined concerning different levels of integration will be pertinent, the focus will be on the epistemic achievement of reliable collective communication by collective agents as such.

7.2   Collective Agency and Reliable Social Communication

This section examines different kinds of reliable collective communication. It is argued that cooperation based on reliable information is a distinctive epistemic goal of collective agency, including attention routines regarding good sources of information, reliable assertion, and cheating.

In one of the earliest and most remarkable experiments concerning animal communication, the ethologist Karl von Frisch (1953) discovered that the bee's waggle dance reliably transmits information about distance and location of food sources that the whole colony uses to feed itself. The bee's waggle dance can be made more dramatic by moving faster, indicating that the food source is particularly good. Thus, the waggle dance not only states publicly that there is food at a particular location, but it also states how much attention the rest of the bees should pay to this information based on the quality of the food source.

Since the time of von Frisch's experiments, psychologists have found abundant evidence of astonishingly reliable communication skills in animals. Although these skills are certainly not equivalent to human language, copious evidence makes it clear that animals must reliably communicate factual information collectively. In the case of bee communication, success in tracking relevant locations does not serve the purposes of a single bee or just a select set of bees. Bee communication, rather, benefits a whole community and it is done for the purpose of the whole colony as such. This is compatible with the community promoting the self-oriented interests of each of its members, such as feeding and reproducing.

Theorists have proposed formal models that seem to be implemented in animal collective communication and decision-making. Work by Robert Axelrod (2006) shows that cooperation under certain circumstances, such as monitoring for cheaters (as in "tit-for-tat" scenarios), is the best strategy among all available strategies to further the interest of decision-makers with limited information. Reliable information transmitted among members of a group enhances cooperation, develops trust, and allows the group to evolve in new ways that give it an evolutionarily and competitive advantage. The idea here is not that groups evolve for the benefit of their species, which would be incompatible with selfish evolutionary individual reproduction. Rather, groups help individuals that cooperate with other members of the group enhance their chances at reproduction and the satisfaction of needs, even if their motivations are selfish. More important, the skills required for (a) detection of cheaters, (b) retaliation against cheaters, and (c) cooperation with "good citizens" depend on reliable group communication.

There is the temptation to bring a traditional dichotomy from political science to bear on these issues: individualism and collectivism. Surely in humans things are much more interesting than in bees, and reliable communication is just one of the most basic aspects of group evolution and collective forms of agency. The ethical dimensions of collective agency, for instance, seem to go beyond these basic communication skills. Perhaps, as in the collectivist understanding of human groups, society and history come first and the individual can only develop from such a background. For the opposite view, individualism, individual agency takes a primordial role and only then can collective agents emerge. We are not going to address this issue here. But we believe that the distinction between moral and epistemic individual agency can be extended to collective agency, and that the dichotomy between collectivism and individualism is cast under a different light based on the arguments below. In fact, we shall claim that drawing the distinction between moral and epistemic agency clarifies the conceptual landscape with respect to both individual agency and collective agency.

Here is how the AAM explains reliable collective communication – a distinctly epistemic achievement. Relevant actions may be specified independently of a social practice (e.g., transmitting information about location and quality of a food source without dancing with a certain intensity) or by specific reference to a social practice (e.g., identifying cheaters by "taking turns" and monitoring cheating behavior in a collective way, rather than identifying cheaters based on the information of a few experts). In either case, attention must be allocated to the right cues, properly anchored (is this performance about food or about cheating behavior?) and generate reliable motivations to act and assert. Critically, the collective depends on reliable assertions and interpretations of assertions to succeed. Collective communication and decision-making are paradigmatically epistemic achievements. Here we characterize collective communication in terms of collective agency that aims at fact-dependent coordination and the achievement of truth (or assertable content). Among the evidence that shows that groups can benefit individuals and display robust forms of epistemic agency is the research on group evolution. Suppose that there is a group selection advantage between two sets of individuals playing a game. A by herself would never win against B, but A and A' would win against B and B'. Assume the same holds for A' and B'. What explains the sudden success of A and A' when they act as a group? There could be two reasons. First, A and A' may have better means of communication and a more reliable way of obtaining information. Second, it could be that B' is friends with A' and based on her obligations to a friend she thwarts B in her efforts to succeed. An assumption of game theory is that the rules of the game hold in the same way for all players and that their decision-making is guided by those rules and the limited information they have available, rather than by other preferences. Without claiming that one can make a clear-cut distinction between epistemic and moral motivations in decision-making, it is clear that the first case requires epistemic, rather than moral agency. In other words, the first case requires capacities for attending and asserting the right information.

Two other aspects of this case are important for the topic of epistemic constitution and cognitive integration. If A and A' reliably succeed in wining against B and B' by cooperating and sharing information, then they will have an advantage as a group against other collectives. For the totality of members, individual and collective, that play the game, A and A' will become an important source of information about how to play and strategize. Other players will flag them as a reliable source of information, and the game will benefit from the overall improved performance. In the long run, other players may evolve better strategies and increase the accuracy of information because of A and A'. Also in the long run, the game will benefit from having players like A and A' who reduce the possibility of manipulation based on strictly family- or friend-based advantages. So the good constitution of A and A' benefits them, the game, and players who, like them, play by the rules.

The formal models offered to explain strategies for game theory show that members of groups must have sophisticated communicative and cooperative skills. Moral agency may require capacities to attend to relevant stimuli, but only the epistemic capacities to attend and respond to stimuli must be fact involving. In the case of collective agents, these capacities can improve in ways that individual agents cannot achieve. When social agents gather information reliably and improve their epistemic performances, higher forms of integration become possible. From the thin requirements of integration as aggregation and compliance with formal rules to the more robust forms of integration based on motivations and attention routines, the epistemic life of every agent becomes more complex by interacting with collective agents or by being a member of a collective. We proceed to discuss how the crucial problem of acquiring and sharing accurate information demands satisfying a *collective* need to express assertable contents – the kind of need that is at the core of the AAM.

7.3   Social Epistemology and Collective Assertion

This section examines some ways in which collective assertion manifests forms of collective agency. A key example discussed is how reliable collective assertion is critical in solving Friedrich Hayek's "economic problem." Several analogies are drawn with individual psychological agency, including the importance of thresholds in the absence of full access to total evidence.

As argued above, a critical aspect of successful collective action is efficient and reliable communication. This kind of communication has been confirmed across many species from bees and corvids to monkeys. There are even explicitly semantic aspects of communication in animal cognition that require higher degrees of cognitive integration, such as the contents of the alarm calls of many animals, including vervet monkeys, who run into bushes when an eagle alarm is produced, jump into trees when a leopard alarm is sounded, and stand bipedally and peer into grass when the alarm is about a snake. A system of mutual confirmation and reliance on such alarms maintains the safety of the community. An error in collective monitoring or in the reliability of the information will end tragically for members of the collective.

Human collective action is without a doubt the most complex of all species. Another source of complexity is that human collective action interfaces epistemic collective agency with moral collective agency. This complexity in cognitive integration, however, does not mean that the basic principles of reliable information and success in attending and asserting the right information are fundamentally the same in both types of agency. As we explain below, in some cases, collective moral agency may jeopardize either reliability or properly epistemic attentiveness, reducing, or eliminating epistemic performance. Before we explain these cases, we need to focus on how successful communication guides human collective agency.

A form of human collective communication that has become globally structured and depends on epistemic collective agency is economic behavior. Here one finds an unprecedented level of integration of information and regulation, constant collective monitoring, collective attentiveness to specific types of social behavior, and international collaboration for global solutions. But the basic *needs* underlying successful communication, the kind one finds in animals, remain the same, albeit within a much more complex system. To appreciate this, it is useful to understand the basic problem underlying economic transactions. In his influential paper "The Use of Knowledge in Society," Friedrich Hayek (1945) describes such problem as follows:

The peculiar character of the problem of a rational economic order is determined precisely by the fact that the knowledge of the circumstances of which we must make use never exists in concentrated or integrated form, but solely as the dispersed bits of incomplete and frequently contradictory knowledge which all the separate individuals possess. The economic problem of society is thus not merely a problem of how to allocate "given" resources – if "given" is taken to mean given to a single mind which deliberately solves the problem set by these "data." It is rather a problem of how to secure the best use of resources known to any of the members of society, for ends whose relative importance only these individuals know. Or, to put it briefly, it is a problem of the utilization of knowledge not given to anyone in its totality. (519–520)

Hayek's account of the economic problem demonstrates the importance of epistemic skills for monitoring and tracking relevant information in a world in which no one has all the information about the motivations of buyers and producers but in which collective action and planning is required. As Hayek emphasizes, it is important not to conceive of the problem of distributed knowledge in terms of idealizations concerning optimal solutions to complete bodies of "data" or total evidence. As we emphasized in previous sections of the book, this criticism has also played an important role in epistemology and in philosophy of language, moving from models about ideal agents and abstract entities (e.g., bodies of total evidence or collections of propositions) toward the specific interests, motivations, and goals of agents.

Bees solve a problem of distributed knowledge regarding how to identify good sources of food with a system of reliable communication in which certain types of dances are interpreted as if they were *assertions* (with all the caveats about the nature of belief and propositional content that must qualify this analogy). Analogously to Hayek's description of the economic problem, no single bee has all the data concerning available food in the vicinity of a hive, so the hive must rely on scouts that travel to find food and come back with information. If the dances were not interpreted in the "assertive" mode, the hive would ignore such behavior. But it has been shown that such dances are systematically followed by collective action and by attentive *rankings* of dances – the more intense the dance the better the food source.

Clearly, although things are very different with the human version of the economic problem, there are striking similarities. Collective agency is not centralized in the case of economic exchanges. Although some economic agents dominate global markets, these dominant agents do not determine the demand of goods, which depends on individual interests and expectations. Identifying information concerning demand and how individuals interact with each other based on their interests is something that requires constant collective monitoring. Prices in the market serve as collective means of communicating and coordinating information for the members of the economy so that they can individually use this information according to their interests and plans. Prices are a kind of *social-factive form of assertion*, which depends on collective coordination. In the ideal scenario, prices convey information reliably about how users of distributed economic knowledge cooperate.

The fact that accuracy is crucial for prices to count as successful statements of the value of a product requires reliability at many levels. The collective monitoring of markets and products at such large scales has generated the need for institutionalizing collective agents devoted to such tasks. Collective agents have become fundamental sources of reliable information, and in some cases, their statements carry much more weight than the assertions of any individual agent. Institutions also play an important role in verifying and balancing the torrent of information that has become characteristic of human communication. News agencies, academic presses, international, and governmental agencies are subject to a standard of epistemic responsibility that no individual member of society is accountable to. The capacity to distinguish assertions required for collective action from social communication based on gossip, entertainment, superstition, wishful thinking, or even political, religious, or moral preferences, is a virtue of epistemic agents, essentially related to the virtue of relying on good testimony. Many of the collective agents that have a big impact on the distribution and monitoring of reliable information are specialized. The International Monetary Fund specializes in monitoring fiscal issues across the world (a social-factual task) and CERN focuses on finding new evidence concerning particle physics (facts that are independent of social exchanges). Each of them shapes the actions of a vast amount of individual and collective epistemic agents. (Wikipedia is perhaps the most dramatic example of a fully decentralized kind of collective epistemic agency, monitored by users for its reliability.)

Collective epistemic achievements concerning reliability in communication are not necessarily moral achievements – although they may be compatible with moral actions. Cases like laboratory research conducted with prisoners in Nazi camps show that epistemic and moral agency *can* be incompatible. Actions that were once thought to be morally good are now considered paradigmatic cases of immorality, such as witch-hunts, the inquisition, or the slave trade, but it is not easy to explain these changes in moral evaluation strictly in terms of epistemic evaluations. In fact, it would be odd and perhaps even *immoral* to think of ethical progress exclusively in terms of epistemic progress. Adopting high standards of epistemic responsibility need not be morally good and can actually be morally pernicious. For instance, the ultraspecialization characteristic of current scientific research creates public unintelligibility, which translates into a hierarchy of power, with just a few individuals making momentous decisions for vast numbers of human beings. Since the time of Galileo, the relation between science and political power is fraught with problems, with the appearance of the nuclear bombs in Hiroshima and Nagasaki as an illustration of publicly unintelligible scientific research in the service of very concrete political goals. While a misuse or abuse of scientific research does not entail a full dissociation between moral and epistemic normativity, precedents like biomedical research without consent on prisoners show that one does not necessitate the other.

Our main focus, however, is in identifying an epistemically proper form of collective agency. According to the AAM, assertions or assertive-like pronouncements are among the most distinctive features of epistemic agency. In the case of collective agency, these statements should be fact involving and they should also have a proper degree of informational integration from relevant motivation. Arguing by analogy, but also based on empirical research on animal communication and what Hayek calls "the economic problem," we have shown that the need to assert plays the same role in collective and individual agency. In this section, we provided concrete examples of reliable collective communication, including the functioning of economic markets. In the next section, we analyze the role of collective attention in achieving collective epistemic goals.

7.4   Collective Attention and Collective Motivation

This section argues that collective attention is a key aspect of collective motivation. It is argued that collective epistemic agents strategically mask their reliable dispositions to assert in order to achieve higher normative goals (moral ones), and that this is important to understand the fundamental difference between moral and epistemic normativity for collective action.

We shall argue that the functions of perceptual attention (e.g., filtering, inhibiting, and contextualizing information) are also characteristic of collective epistemic agency. Our focus here is on how collective agents must be virtuously insensitive to information in the same way as individual agents. In the previous section, we showed how the collective monitoring of information, for instance in markets, is driven by attention-like routines concerning exchanges between individuals and their motivations. Here, we want to make a more subtle point. The AAM explains not only how collective agents reliably succeed at satisfying basic epistemic needs, such as those involved in reliable communication, but also how collective agents *mask* some of their reliable epistemic dispositions in order to be insensitive to epistemic information that may jeopardize the achievement of other social goods, for example justice.

In particular, there are cases of collective agency in which moral principles are integrated into the epistemic process in order to work as masks – these are epistemically vicious masks (see 1.3) because they prevent the acquisition of reliable information. Fairness in due process trumps the epistemic goal of seeking the truth. Here, the court "masks" its capacities to consider or attend to reliable information not obtained in accordance to Constitutional requirements. Thus, courts filter out or inhibit information that should be considered as relevant from a strictly epistemic point of view.

This way of understanding the constraints on the epistemic processes of collective agents in terms of masks on epistemic dispositions has consequences beyond legal philosophy. One potential area of research that this approach may clarify concerns the controversy surrounding the social impact of the "value-neutral" language of science. Scientific investigation must be curtailed for legitimate social and political reasons. But it is notoriously difficult to strike a balance between scientific and sociocultural forms of human behavior control. On the one hand, scientists should be free to investigate the truth independently of political and moral ideologies. The trial of Galileo by the Inquisition is an example of inappropriate religious interference with the pursuit of truth. On the other hand, science should not become a form of political domination by turning social and moral issues into areas of empirical investigation in which only scientists can participate and make pronouncements. Scientists must collectively debate in order to find appropriate ways of curtailing their scope of inquiry and communicate with the public. Politicians and moral collective agents should inform their views scientifically and at the same time should fight against introducing a scientific perspective where it is not relevant.

The limitations imposed on scientific inquiry may not constitute epistemically virtuous "masks," but they satisfy *more important* normative purposes – moral ones. Should this hold for individual and collective epistemic agents? Perhaps, but not to the same degree, and it is possible that there is a fundamental difference between individual and collective agents with respect to this issue. Because of the intrinsic political power of contemporary forms of collective information gathering, curtailing and impeding attention-like routines conducted by collective agents becomes crucial. This does not seem to be the case with individual epistemic agents whose investigative power and collective influence is more limited.

Going back to legal collective agents, we shall draw an important conclusion from the previous discussion. Protecting the freedom of citizens is a fundamental goal of contemporary legal systems. Legal collective agents need to mask their epistemic dispositions to investigate information because of the rights citizens have (e.g., privacy or bodily integrity). Economic collective agents, because of their more strictly epistemic goals, seem to be much more unconstrained. If economic collective agents frequently masked their capacities to investigate markets for moral reasons, problematic consequences for society at large might ensue. Thus, the AAM provides a framework for understanding a fundamental difference between legal and economic collective agents: the investigative capacities of legal collective agents are masked because of their immediate political restriction of freedom, while those of economic agents are not masked because they either promote freedom or are at least compatible with it. This is an important issue with respect to how to understand the relation between legal and economic collective agents, as well as the justification of legal barriers to commerce and the economic analysis of the law.

Ideally, individual and collective epistemic agents should avoid such exceptions to epistemic responsibility. For instance, they should not let moral values guide their attention with respect to which evidence they accept or reject. They should accept a finding, even if it reveals that an important worldview infused with moral value is false (for instance, the finding that humans have no privileged place in the universe or even as a form of life). The practice of filtering out or ignoring moral and religious values in scientific research is socially good, especially given the value secular societies have because of the enhancement of the freedom of their citizens. As the previous discussion shows, however, this is not so straightforward with legal collective agents.

Because of differences in how collectives attend to contents and assert statements, such as those we highlighted between legal and economic collective agents, it is important to explain in more detail how collective motivations are integrated with epistemic goals. The very idea of collective motivation is problematic. If collective intentions are constitutively determined by the cognitive integration of beliefs and desires of individual members through aggregation, for instance, then one must explain how this integration occurs (List and

Pettit, 2011). If collective intentions are not reducible to beliefs and desires of individual members, then one must explain what is the cognitive nature of irreducibly collective motivation. These views correspond to the thin and thick conceptions of cognitive constitution we addressed at the beginning of this chapter. Depending on the conception of motivation one favors, these views will become more or less problematic. We shall argue that the need-based approach we defended of the AAM is the least problematic and bypasses many of these thorny issues.

According to the cognitivist account, intentions are types of beliefs.[1] An alternative account postulates that intentions necessarily involve motivations, and that a plausible construal of this motivational requirement is that intentions are cognitively integrated beliefs and desires. An influential criticism of the belief and desire construal of intentions argues that integrating beliefs with desires leads to systematically incorrect results regarding how we intuitively understand intentions.[2] Roughly, the criticism is that while one may intend to F and not believe that one will F one must, in general, intend what one believes. Desires, unlike intentions, do not generally obey this principle. Desiring to buy a car while believing that one will not buy it is not irrational or problematic in any way. In fact, this kind of desire as "not believed" is part of our daily activities, plans, and frustrations. But intending to buy a car without believing that one will buy it seems to be irrational and problematic. Most of our attributions of intentional action would fail if intentions were not constitutively determined by beliefs.

We have already argued against an explicit intention view of epistemic motivation for individual epistemic agency and defended the AAM, which is a need-based approach to epistemic motivation. Our current concern is whether the AAM is an adequate view of collective epistemic motivation. If one favors the cognitivist approach to collective intentions and one assumes the constitution as aggregation view, then it seems to follow that collective epistemology requires explicit beliefs that are aggregated (or otherwise integrated) according to explicitly formulated rules for rationality, which as mentioned before, seem to be fundamentally different from the rules of individual rationality. Thus, it seems to follow that under a very standard construal of collective epistemic intentions, the AAM cannot account for collective epistemic achievements. If this argument were correct, collective agents would need to be more reflective and explicit in their motivations and goals than their individual members. We believe this is not a plausible view of collective agency. In the remainder of this chapter, we argue that the AAM should be preferred as the adequate explanation of collective epistemic agency.

---

[1] See Velleman (1989).   [2] See Bratman (1987).

7.5   Reflection, Explicit Judgment, and Reliability

This section examines the type of intention required for normatively praiseworthy performance in collective agents. It is argued that, as in the case of individual agency, reflective and explicit endorsement of reasons or norms is not necessary for virtuous collective agency, and that reliable capacities integrated in a virtuous cognitive constitution are sufficient, even if they are not reflective or explicit.

The AAM postulates that motivations for epistemic agency do not depend on reflective and explicit reasoning. One can model epistemic achievements as if they were the result of explicit reasoning, but the empirical evidence shows that epistemic agents typically satisfy basic epistemic needs without having to engage in reflective or explicit reasoning. In the case of collective agency, one must similarly consider realistic and empirically confirmed cases in order to appreciate the advantages of the AAM. We examined two cases: (a) collective reliable communication in animals and (b) coordinated reliable information to solve the economic problem. A beehive and global markets reliably satisfy collective epistemic needs, but it would be quite challenging to model such processes as the aggregation of explicit beliefs under explicitly formulated rational rules, for similar considerations as those we reviewed in the first chapters of this book. Reliable needs are better suited to explain collective epistemic motivations in these cases. This may or may not be the case with shared *moral* motives, because collective moral motivation *may* require explicit belief aggregation.

It is intuitive to think of intentions as the result of sophisticated and highly integrated cognitive processes that involve satisfying standards of rationality. If so, intentions seem to require a kind of cognitive integration that involves reflective thinking. Consider Sosa's (2009) distinction between two types of knowledge (a non-reflective and a reflective type), which yield two types of knowledge attributions: animal and reflective knowledge. According to Sosa, only reflective knowledge qualifies as the most apt and reliable form of knowledge. Reflective knowledge is a meta-competence that satisfies demanding requirements for cognitive integration, such as metacognition and metarepresentation. Shouldn't these standards apply to collective epistemic agents? How do we even make sense of object-based or first-level animal knowledge for collective agency? To motivate the more minimal account of collective epistemic agency we favor, it is useful to revisit Greco's (2004, 2010) objection that a reflective requirement on knowledge imposes unrealistic psychological demands on epistemic agents. When a child accurately perceives a red object and forms the belief that there is a red object in front of her, she seems to know that there is a red object in front of her and we *should* attribute such knowledge to her. Why would a reflective component be required for her to fully know that there is a red object in front of her? One can ask the same question with respect to beehives, economies, and linguistic communities.

However, reliably detecting features of the environment can be characterized as a form of reflective knowledge. Diana, the huntress, has to be reliably successful in hitting targets, and she also needs to be selective with respect to the type of target she should hit. The capacity to select targets allows her to represent many targets, attend to only the relevant ones, act only with respect to the relevant ones, and refrain from hitting inadequate ones. Diana may do this by reflecting on the relevance of certain actions and by withholding judgment explicitly with respect to those actions she believes are not epistemically adequate. But it is more natural to describe Diana's situation in terms of the AAM. She has reliable skills that are virtuously integrated with (a) her basic epistemic needs, (b) her capacities to act only on relevant contents specified by her attention skills, and (c) her capacities to act only on assertable contents.

Consider the following case, presented in the context of collective agency. Suppose DIANA is the acronym of a NASA project. DIANA's purpose is to identify planets that could foster life, which involves attending to information only about solar systems, planets of the right size and the right distance from their star. Success requires being virtuously insensitive to irrelevant information about the universe. Then, once a planet is located, there is a further filtering of information concerning the chemical composition of the planet. Is DIANA reflecting on which targets she should spot or is she simply selectively processing information? One answer is that when DIANA spots a planet (the equivalent of "hitting a target") her success is due to reliable systems that attend to the right features. An alternative answer is that DIANA is reflecting and assessing deliverances of first-level skills for attending to features, then explicitly judging which are the correct ones based on beliefs and intentions, according to explicit rules of assessment. These are two ways of interpreting what DIANA needs to do in order to succeed: one emphasizes reliability while the other emphasizes explicit reflection.

Now, we can offer an example we used in the case of individual epistemic agency to settle the question of DIANA's epistemic responsibility. Suppose NASA divides the DIANA mission into two project teams. DIANA-1 develops an algorithm that allows the team to come up with fast and very reliable results. Their statements can be vetoed by DIANA-2, a team that asks questions about the results DIANA-1 produces. The final assertion of the whole DIANA team depends on DIANA-2. But DIANA-2 is also in charge of detecting planets that could sustain life. Thus, it could be said that DIANA-1 and 2 should attend to the same features in order to satisfy the same epistemic need: identifying life-sustaining planets. Suppose that DIANA-1 is on average much more reliable in detecting the right planets than DIANA-2. Then, to the extent that the whole team DIANA is reliable, it would depend on the performances of DIANA-1.

Interventions by DIANA-2 would be either irrelevant or *potentially pernicious*. There is still a possibility, however, that in the long run, the reflective assessments of DIANA-2 would improve the chances of selecting planets that most closely resemble Earth, for example. But the driving force behind such improved performance will be DIANA's overall reliability, not her reflective skills. Moreover, although one can think of fine selectivity in terms of judgment, one can also, and more naturally, think of it in terms of non-reflective selective attention, as the AAM proposes. Thus, analogously to the case of individual epistemic agency, the AAM seems to be the best characterization of collective epistemic agency.

Hilary Kornblith (2010) would go even further. He would argue that reflection is a problematic requirement for knowledge because instead of increasing reliability (as Sosa thinks) it actually *reduces* it. This might be one aspect of a larger problem, which we examined before, namely that the reliability of basic skills that require high levels of cognitive integration may be automatic and largely dissociated from explicit forms of action selection and reflection. Going back to the theme of idealized rationality, according to an influential interpretation of the research that fostered behavioral economics, human capacities for decision-making do not comport with the basic normative constraints required for explicit rationality, understood in terms of Bayesian subjective probabilities (Kahneman, 2003, 2011). This research is frequently interpreted as a decisive demonstration that humans produce false (and in many cases, problematically inconsistent) beliefs in a vast variety of circumstances. As mentioned before, this interpretation of psychological experiments is also behind the situationist challenge to virtue epistemology. We will not repeat our arguments against the situationist challenge, but will highlight some consequences of our view that are pertinent to the issue of collective agency.

The large amount of findings supporting the skeptical thesis of human irrationality (understood in terms of deviations from optimal decisions and beliefs based on the axioms of probability) has led Kahneman (2011) to argue that there are two systems or types of reasoning. He says that these two systems (systems 1 and 2) are useful fictions that capture two ways in which the brain engages with problem-solving and truth-evaluation in a variety of situations and tasks. System 1 is a fast, flexible, but apparently unreliable and irrational system that in many cases trumps a slow, consciously taxing, and reflectively reliable system. The fast system evolved to respond quickly to urgent, contextually specific, and typical situations, and is responsible for much of our success as a species. The slow system is more cautious and examines the nature of problems step by step in a more reflective and meticulous manner. Kahneman says it is a mistake to associate human decision-making with system 2 because system 1 trumps system 2 very frequently. System 2 is energy consuming and, paradoxically, weak. These two aspects of system 2 are captured in many experiments in which the quick cognitive deliverances of system 1 prevail over the more principled cognitive processing of system 2. Even training and conscious reflection seem to be of no help.

Maybe system 2 is like DIANA-2 and system one is like DIANA-1. As in the case of humans, system 2 is the only reliable system for abstract reasoning and the explicit assessment of logical and mathematical entailments, but it is not reliable in most contexts in which attention needs to be guided automatically. As mentioned, Gigerenzer (2008) argues that although Bayesian rationality is indeed an implausible idealization of human capacities for decision-making, one could still give an account of human rationality that is highly context dependent and at the same time optimal and reliable. We have argued that this is the right way of understanding how attention and assertion operate reliably, cognitively integrated with epistemic motivation. As mentioned at the beginning of this chapter, there is the possibility that collective agents should be accountable to idealized forms of rationality. Even if this were the case, the AAM helps understand collective agency in insightful and more plausible ways.

7.6   Complex Collective Agency

This section argues that the present account can be used to explain complex forms of collective agency. In particular, it shows that legal systems are intricately complex, in the sense that they demand different kinds of cognitive integration and the imposition of moral masks at least at the judicial level. Individual and collective agency are shown to have a layered structure in the constitution of legal systems, but reliable collective communication, it is argued, is necessary for any legal system to work.

We have concluded that the AAM is also a satisfactory account of collective epistemic agency. We now discuss some consequences of the previous analysis for how complex collectives, such as legal systems, may operate outside strictly epistemic contexts. One cannot conceive of a legal system that requires conscious reflective knowledge of the law in every single behavior that is protected or prohibited by law. But there must be a compromise between a fully "divided" agency in which agents *never* reflect on norms and the type of agency in which agents are *always* required to explicitly judge norms. It may not be a happy compromise (for instance, voluntarily and consciously checking for belief consistency as a necessary condition for intentional action may be out of the question), but whatever the compromise is, it must be at the basis of what justifies moral and legal systems of norms. We cannot, in other words, be constant "strangers to ourselves" when it comes to morality and the law, even if we can be epistemically responsible through implicit and automatic agency. Perhaps the answer to the question "when does a legal system require conscious motivation and agency?" is not as simple as one may think.

At least in the context of *criminal* law, consciously intentional action *is* necessary for punishment. Similarly, conscious intentional action seems to be necessary for moral approval and condemnation. Moreover, the fact that many *attempts* to commit a crime are also criminalized (and not just the actions that would have resulted from these attempts) shows that conscious planning is essentially involved in criminalized behavior and assumed as the target of criminal law. Criminal intent should not be the result of unconscious biases. Unconscious biases can be epistemically adequate but criminal responsibility, like moral responsibility, seems to require conscious beliefs and intentions. This is a reminder that epistemic and moral normativity are not the same thing. In the context of criminalization, the standard theory of intentional action, with all of its assumptions about conscious reflection and belief consistency verification, seems to be crucial.[3]

It must be emphasized that having a criminal law system based exclusively on strict liability and the reparation of harms is not *inconceivable* and, according to some views, may actually be preferable. For instance, a legal positivist may think that the law should not inquire into the conscious intentions and judgments, moral or otherwise, of subjects. Alternatively, some may think that a strict liability system would at least explicitly reveal the intrinsically oppressive nature of criminal laws. Criminalizing intentions to act, according to this latter view, is just a form of further intruding into the lives of citizens, rather than a justified practice, normatively grounded on the prevention of intentional harm to others. In any case, even if criminal legislation requires conscious intentions for action for it to be justified, the type of cognitive integration assumed in theories of intentional action cannot be present in many contexts for action and it cannot be a requirement for the justification of legal systems *in general*. If legal systems operate by assuming that conscious reflection is basic for the justification of rules, and that collective justification proceeds by aggregation, then aggregation will result in a thick, rather than a thin kind of cognitive integration, with robust features similar to character traits, as Fricker (2010) proposes.

Many legal systems presuppose the type of agency and reflective cognition assumed, for instance, in the Rawlsian notion of reflective equilibrium. Many findings show that this assumption is unjustified. But instead of identifying irrationality or supporting skepticism, perhaps what the findings show is that cognitive integration varies in different conditions. If intentions for action have

---

[3] For a theory of criminal intent that follows the traditional approach to intentions and the philosophy of action, see Yaffe (2010). It is important to note, however, that this approach is not entirely uncontroversial, because brain lesions and some psychopathologies seem to be essential to explain many forms of criminal behavior where there is no explicit intention on the part of the criminal, but which are not fully recognized as exceptions to punishment precisely because of the prevailing intentional explicit view.

different types of cognitive integration, some more epistemic than others, then applications of philosophy of action to legal theories must take into consideration these different types of cognitive integration. How to achieve this goal? One possibility is to treat different approaches to legal philosophy as tackling different aspects of intentional action. Contract law, for instance, places a strong emphasis on the free decision of the parties to enter a contract by assuming rights and responsibilities, based on their fully informed and unconstrained voluntary intention to sign the contract. But because of the considerations about reflection mentioned above, such informed and free consent cannot entail the high degree of cognitive integration assumed in theories of intentional action, based on consciously explicit assessments of coherence and consistency.

The law can plausibly require only that the consent of the parties was not *coerced* by threats or that it was not based on purposefully false information. But purposeful manipulation of unconscious biases and inclinations are part of publicity, for instance, and of many of the normal daily transactions contract law regulates and approves. So, the degree of conscious cognitive integration required for contract law is rather minimal (think of cases like the contracts involved in purchasing clothes and food, or the contract one enters into when one uses public transportation). The AAM shows why this is not surprising. Contract law, unlike criminal law, may be guided by an economic analysis of transactions, and we showed that economic transactions depend on reliable communication that does not necessitate reflective assessments of bodies of data.

One may think of cases in which obedience to the law requires almost no cognitive demands, as many areas of family law demonstrate. Criminal law, however, presents a variety of cases in which punishment depends on different *degrees* of cognitive integration, as cases of criminal intent illustrate. In some cases, therefore, our highest capacities for rational and moral reasoning will be required as part of the cognitive integration that led to an intention to act criminally. Some versions of contractualism and natural law (which appeal to our rational and moral natures) fit this description. In many other cases, however, the law requires extremely limited cognitive integration of explicit belief, judgment or reflection, and considerations about power and violence are much more relevant, as positive law theory emphasizes. This means that if one conceives of legal systems as collective agents, then their members would constitute such systems by layers of different requirements for cognitive integration: some more explicit and others more automatic.

In economics, the psychological findings that allegedly show human irrationality have had a very significant impact. In legal theory, however, the focus remains centered on theories of intentional action with high degrees of cognitive integration constrained by the idealized kind of rationality that psychology has disproved, and also on debates concerning the role of morality in legal theories. A legal system certainly requires more than epistemic sensitivity to information about optimal decisions because it assumes forms of moral responsibility and responsiveness to attitudes, such as resentment, remorse, condemnation, and approval. Intentions to act in a way that is responsive to our moral natures require high degrees of cognitive integration and explicit judgment, which include epistemic and moral reasoning. But criminal intent seems to be the only area in which different degrees of cognitive integration correlate with legal consequences, with the most severe types of punishment reserved for the highest degrees of conscious reflective cognition.[4]

In sum, the testimony of an epistemically responsible collective agent (e.g., CERN, the United Nations or NASA) facilitates communication, settles disputes, helps organize common efforts, and optimizes access to resources. A non-trivial epistemic achievement of collective agents is that they help *reduce disagreement* and focus collective attention and action toward common goals. Negatively, reliance on an epistemically irresponsible collective epistemic agent may be disastrous, as the misinformation regarding the inadequate evidence that led to the war against Iraq in 2003 illustrates. In the case of collective agency in legal systems, there are two kinds of highly integrated and complex cognitive integration. One of them concerns integrating information that is morally relevant and constrained by the standards of moral normativity. The other concerns the type of cognitive integration that is epistemic in nature. The most complex cases involve both types of cognitive integration.

In many cases, the expert opinion of a collective agent is not just about truth seeking (i.e., finding evidence of war crimes or weapons of mass destruction), but fundamentally about understanding the political implications of a situation in a deeper, morally conceived way (i.e., what a panel on ethics should decide regarding a scientific practice, such as not informing patients about the consequences of a medical procedure). The need to appeal to moral considerations, for example, in *Brown v. Board of Education*, has decisive implications with respect to the normative constraints on a legal system and its legitimacy.[5] In cases like *Roe v. Wade* or *Brown v. Board of Education*, legitimate disagreements about how to deal with an issue may arise, but exclusively fact-finding considerations cannot override or settle deliberations about human dignity, as evidenced by the legislative principles that emerged from the Nuremberg trials.

---

[4] A democracy will not only require high degrees of cognitive integration, but also reliable information so that the population is well informed about policies and regulations. In a monarchic tyranny, high degrees of cognitive integration occur only in a centralized fashion, with the rest of the population completely decoupled from such epistemic processes, thereby facilitating manipulation and oppression, with no cognitive integration at the public sphere level. Thus, the very idea of a public sphere depends on some level of cognitive integration and epistemic agency, which has clear implications for political philosophy.

[5] For arguments in favor of the view that judicial wisdom involves a moral type of normativity, see, for instance, Dworkin (1986).

Darwin (1871) claimed that the difference between cooperation in animals and humans is one of degree and not of kind. A way in which this approach can be fleshed out is in terms of the AAM and the degrees of cognitive integration for epistemic differences that depend on contexts of normative evaluation. Not any group that cooperates is an agent. Just like Truetemp is not responsible because his temperature-detection ability is not well motivated or properly integrated with his other attention and assertion skills, groups may cooperate and succeed in many tasks and, yet, they may fail to count as an epistemic agent. AAM allows for a variety of epistemic agents. Some agents are highly complex, while others perform only a few tasks reliably. This variety of epistemic agency grounds collective communication and it makes possible complex forms of behavior regulation, including the imposition of moral limitations on collective epistemic inquiry.

Bibliography

Alfano, M. (2013). *Character as Moral Fiction*. Cambridge University Press.

Allport, A. (1987). Selection for action: Some behavioural and neurophysiological considerations of attention and action. In A. Sanders and H. Heuer (eds.), *Perspectives on Perception and Action*. Hillsdale, NJ: Lawrence Erlbaum Associates, pp. 395–419.

Allport, A. (2011). Attention and integration. In C. Mole, D. Smithies, and W. Wu (eds.), *Attention: Philosophical and Psychological Essays*. Oxford University Press, pp. 24–59.

Anand, P. and Hacquard, V. (2013). Epistemics and attitudes. *Semantics and Pragmatics*, 6 (8): 1–59.

Anderson, E. (2007). The epistemology of democracy. *Episteme: A Journal of Social Epistemology*, 3 (1): 8–22.

Andrews, K., (2014). Animal cognition. *The Stanford Encyclopedia of Philosophy* (Fall Edition), E. N. Zalta (ed.), URL http://plato.stanford.edu/archives/fall2014/entries/cognition-animal/.

Anscombe, G. E. M. (1957). *Intention*. Harvard University Press.

Anscombe, G. E. M. (1958). Modern moral philosophy. *Philosophy*, 33: 1–19.

Anscombe, G. E. M. (1962). On sensations of position. *Analysis*, 22 (3): 55–58.

Axelrod, R. (2006). *The Evolution of Cooperation* (Revised Edition). Perseus Books Group.

Bach, K. (1984). Default reasoning: Jumping to conclusions and knowing when to think twice. *Pacific Philosophical Quarterly*, 65: 37–58.

Bach, K. (2008). Applying pragmatics to epistemology. *Philosophical Issues*, 18: 68–88.

Bach, K. and Harnish, R. (1979). *Linguistic Communication and Speech Acts*. MIT Press.

Bacon, W. F. and Egeth H. E. (1997). Goal-directed guidance of attention: Evidence from conjunctive visual search. *Journal of Experimental Psychology: Human Perception and Performance*, 23 (4): 948–961.

Baehr, J. (2011). *The Inquiring Mind: On Intellectual and Virtues and Virtue Epistemology*. Oxford: Oxford University Press.

Bargh, J. A., and Chartrand, T. L. (1999). The unbearable automaticity of being. *American Psychologist*, 54: 462–479.

Battaly, H. (2008). Virtue epistemology. *Philosophy Compass*, 3 (4): 639–663.

Berker, S. (2013a). Epistemic teleology and the separateness of propositions. *Philosophical Review*, 122 (3): 337–393.

Berker, S. (2013b). The rejection of epistemic consequentialism. *Philosophical Issues*, 23 (1): 363–387.

Bermudez J. L. (2003). *Thinking without Words*. New York, NY: Oxford University Press.

Bernstein, N. A. (1950/1996). *Dexterity and Its Development*. Edited by M. L. Latash and M. T. Turvey. Mahwah, NJ: L. Erlbaum Associates.

Blackburn, S. (2001). Reason, virtue, and knowledge. In A. Fairweather and L. Zagzebski (eds.), *Virtue Epistemology: Essays on Epistemic Virtue and Responsibility*, pp. 15–29.

Blackburn, S. (2010). Success semantics. *Practical Tortoise Raising: And Other Philosophical Essays*. Oxford University Press, pp. 181–199.

Blum, L. A. (1986). Iris Murdoch and the domain of the moral. *Philosophical Studies*, 50 (3): 343–367.

Boghossian, P. (2000). Knowledge of logic. In P. Boghossian and C. Peacocke (eds.), *New Essays on the A Priori*. Oxford University Press, pp. 229–254.

Bonjour, L. (1980). Externalist theories of empirical knowledge. *Midwest Studies in Philosophy*, 5 (1): 53–73.

Brandstätter, E., Gigerenzer, G., and Hertwig, R. (2006). The priority heuristic: Making choices without trade-offs. *Psychological Review*, 113 (2): 409.

Bratman, M. (1987). *Intention, Plans and Practical Reason*. Cambridge, MA: Harvard University Press.

Brendel, E. (2009). The epistemic function of virtuous dispositions. In G. Damschen, R. Schnepf, and K. R. Stuber (eds.), *Debating Dispositions: Issues in Metaphysics, Epistemology and Philosophy of Mind*. New York: Walter de Gruyter, pp. 320–340.

Broncano, F. (2014). Daring to believe: Metacognition, epistemic agency and reflective knowledge. In A. Fairweather (ed.), *Virtue Epistemology Naturalized*. Springer International Publishing, pp. 1–9.

Burge, T. (2010). *Origins of Objectivity*. New York, NY: Oxford University Press.

Call, J. and Tomasello, M. (2008). Does the chimpanzee have a theory of mind? 30 years later. *Trends in Cognitive Sciences*, 12: 187–192.

Cappelen, H. (2011). Against assertion. In J. Brown and H. Cappelen (eds.), *Assertion: New Philosophical Essays*. Oxford University Press, pp. 21–47.

Carrasco, M. (2011). Visual attention: The past 25 years. *Vision Research*, 51 (13): 1484–1525.

Carruthers, P. (2006). *The Architecture of the Mind: Massive Modularity and the Flexibility of Thought*. Oxford University Press.

Cave, K. R. and Bichot, N. P. (1999). Visuospatial attention: Beyond a spotlight model. *Psychonomic Bulletin & Review*, 6 (2): 204–223.

Chica, A. B., Bartolomeo, P., and Lupianez, J. (2013). Two cognitive and neural systems for endogenous and exogenous spatial attention. *Behavioural Brain Research*, 237: 107–123.

Conee, E. and Feldman, R. (2001). Internalism defended. In H. Kornblith (ed.), *Epistemology: Internalism and Externalism*. Malden, MA: Blackwell, pp. 231–260.

Copp, D. (2006). On the agency of certain collective entities: An argument from "normative autonomy." *Midwest Studies in Philosophy*, 30 (1): 194–221.

Copp, D. (2007). The collective moral autonomy thesis. *Journal of Social Philosophy*, 38 (3): 369–388.

Craig, E. (1990). *Knowledge and the State of Nature*. Oxford, UK: Oxford University Press.

Darwin, C. (1871). *The Descent of Man and Selection in Relation to Sex*. London: John Murray.

Davidson, D. (1979). Moods and performances. In A. Margalit (ed.), *Meaning and Use*. Dordrecht: Reidel, pp. 9–20.

Davidson, D. (1999). Intellectual biography. In L. Hahn (ed.), *The Philosophy of Donald Davidson*. Library of Living Philosophers. La Salle, IL: Open Court.

de Sousa, R. (1987). *The Rationality of Emotion*. Cambridge, MA: MIT Press.

DeRose, K. (2002). Assertion, knowledge and context. *Philosophical Review*, 111 (2): 167–203.

DeRose, K. (2009). *The Case for Contextualism: Knowledge, Skepticism, and Context*, Vol. 1. Oxford: Oxford University Press.

Dickie, I. (2011). Visual attention fixes demonstrative reference by eliminating referential luck. In C. Mole, D. Smithies and W. Wu (eds.), *Attention: Philosophical and Psychological Essays*. Oxford University Press, pp. 292–322.

Dickie, I. (2015). *Fixing Reference*. Oxford University Press.

Dietrich, F. and List, C. (2008). Judgment aggregation without full rationality. *Social Choice and Welfare*, 31 (1): 15–39.

Ding, N., Melloni, L., Zhang, H., Tian, X., and Poeppel, D. (2015). Cortical tracking of hierarchical linguistic structures in connected speech. *Nature Neuroscience*, doi:10.1038/nn.4186.

Dobrynin, N. (1961). Basic problems of the psychology of attention. In B. G. Anan'yev (ed.), *Psychological Science in the USSR*. Washington, DC: U.S. Dept. of Commerce, Clearinghouse for Federal Scientific and Technical Information, pp. 274–291.

Dokic, J. and Engel, P. (2006). *Frank Ramsey: Truth and Success*. New York, NY: Routledge.

Doris, J. (2002). *Lack of Character: Personality and Moral Behavior*. Cambridge: Cambridge University Press.

Dormashev, Y. (2010). Flow experience explained on the grounds of an activity approach to attention. In B. Bruya (ed.), *Effortless Attention*. Cambridge, MA: MIT Press, pp. 287–333.

Douven, I. (2006). Assertion, knowledge and rational credibility. *Philosophical Review*, 115: 449–485.

Dummet, M. (1981). *Frege: Philosophy of Language* (2nd Edition). Harvard University Press.

Dworkin, R. (1986). *Law's Empire*. Harvard University Press.

Engel, P. (2008). In what sense is knowledge the norm of assertion? *Grazer Philosophische Studien*, 77 (1): 45–59.

Fairweather, A. (2001). Epistemic motivation. In A. Fairweather and L. Zagzebski (eds.), *Virtue Epistemology: Essays on Epistemic Virtue and Responsibility*. Oxford, England: Oxford University Press, pp. 63–81.

Fairweather, A. and Montemayor, C. (2014a). Inferential abilities and common epistemic goods. In A. Fairweather (ed.), *Virtue Epistemology Naturalized: Bridges between Virtue Epistemology and Philosophy of Science: Vol. 366. Synthese Library*. Springer, pp. 123–142.

Fairweather, A. and Montemayor, C. (2014b). Epistemic dexterity: A Ramseyian account of agent based knowledge. In A. Fairweather and O. Flanagan (eds.), *Naturalizing Epistemic Virtue*. Cambridge University Press.

Fairweather, A. and Alfano, M. (eds.), (2017). *Epistemic Situationism*. Oxford: Oxford University Press.

Firth, R. (1981). Epistemic merit, intrinsic and instrumental. *Proceedings and Addresses of the American Philosophical Association*, 55: 5–23. Presidential address delivered at the Annual Eastern Meeting of the American Philosophical Association in December, 1980. Reprinted in Firth 1998, 259–271. Page references are to the 1998 reprint.

Flanagan, O. (1991). *Varieties of Moral Personality*. Cambridge, MA: Harvard University Press.

Fodor, J. A. (1983). *The Modularity of Mind*. MIT Press.

Fodor, J. A. (1987). Modules, frames, fridgeons, sleeping dogs, and the music of the spheres. In Z. W. Pylyshyn (ed.), *The Robot's Dilemma: The Frame Problem in Artificial Intelligence*. Norwood, NJ: Ablex, pp. 139–149.

Fodor, J. A. (2000). *The Mind Doesn't Work That Way*. MIT Press.

Foot, P. (1972). Morality as a system of hypothetical imperatives. *The Philosophical Review*, 81 (3): 305–316.

Foot, P. (1978). Reasons for action and desires. In *Virtues and Vices and Other Essays*. Berkeley, CA: University of California Press, pp. 148–156.

Foot, P. (2002). *Virtues and Vices and Other Essays in Moral Philosophy*. Oxford: Clarendon Press.

Frege, G. (1918–1919/1997). Thought. In M. Beany (ed.), *The Frege Reader*. Malden, MA: Blackwell, pp. 325–345.

Fricker, M. (2010). 10. Can there be institutional virtues?. *Oxford Studies in Epistemology*, 3: 235.

Graziano, M. S. (2013). *Consciousness and the Social Brain*. Oxford University Press.

Gigerenzer, G. (2008). *Rationality for Mortals: How People Cope with Uncertainty*, Oxford University Pres.

Gigerenzer, G. and Gaissmaier, W. (2011). Heuristic decision making. *Annual Review of Psychology*, 62: 451–482.

Gigerenzer, G. and Sturm, T. (2012). How (far) can rationality be naturalized? *Synthese*, 187 (1): 243–268.

Gilbert, M. (1987). Modelling collective belief. *Synthese*, 73 (1): 185–204.

Gilbert, M. (1992). *On Social Facts*. Princeton University Press.

Gilbert, M. (2006). *A Theory of Political Obligation: Membership, Commitment, and the Bonds of Society*. Oxford: Oxford University Press.

Glover, S. and Dixon, P. (2002). Semantics affect the planning but not control of grasping. *Experimental Brain Research*, 146 (3): 383–387.

Glymour, C. (1987). Android epistemology and the frame problem: Comments on Dennett's cognitive wheels. In Z. W. Pylyshyn (ed.), *The Robot's Dilemma: The Frame Problem in Artificial Intelligence*. Norwood, NJ: Ablex, pp. 63–75.

Goddard, C. (2002). The search for the shared semantic core of all languages. In C. Goddard and A. Wierzbicka (eds.), *Meaning and Universal Grammar – Theory and Empirical Findings*, Vol. I. Amsterdam: John Benjamins, pp. 5–40.

Goldberg, S. C. (2015). *Assertion: On the Philosophical Significance of Assertoric Speech*. Oxford University Press.

Goldman, A. (1992). Epistemic folkways and scientific epistemology. In A. I. Goldman (ed.), *Liaisons: Philosophy Meets the Cognitive and Social Sciences*. Cambridge, MA: MIT Press, pp. 155–178.

Goldman, A. (2015). Reliabilism, veritism, and epistemic teleology. *Episteme*, 12: 131–143.

Goldman, A. and Olsson, E. (2009). Reliabilism and the value of knowledge. In A. Haddock, A. Millar, and D. Pritchard (eds.), *Epistemic Value*. Oxford: Oxford University Press, pp. 19–41.

Goodale, M. A. (2010). Transforming vision into action. *Vision Research*, 10 (1016): 7–27.

Graham, P. (2011). Psychological capacity and positive epistemic status. In J. G. Hernandez (ed.), *The New Intuitionism*. Continuum International Publishing Group, pp. 128–150.

Graham, P. (2014). Functions, warrant and history. In A. Fairweather and Flanagan, O. (eds.), *Naturalizing Epistemic Virtue*. Cambridge: Cambridge University Press, pp. 15–35.

Graham, P. J. (2012). Epistemic Entitlement. *Noûs*, 46: 449–482.

Greco, J. (2004). How to preserve your virtue while losing your perspective. In J. Greco (ed.), *Ernest Sosa and His Critics*. Oxford: Blackwell, pp. 96–105.

Greco, J. (2010). *Achieving Knowledge: A Virtue-Theoretic Account*. New York, NY: Cambridge University Press.

Greco, J. and Turri, J. (2011). *Virtue Epistemology*. MIT Press.

Grice, H. P. (1989). *Studies in the Ways of Words*. Cambridge, MA: Harvard University Press.

Grimm, S. R. (2009). Epistemic normativity. In A. Haddock, A. Millar, and D. Pritchard (eds.), *Epistemic Value*. Oxford: Oxford University Press, pp. 243–264.

Gruber, M. J. (2014). States of curiosity modulate hippocampus – Dependent learning via the dopaminergic circuit. *Neuron*, 84 (2): 486–496.

Hacking, I. (2014). *Why Is There Philosophy of Mathematics at All?* Cambridge University Press.

Haddock, A., Millar, A., and Pritchard, D. (eds.). (2009). *Epistemic Value*. Oxford University Press.

Haladjian, H. H. and Montemayor, C. (2015). On the evolution of conscious attention. *Psychonomic Bulletin and Review*, 22 (3): 595–613.

Harman, G. (2000). The nonexistence of character traits. *Proceedings of the Aristotelian Society*, 100: 223–226.

Hawthorne, J. (2004). *Knowledge and Lotteries*. Oxford University Press.

Hawthorne, J. and Stanley, J. (2008). Knowledge and action. *Journal of Philosophy*, CV: 571–590.

Hayek, F. A. (1945). The use of knowledge in society. *American Economic Review*, 35 (4): 519–530.

Hazlett, A. (2014). Expressivism and convention relativism about epistemic discourse. In A. Fairweather, and O. Flanagan (eds.), *Naturalizing Epistemic Virtue*. Cambridge: Cambridge University Press, pp. 223–246.

Henderson, D. and T. Horgan (2009). Epistemic virtues and cognitive dispositions. In K. Steuber, G. Damschen, and R. Schnepf (eds.), *Debating Dispositions: Issues in Metaphysics, Epistemology and Philosophy of Mind*. Berlin: de Gruyter, pp. 296–319.

Henderson D. and T. Horgan (2011). *The Epistemological Spectrum*. Oxford University Press.

Hommel, B. (2010). Grounding attention in action control: The intentional control of selection. In B. Bruya (ed.), *Effortless Attention*. Cambridge, MA: MIT Press, pp. 121–140.

Hookway, C. (2001). Epistemic akrasia and epistemic virtue. In A. Fairweather and L. T. Zagzebski (eds.), *Virtue Epistemology: Essays on Epistemic Virtue and Responsibility*. Oxford University Press, pp. 178–199.

Inan, I. (2012). *The Philosophy of Curiosity*. New York, London: Routledge.

Inan, I. (2014). Curiosity, belief and acquaintance. In *Virtue Epistemology Naturalized*. Springer International Publishing, pp. 143–157.

Jones, W. (1997). Why do we value knowledge? *American Philosophical Quarterly*, 34: 423–439.

Kahneman, D. (2011). *Thinking, Fast and Slow*. Farrar, Straus and Giroux.

Kahneman, D. (2003). Maps of bounded rationality: Psychology for behavioral economics. *The American Economic Review*, 93 (5): 1449–1475.

Kahneman, D. and Tversky, A. (1979). Prospect theory: An analysis of decision under risk. *Econometrica: Journal of the Econometric Society*, 47 (2): 263–291.

Klein, P. (2003). How a Pyrrhonian skeptic might respond to academic skepticism. In S. Luper (ed.), *The Skeptics: Contemporary Essays*. London: Ashgate Press, pp. 75–94.

Koch, C. and Crick, F. (2001). The zombie within. *Nature*, 411 (6840): 893.

Kornblith, H. (1993). Epistemic normativity. *Synthese*, 94 (3): 357–376.

Kornblith, H. (2000). The contextualist evasion of epistemology. *Philosophical Issues*, 10: 24–32.

Kornblith, H. (2002). *Knowledge and Its Place in Nature*. Oxford University Press.

Kornblith, H. (2010). What reflective endorsement cannot do. *Philosophy and Phenomenological Research*, 80 (1): 1–19.

Korsgaard, C. M. (1996). *The Sources of Normativity*. O. O'Neill (ed.). Cambridge University Press.

Kvanvig, J. L. (2005). Truth and the epistemic goal. In M. Steup and E. Sosa (eds.), *Contemporary Debates in Epistemology*. Malden: Blackwell, pp. 285–295.

Kvanvig, J. L. (2009). Assertion, knowledge and lotteries. In P. Greenough and D. Pritchard (eds.), *Williamson on Knowledge*. Oxford: Oxford University Press, pp. 140–160.

Kvanvig, J. L. (2011). *Norms of assertion*. In J. Brown and H. Cappelen (eds.), *Assertion: New Philosophical Essays*. Oxford: Oxford University Press, pp. 233–250.

Lackey, J. (2007). Why we don't deserve credit for everything we know. *Synthese*, 158 (3): 345–361.

Lackey, J. (2008). *Learning from Words: Testimony as a Source of Knowledge*. Oxford University Press.

Lahroodi, R. (2007). Collective epistemic virtues. *Social Epistemology*, 21 (3): 281–297.

Liberman, A. M., and Whalen, D. H. (2000). On the relation of speech to language. *Trends in Cognitive Sciences*, 4 (5): 187–196.

Lehrer, K. (1990). *Theory of Knowledge*. Boulder, CO: Westview Press.

Leontiev, A. N. (1978). *Activity, Consciousness, and Personality*. Translated by M. J. Hall. Englewood Cliffs, NJ: Prentice-Hall.

Lepock, C. (2014). Metacognition and intellectual virtue. In *Virtue Epistemology Naturalized*. Springer International Publishing, pp. 33–48, 143–157.

Lewis, D. (1997). Finkish dispositions. *The Philosophical Quarterly*, 47: 143–158.

List, C. (2012). Collective wisdom: A judgment aggregation perspective. In H. Landemore and J. Elster (eds.), *Collective Wisdom: Principles and Mechanisms*. Cambridge: Cambridge University Press.

List, C. and Pettit, P. (2011). *Group Agency: The Possibility, Design, and Status of Corporate Agents*. Oxford: Oxford University Press.

Littlejohn, C. and Turri, J. (eds.). (2014). *Epistemic Norms: New Essays on Action, Belief and Assertion*. Oxford University Press.

MacFarlane, J. (2007). Relativism and disagreement. *Philosophical Studies*, 132: 17–31.

MacFarlane, J. (2011). What is assertion? In J. Brown and H. Cappelen (eds.), *Assertion*. Oxford: Oxford University Press, pp. 79–96.

MacFarlane, J. (2014). *Assessment Sensitivity: Relative Truth and Its Applications*. Oxford University Press.

Maitra, I. and Weatherson, B. (2010). Assertion, knowledge, and action. *Philosophical Studies*, 149: 99–118.

Manser, M. B., Bell, M. B., and Fletcher, L. B. (2001). The information that receivers extract from alarm calls in suricates. *Proceedings of the Royal Society of London, Series B*, 268: 2485–2491.

Mantel, S. (2013). Acting for reasons, apt action, and knowledge. *Synthese*, 190 (17): 3865–3888.

Mellor, D. H. (ed.). (1990). *F. P. Ramsey: Philosophical Papers*. Cambridge, UK: Cambridge University Press.

Mellor, D. H. (1991). *Matters of Metaphysics*. Cambridge, UK: Cambridge University Press.

Millikan, R. (2000). *On Clear and Confused Ideas: An Essay about Substance Concepts*, Cambridge: Cambridge University Press.

Misak, C. (2016). *Cambridge Pragmatism: From Peirce and James to Ramsey and Wittgenstein*. Oxford: Oxford University Press.

Mitova, V. (2011). Epistemic motivation: Towards a metaethics of belief. In A. Reisner and A. Steglich-Petersen (eds.), *Reasons for Belief*. Cambridge University Press, pp. 54–74.

Mole, C. (2006). Attention, self, and *The Sovereignty of Good*. In A. Rowe (ed.), *Iris Murdoch: A Reassessment*. Basingstoke: Palgrave Macmillan, pp. 72–84.

Mole, C., Smithies, D., and Wu, W. (eds.). (2011). *Attention: Philosophical and Psychological Essays*. Oxford University Press.

Moltmann, F. (2014). Propositions, attitudinal objects, and the distinction between actions and products. *Canadian Journal of Philosophy*, 43 (5): 679–701.

Montemayor, C. (2014). Success, minimal agency, and epistemic virtue. In A. Fairweather (ed.), *Virtue Epistemology Naturalized: Bridges Between Virtue*

Epistemology and Philosophy of Science: Vol. 366. Synthese Library. Springer, pp. 67–82.

Montemayor, C. and Haladjian, H. H. (2015). *Consciousness, Attention, and Conscious Attention.* MIT Press.

Montmarquet, J. A. (1993). *Epistemic Virtue and Doxastic Responsibility.* Rowman & Littlefield.

Morton, A. (2012). *Bounded Thinking: Intellectual Virtues for Limited Agents.* Oxford University Press.

Murdoch, I. (1970). *The Sovereignty of Good.* New York: Schocken Books.

Nanay, B. (2013). Success semantics: The sequel. *Philosophical Studies*, 165: 151–165.

Neta, R. (2014). The epistemic ought. In A. Fairweather and O. Flanagan (eds.), *Naturalizing Epistemic Virtue.* Cambridge: Cambridge University Press, pp. 36–52.

Olin, L. and Doris, J. M. (2014). Vicious minds. *Philosophical Studies*, 168 (3): 665–692.

Owings, D. H. and Hennessy, D. F. (1984). The importance of variation in sciurid visual and vocal communication. In J. O. Murie and G. R. Michener (eds.), *The Biology of Ground-Dwelling Squirrels.* Lincoln: University of Nebraska Press, pp. 169–200.

Paul, L. (2014). *Transformative Experience.* New York, NY: Oxford University Press.

Pavese, C. (2015). Practical senses. *Philosophers' Imprint*, 15 (29): 1–25.

Peirce, C. S. (1992). *The Essential Peirce: Selected Philosophical Writings*, Vol. I. N. Houser and C. Kloesel (eds.). Indiana University Press.

Petitto, L. and Marentette, P. (1991). Babbling in the manual mode: Evidence for the ontogeny of language. *Science*, 251 (5000): 1493–1496.

Petitto, L. A., Berens, M. S., Kovelman, I., Dubins, M. H., Jasinska, K. and Shalinsky, M. (2012). The "Perceptual Wedge" hypothesis as the basis for bilingual babies' phonetic processing advantage: New insights from fNIRS brain imaging. *Brain and Language*, 121 (2): 130–143.

Plantinga, A. (1993). *Warrant: The Current Debate.* Oxford: Oxford University Press.

Proust, J. (2012). Mental acts as natural kinds. In A. Clark, J. Kiverstein and T. Vierkant (eds.), *Decomposing the Will.* Oxford: Oxford University Press, pp. 262–282.

Pritchard, D. (2009). Knowledge, understanding and epistemic value. *Royal Institute of Philosophy Supplement*, 64: 19–43.

Pritchard, D. (2012). Anti-luck virtue epistemology. *Journal of Philosophy*, 109: 247–279.

Pylyshyn, Z. W. (ed.). (1987). *The Robot's Dilemma: The Frame Problem in Artificial Intelligence.* Ablex.

Pylyshyn, Z. W. (2003). *Seeing and Visualizing: It's Not What You Think.* Cambridge, MA: MIT Press.

Quine, W. V. O. (1969). *Epistemology Naturalized. In Ontological Relativity and Other Essays.* New York, NY: Columbia University Press.

Ramsey, F. P. (1927). Facts and propositions. *Proceedings of the Aristotelian Society*, 7 (1):153–170.

Ramsey, F. P. (1931). Knowledge. In R. B. Braithwaite (ed.), *The Foundations of Mathematics and Other Essays.* New York, NY: Harcourt Brace, pp. 258–259.

Rescorla, M. (2009). Assertion and its constitutive norms. *Philosophy and Phenomenological Research*, 79 (1): 98–130.

Richard, M. (2004). Contextualism and relativism. *Philosophical Studies*, 119: 215–242.

Rosenbaum, D. A. (2002). Motor control. In H. Pashler (Series ed.) and S. Yantis (Vol. ed.), *Stevens' Handbook of Experimental Psychology: Vol. 1. Sensation and perception* (3rd Edition). New York, NY: Wiley, pp. 315–339.

Rudder-Baker, L. (2013). *Naturalism and the First Person Perspective*. Oxford University Press.

Sahlin, N. E. (1990). *The Philosophy of F. P. Ramsey*. Cambridge, UK: Cambridge University Press.

Salmon, W. C. (1998). *Causality and Explanation*. New York, NY: Oxford University Press.

Schlenker, P. (2010). Local contexts and local meanings. *Philosophical Studies*, 151: 115–142.

Searle, J. (1969). *Speech acts: An Essay in the Philosophy of Language*. Cambridge: Cambridge University Press.

Searle, J. R. (1985). *Expression and Meaning: Studies in the Theory of Speech Acts*. Cambridge: Cambridge University Press.

Seyfarth, R. M., Cheney, D. L., and Marler, P. (1980). Monkey responses to three different alarm calls: Evidence of predator classification and semantic communication. *Science*, 210 (4471): 801–803.

Seyfarth, R. M. and Cheney, D. L. (1990). The assessment by vervet monkeys of their own and another species' alarm calls. *Animal Behaviour*, 40 (4): 754–764.

Sinnott-Armstrong, W. (ed.) (2007). *Moral Psychology (Vol. 2). The Cognitive Science of Morality: Intuition and Diversity*. Cambridge, MA: MIT Press.

Smith, P. (2003). Deflationism: The facts. In H. Lillehammer and G. Rodriguez-Pereyra (eds.), *Real Metaphysics*. New York, NY: Routledge, pp. 43–53.

Smithies, D. (2011). Attention is rational-access consciousness. In C. Mole, D. Smithies and W. Wu (eds.), *Attention: Philosophical and Psychological Essays*. Oxford: Oxford University Press, pp. 247–273.

Sosa, E. (2000). Skepticism and contextualism. *Philosophical Issues*, 10: 1–18.

Sosa, E. (2007). *A Virtue Epistemology: Apt Belief and Reflective Knowledge (Volume I)*. New York: Oxford University Press.

Sosa, E. (2009). *Reflective Knowledge: Apt Belief and Reflective Knowledge, Volume II*. Oxford: Oxford University Press.

Sosa, E. (2011). *Knowing Full Well*. Princeton, NJ: Princeton University Press.

Sosa, E. (2013). Epistemic agency. *The Journal of Philosophy*, 110 (11): 585–605.

Sosa, E. (2015). *Judgment & Agency*. Oxford University Press UK.

Stainton, R. (2006). *Words and Thoughts*. Oxford: Oxford University Press.

Stalnaker, R. (1978). Assertion. *Syntax and Semantics*, 9: 315–332.

Stalnaker, R. (1984). *Inquiry*. Cambridge, MA: MIT Press.

Stalnaker, R. (2002). Common ground. *Linguistics and Philosophy*, 25 (5): 701–721.

Stanley, J. (2005). *Knowledge and Practical Interests*. Oxford: Oxford University Press.

Stanovich, K. (2011). *Rationality and the Reflective Mind*. New York, NY: Oxford University Press.

Steup, M., Turri, J., and Sosa, E. (eds.). (2013). *Contemporary Debates in Epistemology*. John Wiley & Sons.

Strawson, P. F. (1964). Intention and convention in speech acts. *Philosophical Review*, 73: 439–460.

Sylvan, K. and Sosa, E. (In Press). The place of reasons in epistemology. In D. Star (ed.), *The Oxford Handbook of Reasons and Normativity*. Oxford: Oxford University Press.

Theeuwes, J. (2013). Feature-based attention: It is all bottom-up priming. *Philosophical Transactions of the Royal Society of London B: Biological Sciences*, 368 (1628): 20130055.

Turri, J. (2010). Epistemic invariantism and speech act contextualism. *Philosophical Review*, 119: 77–95.

Turri, J. (2011). Manifest failure: The Gettier problem solved. *Philosophers' Imprint*, 11: 8.

Turri, J. (2013). The test of truth: An experimental investigation into the norm of assertion. *Cognition*, 129: 279–291.

Unger, P. (1975). *Ignorance: A Case for Skepticism*. Oxford University Press.

Velleman, J. D. (1989). *Practical Reflection*. Princeton: Princeton University Press.

Velleman, J. D. (2007). What good is a will? In A. Leist (ed.), *Action in Context*. Berlin: de Gruyter, pp. 193–215.

von Fintel, K. and Gillies, A. (2008). CIA leaks. *Philosophical Review*, 117 (1): 77–98.

von Fintel, K. and Gillies, A. (2011). 'Might' made right. In A. Egan and B. Weatherson (eds.), *Epistemic Modality*. Oxford: Oxford University Press, pp. 108–130.

von Frisch, K. (1953). *The Dancing Bees: An Account of the Life and Senses of the Honey Bee*. Harcourt Brace.

Weiner, M. (2005). Must we know what we say? *The Philosophical Review*, 114: 227–251.

Whitcomb, D. (2010). Curiosity was framed. *Philosophy and Phenomenological Research*, 81 (3): 664–687.

Whyte, J. T. (1990). Success semantics. *Analysis*, 50: 149–157.

Williamson, T. (1994). *Vagueness*. New York, NY: Routledge.

Williamson, T. (1996). Knowing and asserting. *Philosophical Review*, 105 (4): 489–523.

Williamson, T. (2000). *Knowledge and its Limits*. Oxford University Press.

Wittgenstein, L. (1969). *On Certainty*. G. E. M. Anscombe and G. H. von Wright (eds.). Basil Blackwell.

Wolfe, J. M. (1994). Guided Search 2.0 – A revised model of visual search. *Psychonomic Bulletin & Review*, 1 (2): 202–238.

Wright, C. (2001). On being in a quandry. *Mind*, 110: 45–98.

Wu, W. (2011). Attention as selection for action. In C. Mole, D. Smithies, and W. Wayne (eds.), *Attention: Philosophical and Psychological Essays*. Oxford University Press, pp. 97–116.

Wu, W. (2013). Mental action and the threat of automaticity. In A. Clark, J. Kiverstein, and T. Vierkant (eds.), *Decomposing the Will*. Oxford University Press, pp. 244–261.

Wu, W. (2015). Experts and deviants: The story of agentive control. *Philosophy and Phenomenological Research*, 93 (1): 101–126.

Yablo, S. (2014). *Aboutness*. Princeton, NJ: Princeton University Press.

Yaffe, G. (2010). *Attempts: In the Philosophy of Action and the Criminal Law*. New York, NY: Oxford University Press.

Yalcin, S. (2007). Epistemic Modals. *Mind*, 116 (464): 983–1026.

Yalcin, S. (2011). Nonfactualism about epistemic modality. In A. Egan and B. Weatherson (eds.), *Epistemic Modality*. Oxford University Press, pp. 295–332.

Zagzebski, L. (1996). *Virtues of the Mind*. Cambridge: Cambridge University Press.

Zagzebski, L. (2000). From reliabilism to virtue epistemology. *The Proceedings of the Twentieth World Congress of Philosophy*, 5: 173–179.

Zuberbühler, K. (2000). Referential labeling in Diana monkeys. *Animal Behaviour*, 59 (5): 917–927.

Index

AAA model, 102
AAM. *See* attention-assertion model
abilities, epistemic. *See* epistemic abilities
aboutness, 130–131
ACC. *See* agential cognitive constitutions
action
  assertion and, 90–93
  attention modulated for, 17, 21
  epistemic, 100–104
  intentional, 15–16, 77
  judgment as, 87
  mental, 100–104
  norm of, 91
  real content and, 91
activity theory, 5
affirmations
  alethic, 64
    epistemic agency and, 98, 103–104
    judgment and, 98–99
  intermediate, 99–100
agency. *See also* epistemic agency
  attention and, 29
  automaticity and, 16
  cognitive, 20
  cognitive constitution and, 33, 67–68
  credit for success and, 44
  epistemic psychology and, 3
  integration as hallmark of, 109
  intentional actions and, 15–16
  as knowledge requirement, 27
  language and, 109–111
  in VTEP, 14, 15
agential cognitive constitutions (ACC), 17–18
aggregation-integration, 158–159
  decisiveness, 159
  systematicity, 159
  universality, 159
akrasia, 127
alethic affirmation, 64. *See also* Sosa, Ernest
  epistemic agency and, 98, 103–104
  judgment and, 98–99
Alfano, Mark, 39–40. *See also* situationism

on bounded rationality, 41–42
on inferential situationism, 41–42
on non-skepticism, 39, 41
on virtue reliabilism, 39, 41
Allport, Alan, 145
analysis, direction of. *See* direction of analysis
animals, successful communication between, 109–110, 160–163
Anscombe, Elizabeth, 56, 57–58, 105
  on intention, 105–108
  on practical knowledge, 106, 107, 108
  on speculative knowledge, 106
anti-luck intuition
  safety and, 24–25
  TrueTemp and, 23, 24–25
anti-luck virtue epistemology, 12, 26
argument from attention, 27–33
  'attending to' selection in, 28, 29–30
  conscious awareness in, 28
  many-many problems in, 30
assertable beliefs, 147–148
asserting agents, 117
assertion
  AAM and, 118
  action and, 90–93
  assertoric force and, 116
  attention and, 21
  collective, 163–166
  credit and, 123–124
  curiosity and, 146–147
  defined, 116
  dispositions to, 114–118
  as epistemic ability, 122–123
  epistemic motivation and, 59–60
  epistemically virtuous halting and, 117, 128–131
  factivity and, 123–124
    social-factive forms, 165
  grip of, 64–66
  inference in, 117
  MCBs and, 117–118
  motivations of, 64, 65

189

assertion (cont.)
norm of, 58, 86–90
philosophical literature on, 139
Pierce on, 87–89
reliability and, 85–86
retraction of, 128–129
social environments and, 123–124
speech act theory and, 118, 128–129
assertoric force, 116
attention and, 118–123
attitudinal account, 119–120
common ground account, 120–121
constitutive rule account, 122
epistemic abilities and, 120–121
intentions and, 119
veridicality and, 120–121
assertoric utterances, 60, 64, 65
asymmetry, in AAM, 121
attention. *See also* argument from attention
action and, 17, 21
agency and, 29
assertion and, 21
assertoric force and, 118–123
attitudinal account, 119–120
common ground account, 120–121
constitutive rule account, 122
cognitive, 153
as cognitive unison, 29
collective, 166–169
communication and, 17, 21,
112–114
constituents of, 29
creativity and, 151–155
curiosity and, 151–155
dexterity and, 5–7
as epistemic ability, 122–123
in epistemic methodology, 21
epistemic value and, 17
evolutionary thesis for, 37
feature-based, 29
as goal-directed, 69
integration and, 5–7, 29
interest-directed, 142
normative, 57
perceptual, 153
post-voluntary, 6
psychology of, 54
reliability and, 75
schema, 17
selection and, 28, 29–30
self-directed, 54–57
spatial, 32
virtue epistemology and, 55
world-directed, 54–57, 103
attentional inhibition, 148

attention-assertion model (AAM), 17–18
assertion and, 118
asymmetry in, 121
attention schema in, 17
attitudinal accounts and, 119–120
collective communication and, 162
collective motivation and, 169
common ground accounts and, 120–121
communication and, 25–26
constitutive rule accounts and, 122
halting-computational threshold in, 136
halting-factive threshold in, 136
halting-subjective threshold in, 136
virtue reliabilism and, 134–135
attitudinal account, 119–120
authority deference, 19, 20
automatic process, 6
mixed process and, 104–105
automaticity
agency and, 16
defined, 96
of dispositions, 16
epistemic agency and, 96–97
mixed process and, 105
virtue reliabilism and, 96–97
Wu on, 96
Axelrod, Robert, 161

Bach, Kent, 115
Bargh, John, 96
Battaly, Heather, 14, 144
behaviorism, 139
belief, 31
assertable, 147–148
assertion and, 87–89
content of, 89
false, 34
formation of, 70
as functions from desires, 82
hypostatization and, 92
MCBs, 117–118
normative force and, 70
Pierce on, 87–89
stability of, 89
Berker, Selim, 48–49, 50
Bernstein, Nicholai A., 6
blindsighters, 28
"blooming buzzing chaos," 148
Blum, Lawrence, 55
bounded rationality, 39, 41–42
Brendel, Elke, 12

causality, 79–81
explanatory salience and, 74, 76
knowledge attribution and, 79–80

objective information and, 80
  success semantics and, 82–83
    constraints on, 81–85
  virtue reliabilism and, 74–79
Chartrand, Tanya, 96
cognitive agency, 20
cognitive attention, 153
cognitive commitment, 57–58
cognitive constitution, 15
  agency and, 33, 67–68
cognitive integration, 37
  collective communication and, 162–163
  collective epistemic agency and, 156–160
  in democracies, 176
  for epistemic agency, 111
  motivation modulated by, 127
  reliable halting and, 150
cognitive needs, 57–59
cognitive processing, success semantics and,
    81–85
collective agency
  complex, 173–177
    contract law and, 175
    criminal intent and, 174
    criminal law and, 174, 175
    social communication and, 160–163
      AAM and, 162
      cognitive integration and, 162–163
      epistemic constitution and, 162–163
      moral agency and, 163
collective assertion, social epistemology and,
    163–166
collective attention, 166–169
collective cognitive integration, 159–160
collective epistemic agency, cognitive
    integration and, 156–160
collective motivation, 157–158, 166–169
  AAM and, 169
collective wisdom, 159
common ground account, 120–121
common sense, 93
communication, successful
  AAM and, 25–26
  in animals, 109–110, 160–163
  assertion needs in, 60
  attention modulated for, 17, 21, 112–114
  collective agency and, 160–163
    AAM and, 162
    cognitive integration and, 162–163
    epistemic constitution and, 162–163
  dispositions to assert and, 114–118
  economic problem and, 164, 165, 166
  halting-computational threshold in, 136
  halting-factive threshold in, 136
  halting-subjective threshold in, 136

  inferential knowledge and, 46–47
  MCBs and, 117–118
communicative presumption (CP), 118
complex collective agency, 173–177
  contract law and, 175
  criminal intent and, 174
  criminal law and, 174, 175
computational theory of the mind, 66, 149
conscious awareness, 28
consequentialism. See epistemic
    consequentialism
constitution
  ACC, 17–18
  cognitive, 15
  epistemic, 162–163
constitutive rule account, 122
content
  of belief, 89
  real, 91
  as theory, 82–83
  truth and, 133–134
contextualism, 74–79
  MacFarlane on, 132–133
  problems with, 77–78
  skepticism and, 136–137
  truth evaluation in, 132
  Yalcin on, 132–133
contract law, complex collective agency
    and, 175
controlled process, 104–105
CP. See communicative presumption
Craig, Edward, 84–85
creativity
  attention and, 151–155
  curiosity and, 151–155
credit
  assertion and, 123–124
  for success, 34
    agent-based, 44
criminal law, complex collective agency and,
    174, 175
culpable masking, 34–35
curiosity. See also epistemically virtuous
    curiosity
  attention and, 151–155
  basic principles of, 141–143
  creativity and, 151–155
  degrees of, 141
  halting thresholds and, 143–148
  as intellectual virtue, 138
  interest-directed attention and, 142
  norm of assertion and, 146–147
  objectual, 141
  propositional, 141
  referential forms of, 154

curiosity (cont.)
  as vice, 138
  virtuous insensitivity and, 148–151

DA. *See* direction of analysis
Davidson, Donald, 85
decisiveness, 159
deductive inference, 47
deference
  authority, 19, 20
  epistemic, 21
democracy, cognitive integration and, 176
Descartes, René, 152–153
desire, beliefs and, 82
deSousa, Ronald, 148
dexterity
  attention and, 5–7
  integration and, 5–7
  requirements for, 6
Dexterity and its Development (Bernstein), 6
Dickie, Imogen, 4, 25–26, 54, 57–58, 94–95
  assertion defined by, 116
  on unattended peripheral vision, 28
direction of analysis (DA), 14–15, 16, 17
dispositions
  credit for success of, 34
  culpable masking and, 34–35
  distinctions between states as cause of and
    manifestation of, 73
  epistemic abilities and, 33–38
    comparisons between, 36–38
  manifestation of, 33–34
  non-culpable masking and, 35–36
  successful communication and, 114–118
  virtuous masking and, 36
Dummett, Michael, 60

economic collective agents, 168
economic problem, need for successful
    communication and, 164, 165, 166
epistemic abilities, 6
  assertion as, 122–123
  assertoric force and, 120–121
  attention as, 122–123
  dispositions and, 33–38
  language and, 134
epistemic action, 100–104
epistemic agency, 1. *See also* assertion
  alethic affirmations and, 98, 103–104
  automaticity and, 96–97
  cognitive integration for, 111
  cognitive needs and, 57–59
  collective, 156–160
  conscious awareness and, 28
  functionings and, 98

in *Judgment and Agency*, 98–100
  language and, 115
  as luck-eliminating, 26, 95–96
  motivational states and, 53–54
  needs in, 60–64
  self-directed attention and, 54–57
  Sosa on, 98–100
  TrueTemp and, 21–24, 97
  virtuous insensitivity and, 68
  world-directed attention and, 54–57
epistemic consequentialism, 48–52
epistemic constitution, 162–163
epistemic deference, 21
epistemic immoderateness, 144
epistemic luck, 26
epistemic methodology. *See* methodology
epistemic modals, 128–131
  aboutness in, 130–131
  virtuous insensitivity and, 129, 130
  virtuous sensitivity and, 129
epistemic motivation, 16, 53
  assertion and, 59–60
epistemic naturalism. *See* naturalism
epistemic psychology, 1
  agency and, 3
  explanatory power of, 2–3
  virtue epistemology and, 3–4
  virtue reliabilism and, 3
epistemic Ramsey success (ERS), 83–84, 108
  reliability for, 83
epistemic situationism, 4–5
epistemic value, 3
  attention and, 17
epistemically responsible halting
    thresholds, 147
epistemically virtuous curiosity, 138–140
epistemically virtuous halting, 117
  epistemic modals, 128–131
    aboutness in, 130–131
    virtuous insensitivity and, 129, 130
    virtuous sensitivity and, 129
  virtuous insensitivity and, 150
epistemology. *See also* meta-epistemology
  NVE, 18–19
  situationism in, 4–5
ERS. *See* epistemic Ramsey success
ethics
  meta-epistemology and, norms of, 60–64
  virtue theories in, 54–57
etiology
  as 'because of' relation, 72–74, 75–76,
    81–82
  of success, 73–74
    contextualist etiology and, 74–79
    Gettier cases, 72–73

exemplarist virtue theory, 73
explanatory salience, 74, 76
explicit intentions, 15–16

factivity, assertion and, 123–124
  social-communicative, 124
false beliefs, 34
feature-based attention, 29
"The Fixation of Belief" (Pierce), 87–88
Foot, Philippa, 4, 52, 54, 62
frame problem
  computational theory of the mind and,
    66, 149
  virtuous insensitivity and, 66–69, 148–149
freedom, 98–99
Frege, Gottlob, 64–66, 86–88
  on assertoric utterances, 65
Fricker, Miranda, 157, 159–160
functionings, judgment as distinct from, 98

Gettier cases, 72–73
Gigerenzer, Gerd, 39, 42–43, 143
Gilbert, Margaret, 157
Goldberg, Sanford, 118–119
Graziano, Michael, 17
Greco, John, 37
  on causality, 79–81
  contextualist etiology of, 74–79
    problems with, 77–78
  explanatory salience for, 74, 76
  reliability and, 75
  virtue reliabilism and, 81
Grimm, Stephen, 70

Hacking, Ian, 92
halting thresholds. See also epistemically
    virtuous halting
  curiosity and, 143–148
  epistemically responsible, 147
  halting-computational, 136
  halting-factive, 136
  halting-subjective, 136
  virtue of reliable sating and, 144–145
Hayek, Frederick, 164–165
hypostatization, 92

Inan, Ilhan, 141, 151
inference, 39–41
  in assertions, 117
  deductive, 47
inferential knowledge, 46–47
inferential situationism, 41–42
integrated representations, 100
integration
  agency and, 109

aggregation-integration, 158–159
attention and, 5–7, 29
  cognitive, 37, 111
  dexterity and, 5–7
  processes required for, 7
intellectual virtues, 12–13
Intention (Anscombe), 105
intentional actions, 15–16, 77, 100
intentions
  assertoric force and, 119
  explicit, 15–16
  R-intentions, 118
  standing static, 102–103
interest-directed attention, 142
intermediate affirmations, 99–100
intuition
  anti-luck
    safety and, 24–25
    TrueTemp and, 23, 24
  stability of, 113
isomorphism. See normative isomorphism

Jackson, Frank, 153
James, William, 30, 148
judgment. See also Sosa, Ernest
  as action, 87
  alethic affirmation and, 98–99
  functionings as distinct from, 98
  non-luckiness and, 99
  reflection and, 170–173
  reliability and, 170–173
Judgment and Agency (Sosa), 4, 9, 31, 58–59,
    95, 98
  epistemic agency and, 98–100

Kant, Immanuel, 69
knowledge. See also argument from attention
  agency as requirement for, 27
  argument from attention for, 27–33
    'attending to' selection in, 28, 29–30
    conscious awareness in, 28
    many-many problems in, 30
  as assertion norm, 139
  'because of' requirement for, 72–74, 75–76,
    81–82
  inferential, 46–47
  of logic, 47
  many-many problems and, 30
  non-reflective, 170–171
  norm of action and, 91
  practical, 106, 107, 108
  reflective, 170–171
  speculative, 106
  of syntax, 44–47
    situationalism and, 45–46

knowledge (cont.)
  virtue reliabilist theory of, 1
  in VTEP, 15–16
knowledge attribution, 79–80
Kornblith, Hilary, 56, 172
Korsgaard, Christine, 4, 52, 54, 61
  on problem of normative force, 61

language
  acquisition of, 110
  agency and, 109–111
  CP and, 118
  epistemic abilities and, 134
  epistemic agency and, 115
  flexibility of, 115
Lepock, Chris, 101
List, Christian, 157
logic, knowledge of, 47
luck. *See* anti-luck intuition; anti-luck virtue
  epistemology; epistemic luck

MacFarlane, John, 127–128, 129–130
  on contextualism, 132–133
manifestation of dispositions, 33–34
Mantel, Susanne, 101–102
many-many problems, 30
masking
  culpable, 34–35
  non-culpable, 35–36
  situationism and, 35
  virtuous, 36
MCBs. *See* mutual contextual beliefs
Mellor, D. H., 46–47
Meno problem, 50
mental action, 100–104
  meta-cognition and, 101
meta-cognition, 101
meta-epistemology
  cognitive needs and, 57–59
  ethical norms and, authority of, 60–64
  motivational states and, 53–54
  self-directed attention and, 54–57
  world-directed attention and, 54–57
methodology, in epistemology, 18–26
  attention studies in, 21
  epistemic deference in, 21
  epistemic naturalism and, 18
    cognitive agency and, 20
  through knowledge-first approach, 18
Millikan, Ruth, 36–38
mixed process
  automatic process and, 104–105
  automaticity and, 105
  as controlled process, 104
  personal success and, 104

sub-personal success and, 104
Mole, Christopher, 4, 29, 56–57
Moltman, Friederike, 134–135
moral psychology, 2, 55
morality
  Foot on, 62
  Murdoch on, 55
Morton, Adam, 43, 143, 151
motivation
  of assertion, 64, 65
  cognitive integration and, 127
  collective, 157–158, 166–169
    AAM and, 169
  epistemic, 16, 53
    assertion in, 59–60
  meta-epistemology and, 53–54
  praiseworthy, 58
motivational virtue epistemology, 11–12
  intellectual virtues in, 12–13
Murdoch, Iris, 4, 52, 54, 56
  on attentional anchoring, 55
  on ethics, 54–57
  on morality, 55
mutual contextual beliefs (MCBs), 117–118

naturalism, epistemic
  authority deference in, 19, 20
  defined, 19
  in epistemic methodology, 18
    cognitive agency in, 20
  Quine and, 19–20
naturalized virtue epistemology (NVE), 18–19
non-culpable masking, 35–36
non-motivational virtue epistemology, 12
  intellectual virtues in, 12–13
non-reflective knowledge, 170–171
non-skepticism, 39, 41
norm of action, 91
norm of assertion, 58, 86–90
normative attention, 57
normative force, 69–71
  assertion and, 58, 86–90
  belief and, 70
  of epistemic norms, 63
  problem of, 61
  in virtue reliabilism, 48–49
normative isomorphism, 49, 50
NVE. *See* naturalized virtue epistemology

objectual curiosity, 141
On Certainty (Wittgenstein), 92

passivity, 98–99
perceptual attention, 153
performance normativity, 31

personal success. *See also* Sosa, Ernest
    in mixed processes, 104
    sub-personal success compared to, 98–100
The Philosophy of Curiosity (Inan), 141
Pierce, Charles Sanders, 85–86, 87–88
    on assertion
        action and, 90–93
        belief and, 87–89
    hypostatization and, 92
post-voluntary attention, 6
practical knowledge, 106, 107, 108
praiseworthy motivations, 58
Principles of Psychology (James), 148
Pritchard, Duncan, 22–23
problem of normative force, 61
process
    automatic, 6
        mixed process and, 104–105
    controlled, 104–105
    mixed
        automatic process and, 104–105
        automaticity and, 105
        personal success and, 104
        sub-personal success and, 104
    reliabilism, 48, 61
process reliabilism, 48
propositional curiosity, 141
Proust, Joelle, 101
psychology. *See* epistemic psychology; moral
    psychology
Pyrrhonian skepticism, 144

Quine, W. v O., 19–20

Ramsey, Frank, 4, 17, 24, 82. *See also* success
    semantics
    on assertion
        action and, 90–93
        reliability and, 85–86
    ERS, 83–84, 108
        reliability for, 83
    philosophical influences on, 85–86, 88–89
    reliability and assertion, 85–86
Ramsey effect, 85
Ramsey principle, 89
Ramsey success, 17, 24
rationality. *See* bounded rationality; reason
reason, types of, 172–173
reflective knowledge, 170–171
Reid, Thomas, 93
reliabilism, 37. *See also* virtue reliabilism
    Anscombe on, 57–58
    process, 48, 61
    success semantics and, 78
reliability

assertion and, 85–86
attention and, 75
for ERS, 83
explicit judgment and, 170–173
Greco and, 75
reflection and, 170–173
reliable halting, 150
responsibilism, 42. *See also* virtue
    responsibilism
retraction
    of assertions, 128–129
    virtuous sensitivity and, 132–136
R-intentions, 118

safety, anti-luck intuition and, 24–25
self-directed attention, 54–57
semantics. *See* success semantics
sensitivity. *See* virtuous insensitivity
Simon, Herbert, 39
situationism, 38–44
    cognitive, 39
    epistemic, 4–5
    inferential, 41–42
    knowledge of logic and, 47
    knowledge of syntax and, 45–46
    masking and, 35
    non-skepticism and, 39, 41
    virtue reliabilism and, 39, 41
skepticism. *See also* non-skepticism
    contextualism and, 136–137
    Pyrrhonian, 144
Smith, Peter, 82–83
Smithies, Declan, 4
social environments, assertion and, 123–124
Sosa, Ernest, 4, 9, 31, 58–59, 95, 98, 119
    AAA model, 102
    on alethic affirmation, 64
    on belief, 31
    on epistemic agency, 98–100
    on freedom, 98–99
    on passivity, 98–99
    on performance normativity, 31
    on virtue reliabilism, defense of, 11, 31, 48
Sources of Normativity (Korsgaard), 61
spatial attention, 32
speculative knowledge, 106
speech act theory, 118, 128–129
Speech Acts, 16
Stalnaker, Robert, 120–121, 135
standing static intentions, 102–103
Stanley, Jason, 90
stopping rules, 143
Strawson, Galen, 21–22
sub-personal success. *See also* Sosa, Ernest
    in mixed processes, 104

sub-personal success (cont.)
  personal success compared to, 98–100
success conditions
  etiology of, 73–74
  virtue reliabilism and, 51
  VTEP and, 16–17
success semantics, 17, 24, 82
  causality and, 82–83
    constraints on, 81–85
  cognitive processing and, 81–85
  content and, 82–83
  contextualist etiology and, 74–79
  ERS and, 83–84
  Gettier cases and, 72–73
  reliabilism and, 78
  truth and, 82–83
syntax, knowledge of, 44–47
  situationalism and, 45–46

TrueTemp
  anti-luck conditions and, 23, 24–25
  epistemic agency and, 21–24, 97
  Pritchard on, 22–23
  virtue reliabilism and, 21–22
truth
  content and, 133–134
  in contextualism, 132
  success semantics and, 82–83

unattended peripheral vision, 28
universality, 159

veridicality, 120–121
virtue epistemology, 1
  anti-luck, 12, 26
  attention and, 55
  claims about, 26
  epistemic psychology and, 3–4
  epistemic situationism as challenge to, 4–5
  epistemic values and, 3
  motivational, 11–12
    intellectual virtues in, 12–13
  non-motivational, 12
    intellectual virtues in, 12–13
  normative conditions in, 34
  NVE, 18–19
  virtue responsibilism and, 3–4, 11–13
virtue of reliable sating, 144–145
virtue reliabilism, 3–4, 11–13
  AAM and, 134–135
  Alfano and, 39–40, 41
  automaticity and, 96–97

causality and, 74–79
  epistemic psychology and, 3
  Greco and, 74
  inference in, 39–41
  knowledge and, 1
  normativity in, 48–49
  Sosa defense of, 11, 31, 48
  success ratio for, 51
  TrueTemp and, 21–22
virtue responsibilism, 3–4, 11–13
virtue theoretic epistemic psychology (VTEP),
    3, 13–17. See also epistemic psychology
  agent-based norm in, 14, 15
  cognitive constitution in, 15
  DA for, 14–15, 16
  intentional actions and, 15–16
  knowledge and, normativity of, 15–16
  right to left reading of, 13–14
  success conditions and, 16–17
virtuous curiosity. See epistemically virtuous
    curiosity
virtuous halting. See epistemically virtuous
    halting
virtuous insensitivity, 56, 60
  curiosity and, 148–151
  epistemic agency and, 68
  epistemic modals and, 129, 130
  epistemically virtuous halting and, 150
  frame problem and, 66–69, 148–149
  psychological processes and, 137
virtuous masking, 36
virtuous sensitivity, 129
  psychological processes and, 137
  retraction and, 132–136
von Frisch, Karl, 160–161
VTEP. See virtue theoretic epistemic
    psychology

whole organism states, 145
Williamson, Timothy, 86, 135
Wittgenstein, Ludwig, 85–86, 92
world-directed attention, 54–57, 103
Wu, Wayne, 4, 6, 29
  on automaticity, 96
  on many-many problems, 30
  on mental action, 100–104

Yablo, Stephen, 130–131
Yalcin, Seth, 127–128
  on contextualism, 132–133

Zagzebski, Linda, 58, 73

CPSIA information can be obtained
at www.ICGtesting.com
Printed in the USA
LVHW042322040119
602794LV00020B/475/P